The Poverty of Nations

The Poverty of Nations

A Guide to the Debt Crisis – from Argentina to Zaire

Edited by
Elmar Altvater
Kurt Hübner
Jochen Lorentzen
Raúl Rojas

Translated by Terry Bond

Zed Books Ltd
London and New Jersey

The Poverty of Nations was first published in German under
the title *Die Armut der Nationen: Handbuch zur Schuldenkrise
von Argentinien bis Zaire* by Rotbuch Verlag, Berlin, in 1987;
updated edition, 1988. First published in English by Zed Books Ltd,
57 Caledonian Road, London N1 9BU, UK, and 165 First Avenue,
Atlantic Highlands, New Jersey 07716, USA, in 1991.

Cover designed by Andrew Corbett.
Typeset by EMS Photosetters, Thorpe Bay, Essex.
Maps by Keith Addison.
Printed and bound in the United Kingdom
by Biddles Ltd, Guildford and King's Lynn.

A catalogue record for this book is
available from the British Library

ISBN 0 86232 948 5 Hb
ISBN 0 86232 949 3 Pb

Contents

Tables

Figures

Maps

Part I
The Debt Crisis
Structure and Trends

1. The Causes and Course of the International Debt Crisis

Elmar Altvater/Kurt Hübner

The cards are reshuffled

August 1982 marked a watershed in the history of the capitalist world economy. That which representatives of official institutions and governments had until then dismissed as the product of a fevered imagination became reality: Mexico, the Third World's most heavily indebted nation, declared her inability to pay her debts. Despite every ground-plan previously laid for dealing with this most serious of situations, the management of the crisis was characterized by improvisation and chaotic decision-making structures. As a result it would henceforth prove impossible to regard the shrewd question posed by the US economist Hyman P. Minsky, 'Can it happen again?', as purely academic. It was, however, still possible to avoid an overt financial crisis such as the one which had occurred in the 1930s. Within 72 hours creditor banks and public institutions had acted jointly to make available to Mexico new loans worth more than US$4 billion. But stability has its price, a price which has hitherto had to be paid first and foremost by the populations of the debtor nations.

Since 1982, the management of the international debt crisis has become almost routine; whereas in the 1970s sums of US$5 billion would still have commanded headlines, the value of loans restructured annually because they cannot be serviced within the prescribed period is now running at US$150 billion. The private banks and public institutions no longer rely on improvisation as they did in the case of Mexico. But like the Mexican crisis in 1982, Brazil's decision in February 1987 to suspend, initially for an indefinite period, the payment of interest on her foreign debts, worth more than US$110 billion, nevertheless triggered hectic activity in private and public institutions and necessitated several crisis meetings. Although intent on subjecting Brazil to a threatening rhetoric on the grounds that her suspension of interest payments is not merely a violation of the international credit world's rules, but also a possible threat to bank profits — the income from interest lost as a result of Brazil's moratorium accounted for 22% of the big US banks' profits for 1986 and in some cases even meant non-liquidity or worse — the private US banks in particular reacted more calmly than they had five years previously. The banks' new self-confidence is founded on developments since the Mexican crisis of

1982. Since then, the flow of private loans to the debtor nations has diminished steadily, with the result that the banks' commitments have reduced in relation to their own capital funds. Whereas in 1982 only just under 50% of all American banks' debts receivable from the Third World nations were covered by those banks' own capital funds, by the end of 1985 the proportion covered had risen to around 80%. Even the particularly vulnerable US big banks were able to improve their balance sheets: whilst in 1982 the proportion of outstanding debts receivable from the four major Latin American debtors (Brazil, Mexico, Argentina and Venezuela) still accounted for 143% of share capital, by the begining of 1987 they accounted for only 74%. During this period the major debtors in Latin America had become net exporters of capital, although not for reasons of economic strength or as a result of an excess of capital but rather in response to the hardship caused by onerous debt commitments.

The banks' strategies for protecting themselves against the consequences of the inability of individual debtors to pay their debts, a possibility for which they have been realistically prepared at least since the Mexican crisis, are many and varied. On the one hand, certain credit institutions have, as far as competition allows, sought to erect buffers capable of neutralizing the threat of lost interest and loan-capital (re)payments by making provisions and creating reserves, and by increasing the margin between interest receivable and interest payable. But the banking system as a whole has also reacted with financial innovations. It has become evident that money and credit are nothing more than commodities which are traded against a price: interest. As has happened on other markets, such as that for cars, a 'used-money and credit market' is now emerging as part of the world monetary and credit markets where debts receivable from Third World nations are offered for sale at a discount and bought up by speculators, just like a Passat with 80,000 kilometres on the clock might be. The banks are able to purge their balance sheets of doubtful debts by disposing of risky debts receivable. Although the speculative buyers are purchasing a high risk, as is the case with factoring, they are also purchasing a high-risk premium: interest is payable on the face value (for example, of 100), whereas the actual purchase price of the debt is far lower. Nor is it only speculators who try to earn themselves the proverbial small fortune in this way. Well-known transnational corporations, too, are interested in the used-credit market. A proportion of the banks' debts receivable from debtor nations is converted into financial stakes in the debtor nations' industries: expropriation through conversion. Such debt-equity swaps are still relatively insignificant but the governments of Mexico and Chile in 1987 approved transactions to the value of at least US$2 billion. For Western concerns this is a good opportunity. They purchase debts from one of the creditor banks at a discount (for example, Mexican debts were being offered for sale at 50–60 cents to the dollar, and Peruvian debts traded at 15–18 cents to the dollar) and exchange these claims at face value, through the debtor nations' central banks, for domestic currency. In this way they are able to make direct investments for a relatively small amount of capital expenditure. For the debtor nations such transactions mean a reduction in their foreign debts to the private banks, although at an extremely high cost: the selling-off of profitable branches of the national economy (obviously no concern would wish to become involved in unprofitable sectors). Although the private creditor banks' books show financial losses from the sale of debts on the used-credit market, the process does, however, permit them to purge their balance sheets and reduce their future provision for risky debts. Of course, the debtor nations are watching developments carefully. They are understandably asking why the discount should benefit speculators engaged in factoring or transnational corporations instead of being used to reduce directly claims on the debtors themselves. We will return to this question later.

Figure 1.1
Discounts for used credit
(selected countries)

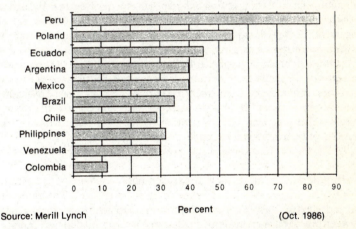

Source: Merill Lynch   Per cent   (Oct. 1986)

Despite the improvement in the banks' strategic reserves, the international financial system is no less fragile today than it was at the beginning of the 1980s. Now, as then, it is vital that the vast majority of debtors remains able and willing to pay. Even today a collective refusal to service debts would inevitably lead to the collapse of the international financial system, and as such a higher degree of flexibility is only available to a few debtors. On the whole, then, debtors have no option but to continue to pay up, that is to remain net exporters of capital in order to preserve the liquidity of the international banking system. Yet instability is not created solely through debtors suspending payments, but also by the way in which the crisis is managed by the private banks themselves. Financial innovations, that is the various new markets within the world monetary markets, are a cause of concern not only to the central banks. They are neither licensed nor certified as roadworthy and consumer-protection bodies will accept responsibility for nothing but tried and tested business methods. Thus the big banks' policy of reducing risks goes hand in hand with an intensification of competition, and this renders the banking system as a whole more fragile. Suppose, for example, that the decision taken in May 1987 by Citicorp, the USA's largest bank, and Chase Manhattan, the third largest bank, to adjust the value of all of their Third World debts receivable downwards and to make provisions worth thousands of millions for the writing off of debts receivable on Third World debtor nations were to become an accepted strategy for dealing with the crisis, this might well set in motion a merry-go-round of concentration. Not only the smaller but also many major credit institutions would be totally unable to raise the funds necessary for such a revaluation. Without government support or the help of the central banks some of the more vulnerable banks might not survive the adjustment of their debts receivable. Though representatives of the banks always reject it emphatically in official statements, the possibility of bankruptcy cannot be completely ruled out. In Japan a consortium of 28 leading Japanese banks was formed with the active support of government agencies for the purposes of counteracting harmful competition and removing themselves from the danger-zone — through adjustments of value and the making of provisions, thereby leaving the other, weaker banks stranded. The consortium intends to take over responsibility for the loans extended to the debtor nations and to adjust the values of those debts in a controlled fashion. It is hoped that fiscal relief will enable some of the debts to be written off in a non-harmful manner.

All of these moves point to the fact that with or without direct government support the international banks are working hard and against the clock in order to survive intact any intensification of the debt crisis which further suspensions of interest payments might trigger.

The rationale and irrationality of foreign debt

The raising of loans in a foreign currency is commonplace on the world market. Foreign-currency loans are extended either for the settlement of international commercial transactions, for the financing of private and government budget deficits, whether for consumption or investment, or are raised purely for speculative reasons (in the expectation of changes in the parity between currencies or interest-rate margins, or of higher yields from, for example, government bonds). The absolute total of external loans therefore has no force of expression whatsoever. From the point of view of a private concern, or even an entire nation, the crucial issue is the relationship which exists between the interest and capital (re)payments on such loans and their current and future yields in terms of net foreign exchange proceeds. The debtors must, of course, have at their disposal present or future income sufficient to enable them to (re)pay the capital and interest (production of funds problem) and to transact the operation in the foreign currency required (transfer problem). Thus a large volume of external loans does not necessarily cause more problems than a small volume. For example, in 1982 Argentina and South Korea had virtually identical external debts of just under US$40 billion. The burden of debt service and therefore the strain placed on the economic reproductive process were nevertheless very different in the two countries. Whereas Argentina had a debt-service ratio of 103%, the corresponding ratio in South Korea was just 21%. Evidently, processes of industrialization oriented towards the world market and backed up by external loans do not automatically have to end in a debt crisis. Since the 1970s, South Korea has been able to increase her national product in real terms by an average of 10% per annum and her exports by 30%. Thanks to this growth dynamic, it has been possible for her to solve both her production of funds and transfer problems simultaneously. So far at any rate this has continued to be possible despite a rapid worsening of the global world economic situation during the 1980s. So, have the governments of other debtor nations failed and backed the wrong development and modernization policies? Have these nations set the debt trap for themselves simply as a consequence of their being corrupt client economies which have used the loans to their own advantage and shuffled off the burden of debt onto the poor population, which is thus plunged from poverty into destitution?

The South Korean experience offers no universally valid answer to this question. The South Korean Government is a dictatorship bent on modernization which has succeeded in spreading the social costs of adjusting to a position in the world economy through repressive political mechanisms without jeopardizing economic efficiency, and in externalizing the remaining costs through an export offensive. Were other debtor nations to back an export offensive with such rigour then the international commodity markets would soon be flooded with a supply of goods for which there was no corresponding international demand with the necessary purchasing power. As has happened on the international markets for raw materials, this would then lead to a fall in prices and/or the introduction of protectionist measures on industrial goods markets. The transfer problem, that is obtaining foreign exchange revenue through the exportation of goods, cannot be solved in this way.

Each nation's debt crisis has a variety of causes, some of which are rooted in national politics. However, the international debt crisis of the 1980s has identifiable causes which are rooted in the very functioning of a capitalist world economy (such as that which emerged after 1945). Within the post-war world order known as the *Pax Americana* the role of the USA was to safeguard the reproductive capacities of the capitalist world economy through economic, political, ideological and military control. At the Bretton Woods Conference of 1944 the US dollar was officially declared the world currency — the currency to which the exchange rates of all other participating currencies would be tied — and as the reserve and intervention currency of the central banks. It had, in practice, deprived sterling of the role during the 1920s. For as long as the dollar remained in short supply and the dollar rate high, the USA profited from having been assigned this role. The US currency's high purchasing power abroad permitted cheap imports and, after the introduction of free convertibility of currencies towards the end of the 1950s, the purchase of favourable terms of stakes in Western European and Third World firms. Eventually Western Europe and Japan accepted the American challenge so talked about in the mid-1960s: in an attempt to make up for lost time, the developed capitalist nations launched an economic attack on the USA. By the early 1970s, having concluded the attack, albeit with dubious success, they had caught up with the USA in terms of technological advance, worker productivity and standard of living. In doing so they had dragged some of the nations of the Third World with them, at least as far as the growth dynamic was concerned. The battle resulted, however, in the institutions set up under Bretton Woods being undermined and the capitalist world economy destabilized. The key events took place in 1971 and 1973: first the unilateral abrogation of the duty to convert paper money into gold (the gold standard) by the Nixon Government; and then the abandonment of the system in favour of a regime of flexible exchange rates.

Whilst in the developed capitalist nations investment fell off sharply, the growth dynamic of the 1950s and 1960s flagged and unemployment soared — all as a consequence of falling profits — many Third World nations (and not only the newly industrialized ones) were able to push their national development models further forward and to achieve high growth rates. The economic crisis in the developed, capitalist world provided them with a unique opportunity to shake off their old dependence and to speed up the processes of industrialization and modernization which they had begun so long before. Conditions, in fact, appeared very favourable. Investment-fatigued concerns from the capitalist metropole and Organization of Petroleum Exporting Countries (OPEC) with their new-found wealth had flooded the international money and credit markets with liquid funds (Metrodollars and Petrodollars). During the 1970s total borrowing on the Eurodollar markets swelled by average rates of increase of around 25% per annum. Moreover, during this period the banks in the developed capitalist world began to organize their businesses on an increasingly transnational basis. Since the late 1960s they had become major sources of finance for the Third World.

A study carried out by the OECD, states explicitly that the expansion of the private banks was, in fact, already underway before OPEC's first rise in crude-oil prices. When investment first flagged in the developed capitalist nations as part of the world economic crisis and profits were parked on the international money and credit markets, the conditions were created for a new, more insistent demand for loans. At no time since World War II had potential debtors been able to obtain funds from the private banks on such favourable terms. If one takes account of fluctuations in the rate of inflation on these markets, then the rates of interest charged in the mid-1970s were actually negative real rates of interest; even in strictly monetary terms the cost of private credit was lower than that of (official) World Bank credit. Thanks to their low interest rates and in particular because they extended largely unconditional credit, the private Euro-banks became the Third World's major lenders. But as well as financing large-scale, often ambitious industrial projects, they financed nepotism, client-economy-style enrichment, an exodus of capital and the expansion of the military and the police, the tools of repression with which the ruling classes hoped to secure their power. Authoritarian indebtedness of this kind was to be found in many countries, including Chile and Argentina. In these countries external loans were not used to finance large-scale industrial or other projects designed to improve the productivity of the national economy. The military dictatorships used them instead to open up domestic markets to imports in order to allow the middle classes a brief, and therefore all the more passionate, frenzy of consumption. The loans raised overseas to finance such orgies of consumption, with which authoritarian regimes attempted to maintain the loyalty of their supporters, led to an exodus of capital. They are still being paid for today with even greater poverty, unemployment and destitution for the majority of the population. Much of the contemporary wealth of such nations, including Argentina, can be found in numbered Swiss bank accounts rather than between Tierra del Fuego and La Plata.

The external debts of the Third World nations rocketed during the 1970s. Whilst in 1972 external loans amounted to around US$100 billion, in the ten years 1973–82 this figure increased to just under US$800 billion. This average growth of more than 20% per annum was matched by average annual increases in the value of exports of 16% and in the Gross Domestic Product (GDP) of 12%. Although the private banks have cut back drastically on their extension of loans since the Falklands (Malvinas Islands) War, an important turning point in terms of the attitudes of the international banks, and in particular since the Mexican crisis of 1982, by 1987 the foreign debt had risen to over US$1,000 billion. The interest alone due on these loans now amounts to just under US$100 billion per annum. In 1977 the corresponding figure was US$15 billion.

The geography of debt

The scale of the debt crisis first becomes apparent, however, when distinctions are drawn between the various debtor nations and regions. The major debtor nations of the Third World are in Latin America, and as such it would hardly seem incorrect to describe the debt crisis not as a global but as a Latin American phenomenon. Yet the debt crisis is not restricted to this one continent. The countries of Eastern Europe and those of Asia and Africa also have huge foreign debts. In fact, in the 1970s the rate of increase in the foreign debt of the 44 nations of southern Africa was actually higher than that for Latin America. At the end of 1985 the low income countries (see Glossary) of this region had average debt ratios of around 400%, ranging from less than 50% (Gabon, Botswana, Lesotho) to more than 1,000% (Sudan, Mozambique, Guinea-Bissau). Many of these countries are indebted not primarily to private banks but to public institutions, yet even public loans impose a great strain on their balance of payments. Since the grant element of new loans halved from 30% to around 15% between 1975/7 and 1983, the servicing of such loans requires a constant transfer of resources. Accordingly, greater efforts have been made to increase the value of exports, but in the face of a serious worsening in the terms of trade an increase in the volume of exports does not mean an increase in foreign currency revenue. Yet the amount of money which these countries needed in order to service their debts between 1980 and 1985 amounted to almost US$50 billion. Despite the scale of this transfer of resources and capital, greater still on the part of the Latin American debtor nations, the IMF refuses to pursue a strategy of reducing a burden which is intolerable for these poor nations; in order to recover the loans extended by the international banks and thereby avert crises in the credit system, debtor nations are offered programmes which amount to no more than a continuation of the transfer. 'Latin America's open arteries', as Eduardo Galeano described the exploitation of Latin America, are not being healed by the IMF but kept open for the purpose of drawing blood.

When looking at the debtor nations of the Third World we must not, however, ignore the fact that the USA, the supreme leader of the world system, has herself now become a debtor nation of the first order. Many nations' inability to pay their debts can be traced back to the USA's attempts to crowd out her competitors from the international credit markets. Under the Reagan Administration the USA has herself become the major debtor in the world economy within the space of just a few years in the hope of eradicating the twin deficits on her current account and national budget (of around US$200 billion per annum); at the end of 1986 the western world's leading economic and political power had net debts of US$66.4 billion. This represents an increase of around US$95 billion between 1984 and 1985; in the space of one year the USA acquired a foreign debt as large as, say, Brazil had done over the previous ten years.

The resulting two-tier credit market has given the debt crisis a certain dynamism, with the 'bad' debtors of the Third World being almost completely excluded from the supply of private credit. Only if they are able to refute the suspicion that they are unable to pay their debts are new loans still extended to the Third World nations, and even then they are subject to a great many conditions. Meanwhile an absurd situation has arisen whereby the Third World nations, badly in debt and constantly on the verge of being unable to pay up, have been forced into becoming net exporters of capital and thus help to satisfy the USA's growing hunger for loans: the poor societies of the southern hemisphere are thus financing the undeservedly high level of consumption enjoyed by WASPS (white anglo-saxon protestants) and yuppies in the USA.

Recently a new form of dependence has begun emerging within the crisis-ridden capitalist world economy, characterized as it is by poor economic growth, a slow expansion in world trade and constantly worsening terms of trade for those debtor nations of the Third World which produce raw materials. This dependence can no longer be interpreted in terms of development theory, for the 'golden ties of credit' do not merely accelerate the economic exploitation of the debtor nations. They have the hidden power to draw the creditors themselves into a whirlpool of financial chaos. The dependence which the two sides in the credit–debtor relationship experience is not identical, but it does ultimately exist; as a result attempts are made to manage the debt crisis so that private banks operating internationally remain intact. This is, of course, only possible at the expense of the debtor nations. Since 1982 the private banks have aimed above all at extricating themselves from the Third World nations' debt crisis in order to strengthen their negotiating position with their debtors. Over the last few years the international banks have been very successful in spreading their losses. Should this trend continue, then it is not impossible that it might have the effect of perpetuating the Third World's new form of dependence.

The management of the debt crisis

International financial and debt crises have a long history. Charles Kindleberger has counted no less than 28 serious financial crises between the development of the capitalist world system in the 'long sixteenth century' and the mid-1970s. All of these crises were overcome — naturally, since no crisis lasts forever — with the help of military and political or economic measures. Here we must distinguish between the annulment of debts receivable by the creditor (the writing off of loans) and the annulment of debts through the suspension of interest or capital repayments by the debtor. One possible compromise between these options is that of rescheduling debts in an attempt to avoid the need for radical steps to be taken outside of the terms of the agreement between the creditor and the debtor, although the costs of rescheduling may be distributed in a highly unequal fashion. The rescheduling of debts has been a central part of crisis management since 1982. Whereas just US$5 billion worth of debts were rescheduled for nine countries in the years 1956–78, this figure rose in the four years 1978–81 to at least US$9 billion. Since the debt crisis of 1982, the value of debts rescheduled has rocketed. In 1986 the total value of medium- and long-term bank debts rescheduled amounted to US$157 billion and the value of public debts to US$33 billion. The arrangements for negotiating the rescheduling of debts have also changed (see Figure 1.2). Until the outbreak of the debt crisis, the overwhelming majority of

Figure 1.2
Restructuring table for the Third World 1980–86
(US$bn)

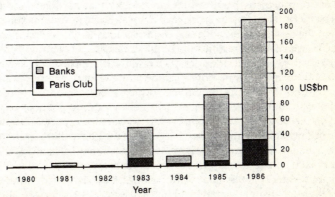

Source: World Bank

debts rescheduled were *public loans* negotiated between the various creditor and debtor governments and multilateral institutions. Loans of this type are negotiated in the Paris Club, which was established in 1956. Although not an institution officially and formally sanctioned under international law, this body has since acquired a major role in the field of international debt management because of the economic and political power concentrated within it. Like the IMF, the Paris Club has over the last few years taken increasing responsibility for setting down markers on the way in which private banks, whose claims on the debtor nations are now much greater than those of the public institutions, manage rescheduling by concluding agreements with the debtor nations on the question of public loans.

During the 1980s the inability of private creditors to impose sanctions has altered the terms under which debts are rescheduled: public and quasi-public institutions now place their capacity for political intervention at the service of those with private interests in the economic security of financial debts receivable. There are three stages to the rescheduling process:

- The debtor nations turn firstly to the IMF, which combines its quantitatively limited ability to extend loans with the imposition of economic policy conditions.
- After the debtor has signed an IMF agreement then a further meeting can be arranged with the members of the Paris Club at which interest rates, periods of grace and currency arrangements for the repayment of public loans are negotiated.
- The agreements concluded during these two rounds of negotiation then form the outline conditions to be negotiated with the private banks and bank syndicates for the rescheduling of private loans.

Without a seal of approval from the IMF and the Paris Club, private loans can only be rescheduled with difficulty, since without that approval the private banks refuse to provide fresh money (see Glossary) to a country which has got into arrears.

The entire process is based on the philosophy that each case should be treated on merit. This strategy is designed to break down the international debt crisis into the debt crises of individual countries and thereby to prevent global approaches which aim at rectification of the system as a whole from becoming viable alternative political strategies. As a result, each rescheduling agreement turns out differently. Some countries are granted particularly favourable conditions (see Chapter 16 on Mexico) whilst other debtors — those, for example, who endeavour to defend themselves against politico-economic attacks on their national sovereignty — are forced to accept rigid conditions relating, for instance, to interest surcharges over and above the market interest rate, the 'spread', the length of the period of grace, the level of charges payable. The idea that it is, in principle, possible for any debtor nation to be one of those treated preferentially in this game has for a long time contributed considerably to the failure of debtors' cartels and collective actions to develop. For the creditors, divide and rule is the key to successful crisis management.

Rescheduling is merely a deferment of outstanding debts until some future date, and even rescheduling on easy terms cannot mean anything more than a temporary reprieve for debtor nations. Those in debt are still required to transfer their resources and their wealth to the creditor nations, albeit over a longer period of time. At best rescheduling enables them to avoid acute liquidity crises. In practice, it means an extension into the future of financial and economic exploitation and dependence, as in the cases of Mexico and Brazil where repayment periods already stretch into the next millennium. This is fatal for a nation's development prospects. Contrary to the theory of the debt cycle — according to which a country gets into debt, uses its loans productively, is able to increase exports and earn foreign currency with which it can clear the debt, then perhaps even pupate into a creditor nation — rescheduling extends into the unforeseeable future the period during which a debtor is forced, prematurely, to be a net exporter of capital. When even a country like Brazil has to transfer more than 5% of her annual GDP abroad against interest payments then the investment and consumption opportunities of such a country are limited accordingly. It is useful to remember that by international agreement the developed industrialized nations are supposed to pay over a flat 0.7% of their GDPs in the form of development aid. They have not done so. Can it be that not even developed nations are in a position to transfer a twentieth of their GDPs to international banks . . . ?

Resources vital to national development are being put aside to service debts from which the private banks in the Western capitalist world are drawing the most benefit. Industry in the First World also profits from this financial despotism, since the debtor nations are forced to throw their products onto the international markets at any price, thereby accelerating the process of predatory exploitation of natural resources at home and abroad. Raw materials and industrial primary products become cheaper and contribute to an increase in the return on foreign investment. The situation is grotesque: were a country like Brazil, for example, to continue to pay off the interest due on her loans for the next five years, then her creditors would have received in their money boxes twice as much as they lent to that country in the 17 years since 1970. Even with an extra period of grace as part of a rescheduling agreement, Brazil's balance of payments would be burdened with interest payments until the end of the millennium, payments which would limit drastically her economic and social room for manoeuvre.

The next move . . . ?

In many cases the huge increase in indebtedness of the 1970s sprang from the attempts of national élites to conceal with loans from overseas banks the contradictions inherent in their development models. Since the early 1980s at least, it has been obvious that the development path taken by the overwhelming majority of these nations was the wrong one and that the consequences of the policies which they pursued are being shouldered by the broad mass of the population. During the first five years of the 1980s the per capita Gross National Product (GNP) of the Third World nations fell by an average of more than 10% (see Figure 1.3). In Latin American countries as a whole (with the exception of Cuba) per capita income fell from US$1,933 (1980) to US$1,782 (1985). Only exports increased during this period; by 1985 their volume was up by almost 20% on its 1980 level. Since the economies of the debtor nations are thus increasingly export-oriented, smaller and smaller proportions of the wealth created are left over for domestic use. It is not only the creditor nations which have profited from the huge debt. Members of the indigenous economic and political élites have stashed away around US$100 billion of flight capital in big US banks and in numbered Swiss accounts.

Figure 1.3
Fall in per capita GNP in Latin America, 1980–85

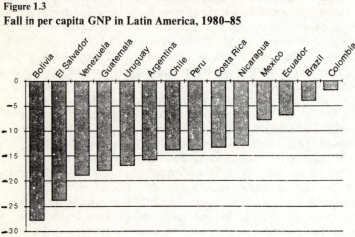

Source: *The Economist*

Of course, the debt crisis can also be seen as an opportunity for debtor nations to revise their development options and to concentrate more on adapted technology and the potential for indigenous development than on the world market. Blocking this process of reorientation are the financial obligations accruing from their loans, obligations which extend well into the twenty-first century. Thus the financial world market and those for goods limit substantially the scope for such alternatives. The selective annulment of debts, lower interest rates and longer repayment periods would allow the debtor nations more room for manoeuvre. But we must realize that national development models can only be restructured successfully if the process is not carried out by the old ruling élites. These have not only used debt as a development model, they are still profiting every time a loan is restructured.

The debt crisis is the result of the superimposition of at least three processes: the crisis which has grown up around national development models; the crisis in the capitalist world economy; and the USA's supremacy crisis. Somewhere in this maze of distortions of varying dimensions is a path which offers a way out. For the moment, however, there is as little sign of the grand design so essential to a reordering of the world economy as of a broad political movement capable of countering the internationalization of capital with an internationalization of opposition and resistance. Participants are still haggling over a multitude of technical solutions aimed at restoring the debtor nations' ability to pay their debts. This step is vital, but not adequate. As Fidel Castro maintains:

Though it would undoubtedly ease the situation for many nations, a solution to the problem of the Third World's external debt would still not by any means be a solution to all development problems. Unless we can conquer once and for all the factors which together add up to an unjust system of economic relations and exploitation — unequal exchange, protectionist measures, dumping, a monetary policy based on the economic power of a few nations, excessive loan interest — that is to say, unless a new world economic order is actually established, then after a few years the situation would be just as bad as, if not worse than, it is now.

2. The Management of International Monetary and Financial Relations During the Crisis

Manfred Nitsch

An outline of the Bretton Woods system

When in July 1944 representatives of 44 countries, including the Soviet Union (although the USSR later failed to join the system), met at the United Nations Monetary and Financial Conference in the small American seaside resort of Bretton Woods, New Hampshire, the world economy was an economy at war with the USA, by far the world's strongest economic power. The USA realized that her interests would be well served if she could take advantage of the general acceptance of the principle of free trade to gain access both to the colonial territories and other spheres of influence and to the domestic markets of the European nations, which had been weakened by World War II. Negotiations to establish a liberal international commercial order took place separately and later resulted in the creation of the General Agreement on Tariffs and Trade (GATT) with its headquarters in Geneva, but at Bretton Woods the USA was concerned to institutionalize the dollar's high standing through the establishment of a monetary and financial order geared to that currency.

The international trade in capital and goods required a world currency or a world monetary order which could guarantee the exchangeability (convertibility) of one national currency into another, so that one nation's surplus trade with a second nation could be used to finance its deficit with a third, thereby enabling the first nation to take full advantage of the international division of labour.

The creators of the Bretton Woods system did not, however, have their sights set exclusively on this one objective, but also on safeguarding full employment through national economic policy measures. Moreover, they regarded the exertion of control over the movement of capital as being totally compatible with the new system — it was not their intention to return to a system as automatic in its operation as the gold standard, a system under which domestic economic policy was submitted to the dictates of foreign trade. On the other hand, they were haunted by the experiences of the 1930s, when the USA had attempted to export unemployment through a programme of competitive devaluation designed to boost exports (a beggar-your-neighbour policy).

The international monetary order drawn up at Bretton Woods — with the USA, the great, supreme economic power, in the background and the IMF, the international organization founded there, in the forefront — was thus intended to guarantee both a multilateral free-trade system with fixed rates of exchange and a high degree of national autonomy as regards economic policy during the post-war period. The role of the IMF was to be to alleviate temporary liquidity squeezes by means of short-term emergency loans and to eliminate structural imbalances through devaluations and revaluations in consultation with the parties concerned. It later emerged, of course, that it was not the dreaded competitive devaluations designed to safeguard full employment which placed the system in jeopardy but rather, at least according to the IMF, the tardy response of countries with balance of payments problems to the pressure to devalue. The governments in such countries preferred to owe money abroad (an option which often enabled them to find short-term solutions to their budget problems) than to restore equilibrium to their balance of payments by using devaluations to raise the price of their imports and boost their exports. John Maynard Keynes, the leader of the British delegation, was unable to win support for his suggestion that surplus countries should bear some responsibility to rectify the situation. As a result, creditor nations were able to accumulate surpluses with impunity, and right at the outset the system acquired a certain degree of bias in favour of the creditors.

Whereas the international monetary system established at Bretton Woods was designed to provide a minimum amount of convertible funds with which to oil the wheels of international trade in the post-war period, the World Bank (or International Bank for Reconstruction and Development (IBRD)), which was also established at Bretton Woods, was set the task of getting international trade moving again through the deployment of longer-term capital. With Europe embarking upon a programme of reconstruction, it was believed that what little capital was available, almost exclusively from the USA, would be in great demand and that interest rates would be extremely high. But since high rates of interest are particularly damaging to investment, that is to reconstruction and development, the World Bank, as an intergovernmental institution with extensive capital funds of its own, would be able to offer extremely secure investments and remain attractive despite its interest rates being low. As far as the extension of credit was concerned, it was hoped that the Bank would learn from others' bad experiences with the extension of purely financial loans and would make funds available exclusively for practical projects which could bring in foreign exchange (import substitution, the promotion of exports or suitable infrastructure). Although later these commercial principles were modified, they were certainly not abandoned.

In the years which followed, the dollar standard proved strong enough and flexible enough to cope with the unprecedented and unexpectedly dynamic expansion in the international traffic in goods and capital and the drive for growth of the 1950s and 1960s. The objective of the Bretton Woods system — to lay the international foundations for the revitalization of international trade and the movement of capital, both predominantly private-sector affairs — was therefore largely achieved.

The management of the system during the 1950s and 1960s

The management of the system required the establishment of certain rules and modes of behaviour. Although Britain and France never totally left the stage, it became accepted, for example, that the dollar was the undisputed number-one currency in international finance and that the US Central Bank, the Federal Reserve System (Fed.) would be the ultimate economic refuge in the event of crisis (lender of last resort). In addition, the economic and political importance of West Germany and Japan increased rapidly during the post-war period, although we should not overlook the smaller countries such as the Netherlands, Belgium, Italy, Sweden, Canada and, last but not least, Switzerland (which, although not a full member of either the United Nations or the IMF and World Bank, has always played an important role as an observer).

Until the beginning of the 1970s the management of the monetary system was primarily a question of discussion and negotiations between governments and international organizations. The private commercial banks were, at that time, of secondary importance. In the 1960s, however, the resources necessary to counterbalance and control speculative movements and to compensate for temporary imbalances in the balance of payments increased to such an extent that the aforementioned countries founded the Group of Ten (G-10) under a special financial agreement known as the General Agreement to Borrow (GAB). At the same time, the dominant positions occupied by the USA and the dollar were weakened by the creation in 1968 of SDRs, the unit of account of the IMF, whose value was tied to that of a basket of several currencies. In addition to normal IMF funds, members of G-10 were able, if necessary, to fall back at short notice on financial resources of up to US$6 billion, which were placed at the disposal of the IMF by other members of the group. Later, in 1983, the Swiss and Saudis joined the group. The amount available was increased to around US$19 billion and the members agreed that loans might also be extended to non-members. G-10 was thus transformed from a private club providing mutual support for its members into a fund within the Fund.

Although the idea for the formation of G-10 originated with staff-members of the IMF, many of the group's major administrative functions were carried out not by the Fund but by its old rival, the Bank for International Settlements (BIS) in Basle, which had been threatened for a time with dissolution and had now passed into obscurity. This institution had been founded in 1930 for the purpose of handling Germany's reparation payments and had, since it was more or less regarded as an international branch of the European Central Bank and the Fed., survived the war as one of the few international organizations in which the Germans and the Allies co-operated right until the end. Many, including the Bretton Woods Conference, felt that it should be dissolved for its collaboration with the Germans. The dissolution was delayed, however, not least because of the legal difficulties which surrounded the question of the succession of the National Bank of the (German) Reich. When the first steps were taken towards the multilateralization of trade within Europe and, after 1950, of money transfers in Europe (through the European Payments Union) under the auspices of the Marshall Plan and the newly established Organization for European Economic Co-operation (OEEC, later, on the inclusion of the other Western industrialized nations, the OECD) the BIS was reactivated. Today it performs an important function as the borrower's bank of the central banks of Europe (with the exception of the USSR, the German Democratic Republic (GDR) and Albania), the USA, Canada, Japan, Australia and South Africa. It also exerts an influence on international finance and its management by dint of its role as a forum for discussion, an information centre, a research centre, and as the secretariat of a multitude of international commissions and groups.

To understand the dynamics and course of the present international debt crisis it is vital to bear in mind the role of Official Development Assistance (ODA) alongside: the currency implications of the debtor nations' inability to pay and of short-term liquidity; the banks' commercial private-sector financial loans; and the loans extended cheaply, although virtually without a grant element, by the World Bank and the regional development banks. In statements issued by the United Nations (UN) on the subject of the development decades since 1961, the organization accepts a figure of 0.7% of the industrialized nations' GDPs as a target net transfer (that is, after deducting repayments) in the form of foreign aid, although the majority of the Western governments have set no date for reaching the target and the governments of Eastern Europe have limited the exercise to the West.

ODA ranges from straight grants in the form of soft loans to loans extended under quasi-commercial terms, and from export credit guarantees, investment incentives and mixed financing (commercial and ODA loans for the same project) to hard bank loans and direct investment.

The structure of debt varies enormously from country to country, but it is nevertheless important for the management of the debt problem not only that each nation should have a general, but not rigid range of debts, but also that there should be a general, but not rigid range between countries. Furthermore, the ongoing target net transfer of 0.7% was envisaged in principle and by common consent as a form of international financial adjustment between North and South, a financial payment requiring no *quid pro quo*. On the one hand, then, the developing nations, and in particular the poorer among them, plead their moral right to ODA. On the other, the international business world would be faced with total decline if it were proposed that the target 0.7% should be used subsequently to convert loans into transfers. Transitional forms such as interest equalization funds, which, if funded through ODA, would ease the commercial burden of interest, have long been propagated and from time to time even used.

Privatization and the renunciation of reform

The 1970s was a decade of unchecked expansion for the international private financial markets and banks (see Part Two). The cautious minimum strategy, adopted by the World Bank in the first few years of the decade, of using foreign capital almost exclusively to finance projects designed to bring in foreign exchange was supplemented and, in terms of its effect on indebtedness, undermined through competition with other donors — not only by soft but generally wholly repayable ODA, but also by hard financial loans from the commercial banks, which cared little about whether the projects they financed brought in foreign exchange.

In general, the hope was cherished, not only in political but in academic circles, that the Petrodollar and other funds which were available on easy terms would enable the newly industrialized countries (NICs) to make a breakthrough in the area of investment which would enable them to become industrial societies of the same calibre as those in the West. The commercial banks were universally praised for their successful recycling.

The hope was dashed by a number of factors: the economic downswing in the industrialized nations: increasing protectionism: the fall in raw-materials prices, disappointment with what was, in the final analysis, only a modest success of the NICs, at least in comparison with that of the industrialized nations, in raising the standard of living of broad sections of the population (if indeed any such rise occurred); and the financial crisis caused by Mexico in the autumn of 1982. There followed a hectic period of crisis management during which each of the participants, either alone or in co-ordination with others in a similar position, attempted to muddle through. The most recent grand design, the great Bretton Woods plan, was dismantled piece by piece without any replacement being found. The proposals put forward by the Brandt Commission in 1980 and 1982 were an attempt at reaching a compromise between the developing nations' demands for a New International Economic Order (NIEO) which actually differed from the old one in several important respects, on the one hand, and representations from those who were intent on free trade and a minimum of international control (*dirigisme*), on the other; the proposals were, however, barely even noted.

Purposeful, popular, negotiated and openly debated reforms were rejected by the majority of the ruling élites, with the result that changes occurred piecemeal. The magic word was adjustment, although the enormous fluctuations in the prices of raw materials and energy, real interest rates and exchange rates, economic expectations, conditions governing access to the world market and the armed conflicts and natural disasters which took place between 1970 and 1986 have made it clear that the world market in no way provides a continuous and reliable yardstick to which it would be worth adjusting.

The ups and downs of the creditors' currencies and their effects on the Third World

The (much-invoked) 'end of Bretton Woods' arrived in 1971, when the USA denounced the gold standard, that is the USA was no longer willing for even central banks to hand over an ounce of gold for US$35 and, thereby, *de facto* to devalue the dollar. The reasons behind this move were the USA's loss of economic importance world-wide, the Vietnam War and all that went with it (in particular inflationary trends and a loss of credibility) and later the Watergate scandal. The universal introduction in 1973 of flexible exchange rates (as opposed to the Bretton Woods' system of fixed exchange rates under which adjustment took place only in the event of serious imbalances) was extolled as an opportunity to free domestic economic policy once again from the restraints imposed upon it by foreign trade and speculation. Instead, these restraints were augmented, since the extension of international liquidity led to exchange rates becoming subject to a greater extent than had previously been the case to the ups and downs (the 'paternoster lift') of speculation; with the partly forced, partly voluntary retirement of the dollar as the world's key currency exchange rates became dependent on the daily changing expectations of those who controlled wealth, on whether the Swiss franc or the Australian dollar, the pound sterling or the deutschmark rose or fell. The table of wealth ownership was rearranged accordingly. Instead of oiling the wheels of trade, currencies became bodies of water which stirred according to the laws governing the markets for enduring commodities, such as those for gold and realty, and in whose tides manufacturing and trading interests threatened to drown.

The West Europeans managed to a certain extent to escape the effects of these disastrous fluctuations by joining forces to create the European Monetary System (EMS) around the deutschmark. Under this system currencies were only to be revalued, upwards or downwards, in the event of serious imbalances, as had been the case world-wide under the Bretton Woods system. Like the Japanese, the West Europeans were also able to hold their own against the USA in sectors particularly threatened by protectionism. The world economic summits which have taken place annually since 1975 and which are attended by the Group of Seven (G-7) — the USA, Britain, France, West Germany, Japan, Canada and Italy, as well as representatives of the European Commission (as observers) — are drawn regularly to a close amid solemn declarations of loyalty by those present to free trade between them. The weaker countries, on the other hand, are engulfed in the ebb and flow of the parity between currencies and the protectionism of G-7.

To prevent cumulative fluctuations from getting completely out of control, the finance ministers and heads of the central banks of the Group of Five (G-5) — G-7 minus Canada and Italy — finally began to meet regularly in the 1980s. Initially the meetings were confidential and no communiqués were issued. Later, public statements were issued and, eventually, after the signing of the agreements known as the Plaza Agreement, named after the New York hotel in which the meeting was held and concluded when the dollar was at its 1985 high, and the Louvre Accord of 1987, concluded when the dollar was at a low, G-5 even began to send off rather outspoken public signals in the direction of the foreign-exchange markets.

Thus the dollar's loss of its role as the world's key currency did not result, for example, in more democratic monetary relations world-wide. The broad convertibility between currencies which were, in principle, equal led instead to speculative regrouping and to a race for stability between the creditor nations.

As far as the international system was concerned, however, this race forced the mighty nations of the world, if they were to avoid the total destruction which the tides can wreak, into a programme of co-operation which boiled down to an intensification of world-wide hierarchization, and led in particular to decisions being taken outside the bodies and organizations responsible under international law.

The BIS and the Fed. — the firefighters of 1982

Just as the world's leading economic nations turned to meetings between politicians as a method of crisis management in the field of monetary policy, the focus shifted to the central banks when it came to dealing with acute debt crises. The Mexican crisis in 1982 clearly illustrated that the IMF was no longer capable of making available large sums — and when banks are threatened with collapse the sums concerned are large — at short notice, since its resources did not run to anything like the private and commercial volumes in question.

When the Mexican crisis erupted it was the Fed. (as the USA's central bank) and the BIS (as the bank and co-ordinating institution above all of the European central banks) which were able to act instantaneously with the IMF to avert the threat of banks collapsing. During the management of the crisis it became clear that the hierarchically graduated funds which backed G-10, G-7, G-5 and, finally, the Fed. and BIS were lodged with the central banks to which these bodies are attached.

The Mexican crisis also revealed a definite weakness in the new methods since, although the central banks and BIS were the natural managers of the crisis, it was only a few weeks before 'the fire brigade rolled up its hoses', as Leutwiler, the then president of BIS, put it, and the bankers, who saw themselves more as engineers than politicians, left the field to those who bore the political responsibility. Since the worst of the crisis was over, however, the latter drew a deep breath and restricted themselves to encouraging the banks to provide further additional payments (fresh money), as suggested in the Baker Plan of 1985. Where necessary, they also helped the banks to gain time by adjusting the value of (writing-down) their outstanding debts, a process which reduced taxable income but meant no remission for the debtor.

Passing the buck between Paris, New York, and Washington

Since the late 1950s it has become usual when a debtor nation is having acute difficulty paying its debts for an informal body made up of government representatives to be convened in Paris to negotiate with the debtor government. This body is known as the Paris Club. The departmental head who bears responsibility within the French Ministry of Finance for the Club convenes the meetings at the request of the debtor nation, and also chairs it. Representatives of the IMF and the World Bank attend as permanent observers, although the unanimous decision of the 1976 UN Conference on Trade and Development (UNCTAD), that it would also invite a representative of the UNCTAD secretariat to the meetings of the Paris Club, is not always upheld.

Negotiations conducted within the Paris Club are invariably concerned first and foremost with extending repayment periods (since 1987 to a maximum of 20 years; the previous maximum was 10 years), partial remissions, interest rates, export guarantees and credits, and new ODA-credits within the scope of Financial Co-operation. There are other groups of creditors, representing other countries, which traditionally meet in Paris and which have a similar function: the 'aid consortia' which have been founded since the 1960s under the auspices of the OECD and the chairmanship of the World Bank for the benefit of the nations on which international development aid is concentrated (for example, India, Turkey and Pakistan). The representatives of governments which belong to these groups also fix public loans.

On the other side of the Atlantic, mainly in New York, the commercial banks, under the chairmanship of one of the largest international commercial banks, the First National City Bank of New York (Citibank or Citicorp after its parent company) form a 'steering committee' for the debtor nation concerned. The committee then maintains contact with the IMF, the World Bank and the Paris Club, and also negotiates directly with the government of the debtor nation.

As a rule the banks are rather flexible in their dealings as long as the debts continue to be acknowledged and while it is still possible to avert a crash. In 1984 they reached an agreement with Mexico (and later with other countries) whereby the previously standard one-year time limit for rescheduling was extended by six months under a multi-year rescheduling agreement (MYRA), and in 1987 they agreed to link repayments to changes in the price of oil. Once again, Mexico was the first to benefit. Nor do the banks reject outright suggestions that repayments should be tied to export income (as proposed and implemented, at least for a while, by Peru) or to increases in the GNP (as put forward by Brazil). They are concerned to play for time in order to adjust the value of their debts.

From the point of view of the debtor, adjustments of value of this kind would, of course, only become significant when the losses were actually realized, hence the acceptance of a proposal put forward in the US Congress in 1986 that institutions supported by the World Bank should purchase such written-down debts at a discount which would be effective for the debtor and that international judges or an international court of arbitration should be able to reduce the debt, as judges are able to do under domestic law in the event of bankruptcy, settlement or the presentation of an insolvent debtor's oath.

The banks' steering committees' ability to act relies, however, on their being able to effect agreement between as many as 400 rival institutions; these days the big banks often feel almost compelled to purchase doubtful debts at a discount from smaller banks which wish to opt out. The big banks are nevertheless reluctant to do this, since they are rightly of the opinion that the pressure on politicians to come up with wholesale solutions will diminish if the big banks, which can most easily be expected to bear losses, are the only ones left.

The attitudes amongst the big banks are determined by competition: it is less a question of which will crash, though even that cannot be ruled out, than of the taking-over of the weaker institutions by the stronger ones.

On the whole, there is intense uncertainty in the credit world among sovereign debtor nations, for although the foundations of the credit system have been supported under international and national law since Bretton Woods, it is only since the 1970s that it has become clear that the 'roof', that is the question of setting an upper limit on the creation of credit, also needs looking at. As at least some of the debtors have since found themselves unable to pay amounts which they owe, the construction of a roof also means reaching agreement over how losses are to be distributed. This is an unpleasant task, and it is therefore not surprising that the buck is constantly passed between governments, the central banks, the commercial banks and the international organizations.

The IMF does not regard itself as the senior in charge of the process, much less as responsible for defining and, if necessary, reforming the rules of the game. Even if it were to join forces with the World Bank, say through the two institutions' joint Development Committee, the resources which it would have at its disposal would still be far from sufficient to enable it to restructure debts itself. It is understandable, therefore, that it should style itself the defender of the broad interests of the creditors, for in this way it can avoid losing the initiative completely to the 'clubs' and 'groups' which support it and work at its side. On the other hand, in order to avoid criticism from the debtors — the developing nations control at least a third or so of the votes on the board of governors — the staff of the IMF, including the managing director, pass themselves off pointedly as technical personnel. These famous faceless men preserve rites of service to a higher cause which are positively reminiscent of religious orders. Unlike in the World Bank, the head of the IMF is known not as the president but as the managing director and is generally recruited not from among prominent politicians or bankers but from within the administration. Since 1974 the committee of 22-member countries which determines IMF policy has been known as the Interim Committee, although it has long ceased to be provisional since the council which it is supposed to serve has never met. It is, moreover, significant that the Interim Committee has no formal jurisdiction whatsoever, its role being purely advisory, with the result that even within the IMF the staff, the board (which, although the senior committee, rarely meets) and the Interim Committee are each able to hide behind the other or behind the 'limitations of the situation'.

The creditors who play this game of hide-and-seek run back and forth between Washington, Paris, New York, Basle and the capital cities of the world acting out what are often schizoid roles. Chronologically, crises tend to conform to the following pattern: as soon as the government of a debtor nation recognizes that within a few months it will be unable to meet the obligations which it has assumed it first gets its iron rations (its currency reserves) to safety, perhaps with an internationally operating Eastern Bloc bank; it then signals to its creditors (banks, governments and international organizations) that it is suspending payments. In return for a promise that it will reach a speedy agreement with the IMF (or, if the debtor government has expressed strong opposition to the IMF at home, with the World Bank), bridging loans are made available to the country by the central banks of the First World, either directly or through the BIS which can use its own funds instead. The central banks each make internal provisions against a crash. In addition, those countries which are involved in continuing negotiations, the success of which may be threatened by the new crisis, are immediately given support (verbal and/or through loans).

Parallel negotiations begin next: between the government and the IMF on the subject of economic-policy measures and quantitative targets, and between the government and the banks' steering committee on the subject of rescheduling. Since each is dependent on the other, the order in which the negotiations are formally concluded is not particularly important. Only when this process has been completed does the Paris Club generally meet; with the rescheduling agreement and the fresh money supplied by banks and governments in the bag, the firefighters can then be paid and word sent out that the crisis has been settled.

On closer inspection the crisis might, however, be more accurately described as deferred than settled, since the volume of debt carried over has not been reduced but, instead, augmented by compound interest.

The role of the debtor nations in the management of the crisis

It is clear from the Brazilian experience early in 1987 just what all this shunting of responsibility between the creditors means for the debtor. During the crisis Finance Minister Funaro travelled to New York, Washington, London, Bonn, Bern and Tokyo, and in each of these capitals the governments referred him to the private banks, the private banks referred him to the governments and both referred him to the IMF, which was also unable to help him with the large sums which he needed. What is more, back in Brazil the IMF was notorious for its policy of setting unreasonable conditions, and the government risked losing its domestic support if it invited the IMF into the country and accepted its terms. Shortly after his return, Funaro was forced to resign and the game began all over again for his successor.

When Western politicians got up onto their soap-boxes to warn that Brazil's new democracy should not be placed in jeopardy, their warnings went unheard as a result of a lack of jurisdiction and an ideological bias in favour of the 'limitations of the situation' in which the IMF found itself. Brazil, as the most heavily indebted Third World nation and as a large country, should have been able to count, more than any other, on receiving some attention.

By dint of the way in which the world's monetary and financial systems are presently structured, the smaller debtors are in a still more hopeless situation. There are no magistrates to commence bankruptcy or settlement proceedings, to get all of the creditors around one table and, in hopeless situations, to restore the credit-worthiness of the debtor — after the debts are discharged and an insolvent debtor's oath has been presented — by turning a new page for him and letting him start again.

The debtor is encouraged instead to convert loans into shares by means of debt-equity-swaps, whereby multinational concerns buy up a bank's debts receivable from a country at a discount and obtain domestic funds from the central bank of the debtor nation against the certificates of indebtedness acquired in this way. They are then able to invest or to buy up indigenous firms. Since in the long term direct investment has, like external loans, to be serviced with foreign exchange, such swaps do not represent any material economic change. In political terms, they are instead the stuff of conflict since they result in the domestic economy being sold off.

Another, more dangerous aspect of the current management (or non-management) of the crisis is that it has become rational from the point of view of the debtor nations for them to appear totally unable to pay their debts in order to get themselves released from debts which they would ultimately be unable to pay and with which previous governments have saddled the country. On the occasion of the first joint annual meeting of the IMF and the World Bank ever to be held on German soil (1988), those attending were reminded of an episode from German history — the savings policy pursued after 1931 by the 'hunger chancellor', Brüning. One of the objectives, if not the major objective, of this policy was to reduce through negotiation the amount of reparations owed by the German Reich. When Germany's intransigent creditors finally agreed to this, Brüning had already been ousted, and Hitler was on the path to power.

The political lessons learned from this episode are exactly what one might have expected: Hitler's campaign against the 'plutocrats' and against 'interest serfdom' earned him a great deal of support, and who knows whether a political merry-go-round *à la* Latin America might not have been set in motion in Germany if Adenauer's Government had not finally been released in 1951/2 from a large part of the country's old debt.

The debtor nations, then, have for a long time been calling for hard-and-fast rules and permanent bodies with responsibility for dealing with questions of indebtedness. We do not yet know what the actual effects of a long-term suspension of payments might be, since there is no case to which we can refer back. When the Bretton Woods Conference took place, problems of overindebtedness and default of payment were still being solved militarily. But what it actually means today for a country like Peru to be placed on the IMF's black-list as being no longer entitled to ('ineligible for') further loans no one knows. In such cases the only proposals on the table are those, and there are many, which serve the interests of the creditors.

The Group of 77 (G-77), which came together on the eve of the first

UNCTAD session in 1964 and now boasts over 100 members, has long been demanding general guidelines for dealing with debt crises. At the fourth UNCTAD meeting in Nairobi in 1976 it succeeded, in the course of an aggressive debate on the NIEO, in introducing a demand for general features in a resolution which was carried overwhelmingly. But in the face of opposition from the creditors, neither the UNCTAD staff, the UNCTAD secretariat, G-77 nor the non-aligned members succeeded in winning support for their demands for the institutionalization of the process and for all aspects, including those of development and protectionism, to be taken into account in the actual handling of debt crises. At most, the creditors condescended to make a verbal admission of joint responsibility and to recognize the 'principle of uniformity of treatment' for all debtors. But in general there was opposition to demands for new rules, to an International Conference on Money and Finance for Development under the auspices of the UN to elaborate and determine those rules, and to the merit rule being adopted by existing institutions. The Paris Club, however, acting on behalf of the creditors, did guarantee equal treatment for all countries.

The Group of 24 (G-24) is made up of eight representatives each from Asia, Africa and Latin America. The group came together in the early 1970s within the G-77 to prepare for the IMF and World Bank annual meeting and has since come up with proposals for the IMF every year. It is the only one of the groups to have earned a certain degree of *succès d'estime* and which is at least able to obtain a hearing.

The eleven members of the Cartagena Group of Latin American debtor nations, which has been meeting for informal discussions since 1985, were apparently so sensitive to pressure, at least until the spring of 1987, that they gave a public assurance to the whole world that they had no intention whatsoever of forming a debtors' cartel; every case was to be treated quite individually.

No one should close his eyes to the fact that both the entire system upon which international monetary and financial relations are currently based and the form of crisis management put to the test during the Mexican crisis function wholly in the interests of leading groups in the industrialized countries and that the status quo is not unattractive to politicians. A permanent Brüning Policy is easily misinterpreted as falling in with a reduction in the room for manoeuvre. It could perhaps even be associated with being sparing of resources and ultimately even with cutting the excessively high rates of population growth. The merry-go-round which this sets in motion on the domestic political front — whereby military *coup* takes over from capitalist democracy, is replaced by right- or left-wing nationalist authoritarianism, which in turn is replaced by right-wing military dictatorship as the caretaker regime before the capitalist democracy, and so on — is chalked up as a 'mentality' or 'not yet ready for democracy and human rights'. There are grounds for reforming the international monetary and financial order in a way which would also serve the well-understood interests of the creditors. But there are grounds too for the view that allowing things to develop in that way could cause a great deal of trouble. Both lines accept that things may simply remain as they are. There is no cause for optimism.

3. The Changing Roles of the IMF and the World Bank

Tatjana Chahoud

The collapse of the Bretton Woods system in 1973 marked a turning-point in the development of the post-war world economy and led to a change in the roles of the two Bretton Woods institutions: the IMF and the World Bank. Whereas before 1973 the IMF had been responsible primarily for overseeing the system's fixed exchange rates (a regulatory function) and providing credit for the settlement of short-term imbalances in the balance of payments (a financing function), after 1973 its duties were limited solely to the financing function. For a while this transformation of the IMF, from a quasi-world central bank into a multilateral credit institution at the same time as private flows of finance were assuming greater importance, threatened to consign the IMF to insignificance.

The IMF and financing the deficit in the 1970s

The turbulence in the world economy during the 1970s, both the first and second crude oil crises and the world economic crisis of 1974–5, had torn big holes in the balance of trade in most of the Third World nations and had increased demand for external financing funds. The existence of readily available Eurodollar loans, the cost of which was lower even than that of World Bank loans, meant generally that it was only those countries which had no private financial options which trod the path to the IMF. According to OECD statistics, the net inflow to private commercial banks had trebled between 1970 and 1980: in 1970 the net transfer was US$7.73 billion, but by 1980 this flow of capital had risen to US$22 billion. Nevertheless, these commercial loans were concentrated on only a very few countries: of the total volume of such loans extended in 1980 US$16 billion was allotted to nine NICs, of which Brazil and Mexico alone received around US$9 billion. Another US$5 billion flowed to middle income countries while the low income countries received only US$0.6 billion in commercial bank loans.

If one looks at the regional distribution of IMF loans during the 1970s, the Latin American states clearly head the table until the middle of 1976. In 1981, however, Latin America's share of IMF drawings was lower than that of any other region (at 560.8 million SDRs), way behind Africa (1,875.9 million SDRs) and Asia (3,299.4 million SDRs). What this reflects is that Latin

America, like the Asian NICs, was largely able to finance its balance of payments deficits without IMF intervention. The IMF's original importance as a body which provided countries experiencing balance of payments difficulties with the necessary seal of approval through emergency loans and rigid austerity programmes, and which thus acted as a catalyst for private and public lenders to help, had been weakened.

The way in which the financial institutions registered the development of *laissez-faire* in the international financial markets was ambivalent. On the one hand it was extolled as a splendid success when it came to recycling Petro- and Metrodollars; on the other it was accompanied by a feeling of positive uneasiness. The OECD's 1979 report, for example, states that:

> The fact that some developing nations have attempted to avoid the onerous terms imposed by the IMF, particularly in the higher-credit tranches, by resorting in the first instance to loans from private commercial banks, has resulted in the emergence of a vicious circle. The high liquidity of the commercial banks has thus led to a weakening of the IMF's role, and a considerable part of its resources remain unused.

Moreover, Eurodollar loans on favourable terms had not only undermined the importance of the IMF but had also brought a worsening of the climate for investment by foreign concerns in Third World countries, since the governments in these countries were now making efforts to promote indigenous concerns and manufacturing sectors and were thus able to raise external loans on favourable terms.

Meanwhile, the IMF had taken on the role of lender of first resort in the less-developed Third World countries. In an attempt to cushion the effects of the crises of the 1970s and as an inducement to the developing nations to make early approaches to the IMF, new credit facilities were introduced and access liberalized. The new facilities included:

- a 50% increase in quotas
- the creation of the so-called Oil Facility (subject to a time stipulation)
- the introduction, agreed in 1974, of extended access (through the Extended Fund Facility, or EFF), with the help of which adjustment programmes were spread over a three-year period instead of the usual one-year programme and
- the so-called Additional Financing Facility (1978–82) for countries with particular structural adjustment problems.

The revision of the IMF's credit guidelines in 1979, to ensure that the social and political priorities of the member countries would be taken into account when drafting the stand-by credit arrangement, was regarded as a particular novelty.

Case studies reveal, however, that often these liberalizations were less than satisfactorily realized. For all that, the industrialized nations had a vital interest in individual elements of the measures: their own trading and financial interests appeared to be more seriously threatened by the lack of the IMF's anticyclical intervention than by the predicted slump in international demand.

The IMF's comeback in the 1980s

Against the background of rather poor economic growth in the industrialized world during the second half of the 1970s, but more importantly also as a consequence of the USA's strivings to restore its own shattered political and economic supremacy through monetarist measures, the world began in 1979 to experience the effects of a fundamental change in economic policy: Keynesian *dirigisme* was abandoned and monetarist economic policies, in the guise of supply-side economics, became the order of the day. This change in US economic policy extended to the Federal Reserve Board's high interest-rates policy and triggered the deepest recession which the world economy had seen for 50 years. The 'growth-cum-debt-strategy' favoured by the IMF and the World Bank began subsequently to falter, and in the summer of 1982 it plunged the majority of the Third World nations, starting with Mexico, into a severe debt crisis.

The restructuring and rescue operations which had now become so urgent made both the commercial banks and public creditors dependent on the conclusion of a stabilization agreement between the IMF and the various national governments. The first to be affected by IMF intervention were the NICs of Latin America. Between the middle of 1982 and the end of 1984, 66 Third World nations (more than half of the IMF's Third World member countries) were forced to yield to rigid austerity programmes. At the same time, the proportion of IMF drawings which carried strict conditionality soared: whereas in 1969 the proportion had been only 50%, by 1984 it had reached almost 90%. At the beginning of 1984 the IMF's director, de Larosière, stated with obvious satisfaction that, '(The) adjustment measures are now really universal . . . Never before have such extensive and yet parallel attempts at adjustment been made.' As far as international private flows of finance were concerned, *laissez-faire* had reached its limits with the liquidity crisis of many of the debtor nations. As the world's financial policeman, the IMF emerged as a crisis manager of the first order, and one which did not shy away from far-reaching intervention in the national political sovereignty of the debtor nations.

The IMF and the covering of risks for private commercial banks

After 1982 a spate of refinancing negotiations took place, during the course of which the IMF acquired not only power and influence over the reconstruction of Third World economies but also an important role in covering the private commercial banks' credit risks. The banks' previous attempts at imposing a certain degree of conditionality upon debtor nations during crisis situations, or at negotiating restructuring procedures with the various governments without IMF intervention, had proved unsuccessful. The Peruvian experience of 1978, for example, had been classified by the commercial banks as an outright failure, and restructuring negotiations conducted with Poland (not yet then a member of the IMF) had likewise pointed up the difficulty of managing a crisis without IMF participation.

In the eyes of the commercial banks, the IMF's role as a force for stability and neutralization (as a lender of last resort) was growing in importance. Emergency loans, with compulsory adjustment programmes attached, reduced the organization's chances of having to acknowledge *de jure* a country's *de facto* inability to pay its debts and so was the only feasible means of ensuring the (re)payment of loan capital and interest.

However, IMF support for the commercial banks had its price. Contrary to previous practice, in 1982 the IMF declared that its loans and stabilization programmes would henceforth be linked to the willingness of the commercial banks involved to make available fresh money themselves. This move, which was supported not only by the major central banks but also by the BIS and the OECD governments, marked the beginning of political intervention in the free banking market. The banks now faced a new and unfamiliar situation — the obligation to provide 'involuntary credit'. Whereas the big US banks *de facto* had no option, the small and medium-sized banks in particular appeared rather unwilling to mobilize fresh money again. In order to make the involuntary extension of credit easier for the banks and to ward off the threat posed by the ongoing practice of cutting and running (curtailments and delays) the IMF backed high-risk premiums for unsecured and new loans. In some cases the spread was huge, and as a result interest charges rose steeply for the debtor nations. The rise in bank profits was a mirror image: the newly fixed spread over and above the London Inter-Bank Offer Rate (LIBOR) earned the banks involved in the Mexican crisis, for example, additional profits of US$500 million, and the banks engaged in business with Brazil were even able to collect additional profits of US$1 billion.

Despite this lucrative incentive, the IMF and the Bank Advisory Committee found mobilizing new bank loans time-consuming and the loans often insufficient. The smaller banks with relatively little committed in the way of loans were particularly stubborn. 'Free-riding', a phenomenon largely unknown in the international banking system before the debt crisis, caused the failure of the first Brazilian restructuring, and the third rescue operation for Mexico in March 1987 likewise revealed that neither the IMF nor the banks' steering committee were yet in the position of being able to solve the problem. In addition to a lack of trust on the part of the lenders (the number of banks involved in Mexico fell from 1,400 to 526, and the number of financial institutions involved in the most recent rescue operation fell still further to 360), the banks' reticence was based also on the calculation that they could obtain higher rates of interest on new loans, for which demand was increasing all the time.

Moreover, as a result of joint pressure from the IMF and the commercial banks, new procedures were laid down for negotiating restructuring. These included an *ex post* guarantee of surety from the government in question in respect of individual debtor concerns in both the public and the private sectors. As had previously been seen in Indonesia, the assumption of public guarantees for individual concerns (here private concerns) proved extremely difficult in some countries, including Mexico. As a rule, however, Third World governments had to yield and guarantee the debt service of private concerns. There is no doubt that this move was a clear case of passing the risks relating to the Western banks' irrecoverable debts on to the populations of the Third World.

It was not only these massive attempts at extortion on the part of the IMF and the banks which were explosive politically. So too was their deliberate interference in the structure of relations between the public and the private sectors. Contrary to the prevailing IMF philosophy of swearing by the magic of the market, the covering by governments of the risks of private commercial banks (bail out) became the top priority. For the banks, bailing out did not, however, rely totally upon close co-operation with the IMF. Both the OECD governments and the BIS also made available short-term interim loans, and in this way it was possible to avert threatened suspensions of interest payments until the IMF stand-by credit arrangement had been finally concluded. Although the support which the banks had received from this creditors' cartel had been effective, at least in the short term, its medium- and long-term effectiveness for the international financial system would continue to be dependent on the effectiveness of measures of adjustment introduced in the various debtor countries.

IMF policy on conditionality and the IMF's measures of adjustment

According to the IMF's own statements, the objective of a conditioned adjustment programme is 'to restore soundness to the balance of payments within the context of price stability and self-financing economic growth and without recourse to measures which restrict the freedom of trade and the free flow of capital'. A glance at the practice to date reveals, however, that the medium-term restoration of equilibrium to the balance of payments ranks above all other objectives. On the assumption that imbalances in the balance of payments are the result primarily of excess demand and distortions in the structure of relative prices, the measures of adjustment are aimed chiefly at curbing demand by limiting credit expansion, reducing the budget deficit and lowering real wages. The devaluation of the national currency of the country concerned is also intended to increase export production and reduce the demand for imports.

The shortcomings of such adjustment programmes are obvious: cutting public-sector spending and controlling demand by means of high interest rates and currency devaluations has a negative effect on the process of capital formation. Investment opportunities for local entrepreneurs are restricted, and vital primary products can no longer be financed, while all obstacles to financial transactions of a speculative nature are removed. This results in falling production, rising costs and rising prices.

Likewise, the insistence on the deregulation of Third World economies according to the motto 'getting the prices right', in other words the stimulation of production and investment through the creation of 'fair market' prices, has consistently shown itself to be dysfunctional according to immanent criteria, among them: structural deficits typically found in Third World economies, such as inadequate transport and marketing systems; a lack of industries engaged in primary production; and insufficient warehousing, all of which continue to be ignored.

In fact, IMF crisis management leads regularly to economic overkill for the debtor economies: the GNP declines, the volume of imports has to be cut and investment falls. The principal victims of failed adjustment policies are the members of the lower social strata. For the majority of the population the so-called elimination of inefficiency in the public sector and the introduction of market-oriented prices policies mean, invariably, mass redundancies, the withdrawal of subsidies on basic foodstuffs and public transport, and cuts in public health services and education. As a result, many countries have seen 'IMF riots' during the 1980s, spontaneous acts of resistance to the economic conditions dictated by the IMF.

On account of its rigid austerity programmes also becoming caught in a huge volley of international criticism, the IMF has recently responded with its own study of the effects of its policies on distribution policy. It refutes cynically an allegation levelled repeatedly at the organization that the abolition of prices fixed by the state and cuts in subsidies on foodstuffs increase social hardship, privation and suffering in the debtor nations, saying:

the application of prices fixed by the state as a means of improving income distribution in favour of the extremely poor is severely limited by objective conditions of poverty. In order to benefit from subsidies one must have the purchasing power necessary to acquire subsidized products in the first place.

Even the former president of the Central Bank of Brazil, C. Langoni, well-known for his adherence to the monetarist Chicago School, has spoken out against the misanthropic ignorance of this policy.

It is totally unjust that the developing nations should bear the whole burden of the process of adjustment through a decline in real income per head. There are indications that the average profit rates of the commercial banks are not falling, but may instead be rising as a result of debt restructuring . . . The accompanying social costs are higher than necessary, even if one takes into account real economic constraints . . . The IMF has not yet been able to find an acceptable way to deal with economic structural problems; such adjustments take time. The Fund is asking too much too soon. Since pressure to embark upon a programme of adjustment materializes so suddenly, there is often a dangerous conflict between the demands made by the Fund and that which is politically and socially acceptable within a country.

This criticism of the IMF has, however, also been voiced by others on the Right. The father of monetarism, Milton Freidman, has objected to any further support for the IMF and has rejected categorically the idea of increasing IMF quotas. He has suggested, moreover, that thought should be given to how the IMF could be dismantled and abolished.

The role of the World Bank since the early 1980s: the Baker Plan

Unlike the IMF, which after an initial loss of importance during the mid-1970s managed to win back and even extend its power and influence in the course of the debt crisis, the World Bank was unable to regain the position which it had lost during that same period and was forced instead to eke out a shadowy existence. At the beginning of the 1980s the Bank was exposed to an ideological offensive led primarily by the Reagan Administration.

The traditionally high proportion of World Bank loans awarded to projects in the public sector (in particular, to infrastructure projects) and its admittedly extremely dubious poverty strategy under President McNamara had long been a thorn in the side of orthodox liberal circles. When A. W. Clausen, formerly director of the Bank of America, was named as the new president of the World Bank in 1981, he initiated a break with previous strategy. 'Redistribution with growth' was dropped and replaced by 'structural adjustment'.

When additional loans were awarded for structural and sector adjustment (1.1% of total lending in 1981, 14% in 1986) and measures were introduced which were aimed at fostering an investment climate attractive to the private sector, the traditional project-orientation of the World Bank turned in the direction of macro-economic intervention. The major cornerstones of the reforms demanded by the World Bank, negotiated with the governments of the Third World in a policy dialogue, and finally made binding in a Letter for Development, were:

- the deregulation of production and trade (i.e. reduction in state intervention);
- increased efficiency in the public sector (i.e. privatization); and
- compulsory promotion of export production (i.e. servicing of overseas debts).

Despite these obvious overlaps with the adjustment policies of the IMF and the continual differentiation of new forms of credit, it was 1985 before the World Bank experienced a noticeable upturn in its fortunes as a result of the initiative put forward by US Finance Minister, James A. Baker.

At the joint annual meeting of the IMF and the World Bank in 1985 Baker announced a new strategy for managing the crisis:

- the international financial institutions, especially the World Bank, should increase total lending substantially;
- the private commercial banks should declare their willingness to make fresh money available; and
- the major problem debtors must commit themselves to increasing the effectiveness of the measures of adjustment and to correcting undesirable trends in economic policy.

At the centre of this initiative stood 17 specially selected debtor nations, to which the Western commercial banks were to extend new loans totalling US$20 billion between 1986 and 1988 at the behest of the OECD governments. In parallel with this, the World Bank and the regional development banks were to increase their annual gross lending to US$9 billion.

As part of the Baker initiative — instead of straightforward adjustment, experts now talk in terms of growth-oriented adjustment (adjustment with growth) — the World Bank evolved a broad range of additional activities. The forms of co-financing (with the help of so-called B loans) introduced in 1983 were developed further and their volume increased. This type of credit couples World Bank transactions with private loans from commercial banks, either by means of the World Bank participating directly in a private loan and extending the life of the loan as a countermove, or by the World Bank guaranteeing private loans and easing the terms (such as interest rates, grace periods) under which they are made.

In 1985 the International Finance Corporation (IFC), a sister organization of the World Bank and one which was making a special effort to develop joint ventures, was revalued upwards when its nominal capital was increased to US$1.3 billion. A year later the IFC recorded a higher percentage increase in funds allocated than that boasted by both the World Bank and the International Development Association (IDA). With the help of a newly established advisory service, it was to back up moves to promote direct investment abroad on a permanent basis. In addition, the IFC was to take on a key role in the conversion, then under discussion, of private bank loans into shareholdings (debt-equity-swaps).

The founding in 1985 of the Multilateral Investment Guarantee Agency (MIGA) resulted in Third World countries being urged to reduce the non-commercial risks faced by multinational concerns. This attempt at safeguarding investment extended to the risk of profit repatriation, the risk of loss, for example on nationalization, the risk of breach of contract, and any risks which might arise as a result of war or internal unrest.

Furthermore, plans were made to extend Structural Adjustment Loans (SALs) and make them more effective: before 1986, 38 SALs had been authorized and another 25 scheduled for 1987/8. So far, however, success in this field has been only moderate. In a recent internal study the World Bank evaluates 15 SALs in 10 countries. In some of the cases the results fall far short of expectations as regards the central elements of the programmes (the promotion of exports, import liberalization, improved efficiency in the public sector). The principal conclusions are remarkable: in order to avoid counterproductive effects in the future all bilateral flows of finance should be subsumed under the World Bank's structural adjustment policies; for the Third World there are plans for the 'internalization' of political reforms during the planning stage through a concerted policy of alliances. Extensive consideration of reform is, however, nowhere to be found in the study.

The entire package known as the Baker Plan is aimed at reducing the risks taken by the commercial banks and foreign direct investors. The costs of the crisis are passed on, in the main, to the population of the Third World through the operation of the structural adjustment policy. Where the commercial banks have been able to win support for fiscal relief, it is the taxpayer in the industrialized world who has been footing the bill.

The Baker Plan has so far failed to achieve its original aim, namely that commercial banks should make available sufficient fresh money. In fact, capital is flowing in the opposite direction: the Third World's net transfer of capital to the industrialized world of around US$30 billion per annum continues.

During the first few decades of the post-war period the development of the world market was characterized by a boom in the international trade in currency and later by the expansion of multinational concerns and the internationalization of money capital. After the outbreak of the debt crisis, itself accelerated by the withdrawal of the commercial banks from Third World business, the IMF and, after some delay, the World Bank attempted to minimize the financial risks and safeguard the profits of the commercial banks through numerous new forms of co-ordination and negotiation, various financial and programme techniques, and extensive loan and inducement packages. The threat of an international financial crash, so serious at the beginning of the 1980s, appeared to have been banished, at least in the short term, with the help of hastily forged creditors' cartels consisting of commercial banks, the IMF, central banks, the BIS and the OECD governments. The accompanying economic overkill and the devastating social consequences of the IMF/World Bank adjustment strategy on the one hand, and the increasing reluctance on the part of commercial banks to supply sufficient fresh money on the other, has since revealed the bankruptcy of this extremely asymmetrical form of crisis management.

The renewed critical deterioration in the position of some of the major debtor nations since the beginning of 1987 would appear to confirm the gloomy predictions made by Darrell Delamaide:

> There will be a second debt crisis, just as there was a second crude oil crisis in the period between 1970 and 1980. And just like the crude oil crisis, the debt crisis is not an economic event. It is political. We are dealing here with tremors caused by massive changes in the balance of power. The real

problem was not solved after the first crude oil crisis, because it was barely perceived at all.

Recommended Reading

Delamaide, D. (1984) *Debt Shock. The Inside Story of the Crisis that Threatens the World's Banks and Stock Markets*, London.

Euromoney, various edns.

Killick, T. (ed.) (1984) *The Quest for Economic Stabilization. The IMF and the Third World*, London.

Payer, Cheryl (1986) 'The World Bank: A New Role in the Debt Crisis?',*Third World Quarterly* 8 (3).

Vries, M. G. de (1986) *The IMF in a Changing World, 1945–1985*, Washington.

Williamson, J. (ed.) (1983) *IMF-conditionality*, Oxford.

4. The Role of the USA in the International Debt Crisis

Claudia Dziobek

In his book *Die Geldverleiher* (*The Money-Lenders*) Anthony Sampson, a popular British economic journalist, documents how in the early 1970s American banks strode forth as pioneers to develop a gold mine — credit dealings with the Third World. They travelled to Latin America, Southeast Asia and Africa to woo politicians and, more importantly, state entrepreneurs for the idea of a great leap forward financed by the dollar, and generously offered their services as lenders. In the initial euphoria, loans were extended relatively indiscriminately, and since these were almost without exception syndicated loans (loans awarded jointly by several banks) the burden of each bank's responsibility was not great.

Only a few years later, when the debtors showed the first signs of financial difficulties during the world economic depression in 1975, did sceptical politicians in Washington introduce into public debate the subject of banking operations with the Third World. The first few debt crises, in Peru, Jamaica and Zaire, were recognized as being symptomatic of the potential riskiness of the entire credit business, although concern centred primarily on the stability of the national and international financial markets and not, for instance, on the process of development within the debtor countries. In actual fact, the debt crisis was seen by the creditors almost exclusively in terms of the financial problem. Developmentalists exercised a remarkable degree of restraint.

According to American tradition, that is according to the customs of a nation which regarded itself as the world's supreme power, the question of debt was classified in the extensive catalogue of global problems and placed on the agenda of the policy-planning institute responsible. The first international plan for dealing with the crisis was developed under the supervision of the central bank, the Fed. Under the rallying call of 'fight inflation', forces were mobilized at the beginning of the 1980s in the USA, Japan and Western Europe. They arrived in the debtor countries via the IMF in the form of austerity policies. When in the mid-1980s the limits of these anti-inflation policies began to appear increasingly clearly on the horizon, that is to say the mountain of debt and all of its attendant problems continued to grow regardless, the Baker Plan was tossed into the ring. It was the product of the Treasury Department and was regarded by the creditor nations as the key to finding a solution to the debt problem.

The USA's internationally acknowledged leading role in the management of the debt crisis must not, however, be permitted to obscure the fact that the USA did not succeed either in reducing the size of the debt or in engineering the recovery of the debtor nations. On the contrary, a technical appreciation of and approach to the crisis was not in any sense the same as making a constructive contribution towards overcoming it. There are at least two reasons for this:

- The methods employed to deal with the crisis displayed considerable shortcomings, since they had been developed from the one-sided perspective of the financial world, without taking into account their consequences for economic and structural policies.
- This lack of success was determined by economic trends within the USA, trends which led to the USA itself being unable to meet its own demands that the world exercise restraint with regard to spending policy. In retrospect, it is clear that as a result of the supply-side economics of the Reagan administration, which came to power in 1980, the USA became the first nation to get out of step with the international wave of financial rehabilitation and instead became the world's largest debtor.

Charged with this burden, official plans for dealing with the crisis put forward in the USA were notable for the fact that they included instructions on how the other creditor nations should act, without checking whether each was willing to co-operate. For example, the Baker Plan provides that Japan and West Germany in particular should pursue expansive growth policies whilst at the same time reducing their trade surpluses. This would both ensure that new loans would flow and at the same time give the debtor nations the opportunity to export themselves out of debt. The other creditors were not, however, keen to take over this leading role, since they regarded the debt problem primarily as an American dilemma, and therefore pleaded their roles as secondary forces in the international set-up.

The US banks and Congress

The first debt crises, in Peru and Zaire in 1975, were taken seriously by the US Congress and recognized as being symptomatic of the avalanche of payment problems which could be expected to follow and which would affect not only the banks, but also governments. Congress' first action was to schedule hearings to which all of the US' top bankers as well as numerous experts from the financial world were invited. Frank Church, Chariman of the Banking Committee and a well-known critic of the multinational oil companies, was the first to go public, and unearthed a wealth of information which even today can still be obtained only with great difficulty in the other creditor countries.

1976 saw the publication of *Financial Institutions and the Nation's Economy* (the *FINE Study*), the first comprehensive report on the subject. In the years which followed, the string of hearings and studies on the subject of debt was neverending. Both the Senate and Congress conducted parallel debates. Since 1987 there has been a Senate Subcommittee for International Debt, whose chair has been taken for the opposition by leading politician Senator Bill Bradley.

At first, the studies focused on the banks' obligation to provide information and on the bodies responsible for monitoring the financial institutions. The Fed., the Comptroller of Currency and US counterpart of the West German Federal Supervisory Office for Credit in Berlin, was questioned in detail about the criteria which it used to control international creditor transactions. The hearings resulted in wide-ranging guidelines on the banks' duty to publish information. Since then, loans which account for more than 1% of a bank's total assets have to be shown separately in that bank's report and accounts. Details of any restructuring negotiations underway and any dodgy loans must also be given for each country.

In addition, the supervising authorities tightened their control over the banks. On several occasions the Comptroller of Currency or the central bank censured individual banks, explicitly referring to risky credit transactions. Such measures must have been interpreted as very unusual steps, for utmost discretion is normally one of the unwritten laws of the credit system, in the USA as elsewhere. Furthermore, the supervising authorities began to compile comprehensive studies and statistics, such as the *Country Lending Exposure Service*, which is now published regularly.

A comparison with the knowledge acquired and interest shown by the corresponding West German institutions and authorities yields astonishing results. In West Germany it was regarded by the Ministry of Finance, the Ministry for Economic Co-operation, the Bundesbank and the supervisory authorities as extremely important that public debate should be stifled. The answers to the numerous questions raised by the Greens in the Bundestag ranged from the conciliatory to the hostile. In principle none of the authorities involved saw any need for concrete action. It was better to rely on American sources or the international financial institutions both for information and for conceptional planning for the crisis.

In fact, unlike the parliamentary bodies of most of the other creditor nations, the US Congress was an important platform on which the public debate over international indebtedness could take place. Looked at as a whole, however, the fierce battle of words between state and banks in the Congress brought few restrictions on the way in which the banks could act. One example of this was the USA's inflexible attitude towards the debtor nations in cases where it was possible for the IMF to protect bank balances and profits. Even in cases of acute conflict, such as the first large-scale debt crises in Mexico and Brazil in the 1980s, the US Treasury Department and central bank always acted in the interests of the banks by making available *ad hoc* bridging-loans which prevented the banks from having to write off debts.

Extraparliamentary management of the debt crisis: the think tanks

While Congress concentrated on procuring information and on punctual directives and instructions for the banks, the actual projection of coherent methods for dealing with the crisis took place at extraparliamentary level. Without exception, the think tanks, which carry out indirect preliminary work for Congress, identified the main areas to be investigated in the field of debt and began to work at an analytical level and to develop strategic plans. Among them were established think tanks such as the ultra-right American Enterprise Institute in Washington, the conservative–liberal Brookings Institute and even the left–liberal (and chronically short of money) Institute for Policy Studies. Other members of the circle included the select opinion-forming universities such as Harvard, Stanford, Chicago and Princeton. The Council on Foreign Relations, a private lobby concerned with American foreign policy, also took an active part in the debate. Its prominent member, Henry A. Kissinger, took an intense interest in the consequences of the debt crisis for inter-American economic and political relations.

Interestingly, the result was an assessment of the debt crisis which differed from the views expressed by the USA in the IMF. The debt crisis in the 1980s was viewed as being extremely critical, and even dyed-in-the-wool *laissez-faire* economists like Rüdiger Dornbusch and Peter Kenen came to the conclusion that only collective debt-relief negotiations between debtors and creditors in conjunction with internationally agreed growth- and free-trade-oriented economic policies offered a solution.

Peter Kenen, Director of Princeton University's International Finance Institute, argued that it was time to look closely at the premises upon which IMF policy was based and to investigate their long-term effects. In a statement to Congress he emphasized that the policy had demanded a great deal of sacrifice of the debtor nations for their overindebtedness, whereas the creditor nations had so far got off lightly. For this reason, he concluded, a proportion of the debts should be annulled. This 'moral argument' was supported politically by the suggestion that years of IMF adjustment programmes were inconsistent with the principle of national sovereignty. In addition, IMF programmes were conceived for the short term and were unsuitable as a long-term solution. He therefore called upon the creditor nations to open up markets, to manage IMF conditionality in a more flexible fashion and above all to orient rehabilitation programmes towards the long term.

Rüdiger Dornbusch and Martin Feldstein came to a similar conclusion. In their analysis they reprimanded the US Government for having raked up the fire of international debt through its own excessive spending policies. Contrary to what the IMF believed, Dornbusch worked on the assumption that austerity policies did not lead to new investment in the Third World and that it could not be taken for granted, either, that flight-capital would return as a result of 'confidence-inspiring monetarism'.

These and other studies reflected concern, still very much alive in the USA, about the possibility of a repetition of the world economic crisis of 1929.

Prevailing opinion on the subject, sustained untiringly for decades by Charles Kindleberger, is that that particular world economic crisis was caused first and foremost by the fact that there was no strong guiding and leading nation capable of taking responsibility for co-ordinating the management of the crisis at international level.

There is also a power vacuum in the current debt crisis, since the USA is neither able, nor willing, to play a leading part in its management. The conservative think tanks repeatedly complained that the Reagan Administration's domestic economic priorities were not in harmony with the economic policy measures required. The restoration of financial soundness to the budget deficit and simultaneous opening up of US markets to the exports forcing their way on to the dollar markets from the debtor nations are rejected by the Government.

The USA: the world's most heavily indebted nation

Since 1982 the USA has been running up more and more debts on the national and international capital markets. Her external debt rose from US$6 billion in 1982 to US$130 billion (net) in 1987 and was expected to reach the US$500 billion mark by the end of the decade. The USA has thus become the world's most heavily indebted nation and is, moreover, now a net debtor for the first time since World War I.

The major reason for this is the Reagan Administration's budget deficit. Attractive interest rates and tax exemptions have been used to induce both wealthy foreigners from Japan and the European Community (EC), and those intent on investing their capital outside their own Third World countries, to purchase American certificates of indebtedness. In 1984 approximately half of the budget deficit was financed by overseas savings.

In terms of its significance, the US debt mountain should be viewed from two angles. On the one hand, the question arises as to whether, as is often asserted, the USA's net indebtedness signals her ultimate demise as a world power. It is too early to assess the long-term effects, but what is certain, although many of those who control wealth overseas have failed to consider it, is that since the USA's debts have been extended in the lenders' own currencies, repayment could be effected in part through devaluing the dollar. The wealthy overseas are now finding themselves in the unfortunate position of being able to see the value of their costly US treasury bonds, expressed in their own currencies, dwindling. In this way they are *de facto* subsidizing the US budget deficit.

Another aspect of the situation is the effect which the US debt is having on international indebtedness as a whole. The USA is now absorbing an increasingly large proportion of the savings available internationally for herself, and this is restricting dramatically the number of new loans which it is possible to extend to the Third World. In addition, the USA is finding herself with less and less room for manoeuvre in her role as the nation chiefly responsible for the international management of the crisis. The strategies provided for by the Baker Plan, which depend on growth and new loans to the Third World, should actually take place without the financial participation of the USA. Yet that situation cannot be allowed to arise, since no other country is prepared to take on the (unpleasant) task of taking overall charge of co-ordinating the crisis at international level. Thus the USA's rapidly increasing external debt is beginning to pose a threat to international financial stability. What this suggests is that the only way out of the dilemma may be for lenders to start annulling debts.

Debt crisis and domestic economic trends in the USA

During the late 1970s the US economy faced one battle after another: rising inflation, persistently high unemployment, the oil-price shocks of 1973 and 1979, and the effects of structural shifts away from the traditional industries in the north of the country to the high-tech munitions industry and service sector in the south. During this period of upheaval there was a great deal of fierce debate on the subject of which economic policy measures would best be able to reform the economy. On one side were the exponents of a concerted structural policy aimed in particular at halting the shift from north to south in favour of a balanced geographical and sectoral distribution of industry; on the other stood those who advocated deregulation and a union-free environment combined with a concerted anti-inflation policy, as the basis for restoring the financial soundness of the economy (and government spending). Under discussion, too, was the question of international competitiveness, which hit the headlines under the catch-phrase 'the Japanese challenge'.

'Supply-led economic policies' was the only banner under which all of the strategies under discussion could be united. The first priority was the fight against inflation, an initiative which was actively backed both by Western Europe and Japan and was, at the same time, declared by the IMF to be the number-one weapon in the battle against the numerous debt crises looming on the horizon. The USA's dependence on oil was countered with generous backing, financed by the private banks, for (speculative) oil drilling on the home front.

After the fall in the world-market price of crude oil, much of this drilling began operating at a loss, and one of the largest US banks, the Continental Illinois, came close to collapse. An increase in speculative transactions and the growth of the USA's internal debt made the financial system extremely vulnerable: the number of banks which have collapsed since the early 1980s is even higher than it was during the world economic crisis in the 1930s (see Figure 4.1).

The government's structural policy was replaced by expansion in the munitions industry which, although it could not prevent the decline of the old industrial centres, did help to get a few states (Massachusetts, Washington State) back on their feet economically. This thoroughly unorthodox mixture of different, and to some extent contradictory, economic policy measures could

Figure 4.1
Bank collapses in the USA, 1934–86

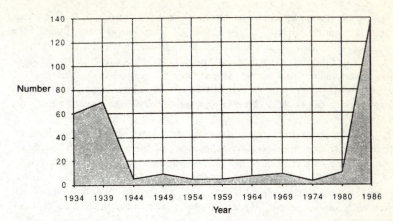

Source: FDIC

only be implemented, however, by the USA taking out a loan overseas and cutting national spending on wages and social programmes. In the mid-1980s the USA was faced with the problem of how to plug her financial holes without turning back history in the process, that is without forcing the redevelopment areas back into decline.

Protectionism and Third World debt

The international debt crisis acts as a catalyst which helps to reveal existing economic problems. In no other creditor country is the link between international indebtedness and economic problems on the domestic scene as manifest as it is in the USA. Whilst until the early 1980s the debt debate centred on purely financial and budgetary matters, it is now becoming apparent that the IMF's strategy, which depends on total repayment, is causing more and more of a trade problem. The export offensive being pursued by the debtor nations as the basis for interest and loan-capital (re)payments is beginning to show up in the USA in the form of a glut of imports, in particular from the Latin American countries. At the same time, the import controls introduced by these countries are having an unfavourable effect on US exports. Around a quarter of US exports go to the less developed countries of the Third World (non-crude-oil-exporting LDCs), and exports now account for a dramatically higher proportion of the USA's national product than they did in the late 1970s. By way of comparison, only around 7% of West German exports go to the Third World.

Most of the USA's exports are foodstuffs, machinery, cars and electrical goods, that is goods produced by the traditional industries. The decline in demand from the debtor nations which has been brought on by austerity is therefore hitting mainly branches of industry which are already among those in crisis in the USA.

The problem is made still worse by the current distribution of total lending. In 1975, US banks still had a 55% share in all Third World loans. By 1984 the figure had fallen to around 40% as a result of increasing reluctance on the part of American banks to extend new loans. Of the loans extended to the most heavily indebted nations, such as Brazil, Mexico, South Korea, Chile and the Philippines, whose exports offer the stiffest competition to American industry, the USA's share is 40–60%. Overall this is an unfavourable situation for the USA.

In addition to having to deal with its own economic weakness, the USA actually has to bear a disproportionate share of the cost of the adjustments made by the creditors. Under the 1987 distribution of trade flows, the USA took around 63% of the exports from the debtor nations of the Third World, the EC 24% and Japan 7%, and only the USA had to tolerate a large trade deficit with these countries. Hence the ever louder calls from within the USA for protectionist measures, particularly against the EC and Japan, must be seen as the USA's refusal to take sole responsibility for the debt crisis internationally.

The dilemma is plain. A continuation of IMF policy is only possible at the expense of the branches of industry mentioned earlier. In the USA there is a conflict of interest between the banks and industry. The conflict is coming to a head among the creditor nations too, for the US Government regards her large trade deficit with the debtor nations as her contribution towards international *détente*. She is now waiting, in vain, for Japan and the EC to follow her lead. But who will force them to do so?

The Bradley Plan: negotiation in place of protectionism

Senator Bill Bradley (Democratic Party) asked the central bank to calculate how the losses which the American export sector expected to sustain compared in percentage terms, with those sustained by the banks when loans are written down. The central bank calculated that a 30% write-down of the loans themselves and the annulment of interest receivable over and above the LIBOR rate would cost the US banks around 3% of their capital base; at 1986 figures there would not be one case in which the loss would exceed the profits earned over the previous three years. What is most remarkable, however, is that the central bank was prepared even to entertain the idea of such a calculation. When questions of this sort are raised the bank normally produces the great unquantifiables, such as financial stability, as a means of avoiding the issue. Statements issued by the central bank on the subject, to the effect that it is not now possible to avoid annulling debts, are the result of a process during which the USA's national priorities and interests with regard to debt have been rethought.

In July 1986, Senator Bradley put forward an alternative to the Baker Plan in which he appealed to American national economic interests and explained the need for debt remission:

Latin America is a major customer of American manufacturing industry. Within the space of two years, between 1981 and 1983, exports of machinery to Latin America fell by 38%, exports of steel and cars by 5%, exports of building materials by 80%, and exports of agricultural machinery by 86% . . . 40,000 Americans have lost their jobs as a result of the fact that the Latin American export market is drying up, and 40,000 more Americans have been unable to find work because Latin America's economic growth has come to a standstill. (Speech to the National Press Club, Washington)

The Bradley Plan was the political upshot of the studies carried out by conservative think tanks. Its first precondition for growth in the heavily indebted countries of the Third World was a staggered remission of debts. Under the plan, a summit meeting of bankers and politicians from both sides would take place annually in order to agree a debt remission package. Debtors would be permitted to participate on condition that they consistently pursued a free trade policy and that they placed no restrictions on foreign investment. In return the creditors would schedule cuts in interest rates of a maximum of 3% and would extend new loans to the value of US$3 billion.

Extraparliamentary debt management: action groups

Since the late 1970s a whole string of action groups has been founded which concern themselves specifically and almost exclusively with the question of the debt crisis. Unlike the aforementioned think tanks, these groups concentrate on networking (direct policy planning), the establishment of contacts for the purpose of concerted action at parliamentary and extraparliamentary level. We will look at three groups which are representative of a whole series of action groups of this kind: the Group of 30, the Institute for International Finance and the Debt Crisis Network.

The Group of 30 was founded in New York in 1978. It describes itself as a private, non-partisan and international organ concerned with budgetary and economic policy. For a while its director was the former head of the IMF, Johannes Witteveen, a clear sign that the group functions to a certain extent as the parlour of the IMF. Its membership includes central bankers; ministers of finance; the directors of various institutes for economic research, for example *Hamburgisches Welt-Wirtschafts-Archiv* — the *HWWA*; the directors of multinational firms, such as International Business Machines (IBM); banks and professors. Of the Third World countries, Brazil, the Philippines and Argentina are represented, as is Hungary.

The group is comparable in its composition with Rockefeller's Trilateral Commission, which likewise enables 'important people' from 'important countries' to confer with each other regularly in an informal setting in order to prepare at that level for more formal international meetings. In this setting it is possible for an exchange of ideas to take place without the conventional decorum which has to be observed within the sub-groups of the IMF or at economic summits. Hence the Group of 30 should be recognized not for the individual articles and publications which it claims as its major task, but rather for the forum which it has created for background discussion, for it is conceivable that as debt negotiations between the IMF and Brazil toughen, as they are doing at the moment, the members' meetings might serve to prevent contact from being broken off and to give Brazil, the debtor nation in question in this instance, the feeling that it is tied into a team of concerned financial managers. The group is financed primarily by the Rockefeller Foundation, American Express, IBM, Shell and several big banks. The list of its sponsors also contains several central banks from the Third World, although this should presumably be regarded as a symbolic gesture. West Germany does not appear on the list, although she is represented by two people (out of a total, in 1987, of 29).

The concerns of the Institute for International Finance can be defined rather more easily. It was founded in Washington in 1984 by 200 commercial banks from the Western world, and sees itself as a services' enterprise and lobbying organization for the member banks. The West German banks involved are the Bank für Gemeinwirtschaft (BfG), the Commerz- und Dresdener Bank, the Vereinsund Westbank, and the Westdeutsche Landesbank (WestLB), but not the Deutsche Bank, which can presumably represent its interests more effectively elsewhere. Like the Group of 30, this institute stresses publicly its role as a provider of information, yet in view of the outstanding work done by the Data Bank Service this cannot really be the establishment's basic objective. In fact, its purpose is instead to establish contact between the world's financial centres and the international financial bureaucracy (the IMF, the World Bank and so on) and at the same time to improve discipline among the banks. The director in 1987, H. Schulmann, as former undersecretary at the Federal Ministry of Finance, himself came from within the financial bureaucracy.

Whilst representing the banks' interests in the international management of debt, the institute has spoken out in favour of continuing and consolidating the IMF's austerity policies and voices confidently the conviction that all debt crises can be solved through sound budgetary and financial policies.

The third federation is the Debt Crisis Network. Founded as an 'informal action group concerned with international indebtedness', the organization unites radical and left–liberal, as well as social democratic individuals and groups. The membership list contains the American Friends Service Committee, the Institute for Policy Studies, the organization grouped around the periodical *North American Congress on Latin America* (*NACLA*), various church groups such as the Mary Knoll Fathers and Brothers and the United Church Board for World Ministries, and, more to the point, also anti-apartheid initiatives and Third World solidarity groups from various parts of the country. Compared particularly with the Group of 30 and the Institute for International

Finance, the Network's financial base is weak, but the personal commitment is all the greater.

The Network sees Third World debt within the context of imperialism: the debts, and in particular the way in which the crisis is managed, illustrate the dominant position occupied by the West. The Network is concerned to promote alternative solutions to the crisis which focus on development (see *From Debt to Development*) rather than on financial policy. It feels, too, that the human costs which accrue as a result of the debt crisis and the intransigence displayed by the creditor nations, i.e. poverty, unemployment, declining standards of living and political destability, should be pointed out. A further matter of concern to the Debt Crisis Network is the promotion of international solidarity. For this reason the Network is also active in its own country with a broad spectrum of progressive organizations and with the trades unions. One of those who emphasize the link between the domestic economy and international indebtedness is the chief economist of the United Auto workers, Steve Beckman, a representative of a branch of industry whose exports have declined as a direct result of the austerity policies being pursued in Latin America. A study of automobile workers has concluded that between 1980 and 1983 around 1.1 million jobs in the USA fell victim to the debt crisis in this manner. The Women's Division of the United Methodist Church is another group which stresses the connection between Third World indebtedness and problems at local level.

The Debt Crisis Network co-ordinates activities, publishes a newsletter, is building up its international contacts and making efforts to win support at parliamentary level for its jointly elaborated alternative solution. It maintains international contacts with many Third World nations, as well as emancipatory movements in the creditor countries (including the Greens in West Germany).

The Network has summarized its demands in a 10-point programme: the annulment of debts owed by the poorest countries, a boycott on lending to the racist regime in South Africa, a re-orientation of IMF programmes and the IMF's adoption of criteria relating, for example, to job creation and improvements in social living conditions. Moreover, the Network is calling for large numbers of debts to be remitted as a medium-term solution. US bilateral financing should, it says, be provided primarily to the poorer social strata and for projects which encourage self-help. Military aid and 'security equipment' should be replaced with programmes designed to aid development.

The Network has made direct demands on the US Government, including several for tighter public supervision of the banks, cuts in budgetary spending in the munitions sector and a rise in corporate tax. In addition, it demands a 'managed trade system', which would promote investment at home rather than abroad, and concerted industrial policies designed to maintain and modernize American industry and create jobs fit for human beings. Finally, maintains the Network, small and medium-sized firms in the USA should be freed from their debts through a concerted agricultural policy aimed at strengthening their position in relation to that of non-producing agricultural service enterprises.

The demands made by the Debt Crisis Network are more radical than those made by the other groups and institutes concerned with the problem of indebtedness. Nevertheless, the Network is totally in step with trends which are now gaining in popularity throughout the whole of the USA.

During the second half of the 1980s, US groups involved in the management of the crisis clearly began undergoing a gradual reorientation. This reorientation is taking place as a result of America's reassessement of her national economic interests. The radical representatives of the Debt Crisis Network also began moving ahead on the basis of linking the USA's own priorities with those of the debtor nations. Investigation has led to the claim that it is now in the interests of the creditors, and in particular of the USA, for debts to be annulled.

This position is not yet official policy. The Baker Plan is still being held up as the only sensible and economically rational way of proceeding. It is to be expected that the ideas contained in the Bradley Plan will first be appraised in terms of their effect on foreign policy, for even though the annulment of debts is in the national interest, even a government led by Democrats would undoubtedly suggest internationally that this should be implemented as an act of mercy towards the debtor nations only if accompanied by appropriate political counterdemands.

Recommended Reading

Debt Crisis Network (ed.) (1985) *From Debt to Development* mimeo.
Dornbusch, Rüdiger (1987) 'Weg mit den Schulden', *Wirtschaftswoche* 12.
Group of 30, Annual Report, Two World Trade Center Suite, 9639 New York, NY 10048.
Newsletter, c/o Institute for Policy Stuides, 1901 Q Street, NW, Washington DC, 20009, quarterly since 1986.
US Congress (1976) Committee on Banking, Currency, and Housing: FINE. Compendium of papers prepared for the FINE Study, Book II, Pt 4. International Banking. 94th Congress, Second Session.
——— (1983) Committee on Banking, Housing, and Urban Affairs: Hearing Before the Subcommittee on International Finance and Monetary Policy. International Debt. 96th Congress, first session.
——— (1985) Hearings Before the Subcommittee on Economic Stabilization. The Costs of Foreign Debt for the United States and the Third World. 99th Congress, first session. See statements of C. F. Bergsten, M. Feldstein, R. Prebisch, and others.
Sampson, A. (1982) *Die Geldverleiher. Von der Macht der Banken und der Ohnmacht der Politik*, Reinbek.

5. West Germany in the International Debt Crisis

Alex Schubert

Since the outbreak of the international debt crisis, economic development in West Germany has been partly responsible for the intensification of trends towards economic crisis world-wide. West Germany, or at least the West German Government, has neither seized nor backed any initiative to check the threat of a world-wide economic recession. Yet with the aid of the conservative policies being pursued by the West German Government the West German economy has taken full advantage of the options and opportunities open to the nation as a result of the debt crisis. The international competitiveness of individual firms, and indeed of the whole economy, has been strengthened. On the world monetary market in particular, the West German economy played a greater role in the second half of the 1980s than it did before the outbreak of the crisis in 1982.

Surplus current-account balances and huge capital exports

The size of West Germany's current-account surpluses is a visible expression of her strong competitive position world-wide (see Table 5.1). Between 1982 and 1986 the value of West Germany's exports increased from DM427 billion to DM526 billion. Imports, on the other hand, increased by DM49 billion, from DM365 billion to DM414 billion. The balance on the country's current account reflected this leap and grew from DM9.9 billion to DM77.8 billion, an increase of some 700%. In 1986, West Germany had the largest current-account surplus of any OECD country with the exception of Japan (US$88 billion).

Until the end of 1985 these surpluses were accompanied by a West German deficit on both short-term and long-term capital transactions. Between 1983 and 1986, Germany's debts receivable from overseas increased by around DM160 billion. In 1986, clearly influenced by the unabating strength of the West German economy, foreign investors began to transfer capital to West Germany and invest it there on a long-term basis and on a large scale. In 1986, when the deutschmark shot up in value, more than DM41 billion of long-term capital streamed into the country. By increasing short-term capital exports to DM106 billion (more than twice the value of short-term net capital exports for the previous ten years!), German investors were able to extend considerably their private assets overseas.

Table 5.1
West German balance of payments position
1982–6 (DM billion)

Position	1982	1983	1984	1985	1986
A. Current Account					
1. Foreign trade					
Exports	427.7	432.3	488.2	537.2	526.4
Imports	365.2	378.5	421.4	451.1	414.2
Balance	+62.6	+53.8	+66.8	+86.0	+112.2
Current Account balance	+ 9.9	+10.6	+19.9	+38.8	+ 77.8
B. Balance of Capital Transactions					
1. Long-term capital transactions					
a) German investment					
overseas (increase: –)	–29.1	–36.5	–42.0	–58.4	
Direct investment	– 6.8	– 8.1	– 9.4	–10.8	
Foreign bonds	–11.4	–10.4	–15.7	–31.3	
Overseas credits					
and loans	– 8.7	–14.7	–14.3	–13.4	
Other capital					
investments abroad	– 2.3	– 3.3	– 2.6	– 2.9	
b) Foreign investment in					
West Germany					
(increase: +)	+14.2	+29.5	+26.3	+52.1	
Balance of long-term capital					
transactions	–14.9	– 7.0	–15.7	– 6.3	+ 41.2
2. Short-term capital transactions					
(net capital exports: –)					
a) Business enterprises					
and private	+ 1.5	– 7.2	–14.7	–13.0	– 46.4
financial loans	+ 3.6	– 1.0	– 5.5	– 9.7	
business loans	– 2.1	– 6.3	– 9.1	– 3.3	
b) Public funds	+ 0.7	– 3.3	– 1.8	+ 0.2	– 1.2
c) Credit institutions	+ 8.1	+ 1.8	+ 0.1	–27.7	– 59.1
debts receivable	+ 4.3	+ 5.3	–17.8	–33.4	
liabilities	+ 3.8	– 3.6	+17.8	+ 5.7	
Balance of short-term capital					
transactions	+10.3	– 8.7	–16.4	–40.5	–106.7
Balance of capital					
transactions	– 4.6	–15.8	–32.0	–46.8	– 65.5

Source: Deutsche Bundesbank (*DBB*)

Expansion in the overseas activities of West German banks and businesses

The aforementioned increase in Germany's overseas assets led to an impressive expansion in the overseas activities of West German banks. At the end of 1982, at the time of the outbreak of the international debt crisis, German credit institutions had active capital overseas amounting to DM199 billion; by the end of 1986 this figure had risen to DM353 billion. Within the space of four years it had increased by DM145 billion, or by 70%. Even when this was combined with an increase in overseas liabilities from DM155 billion to DM193 billion, the increase in net capital exports still amounted to more than DM100 billion. The overseas branches of West German banks, which were active primarily in the free banking zones overseas, had a not inconsiderable influence on this. Between 1982 and November 1986 the volume of their business increased from DM137 billion to DM201 billion, or by 46%.

But the banks were not solely responsible for this considerable expansion in the value of West German wealth invested overseas; other West German concerns also played their part. Since 1983 the world has witnessed the intensification of a trend which began in the mid-1970s:

The mid-1970s saw a fundamental change in the capital interrelations between (German) firms and foreign countries. Until then foreigners had invested far more capital each year for the purposes of acquiring business assets in the German economy than West Germans had spent on acquiring business assets overseas. Since 1975, however, the scale of West Germany's overseas investment (through the acquisition of new interests and extension of existing interests) has increased far more than overseas investment in West Germany. Between 1984 and 1986 Germany's net outflow of direct investment amounted to more than DM10 billion per annum. At the end of 1985 German participatory assets in overseas subsidiaries and branches (including such credits and loans as had been extended in direct relation to existing overseas interests) thus exceeded, at DM131 billion, the value of business assets in West Germany which were owned by foreigners (DM88 billion) by almost a half. At the end of 1976, when more precise figures first became available, the relationship between the two types of assets had been the reverse — although volumes were obviously smaller — (DM43.5 billion to DM63.5 billion). Deutsche Bundesbank (DBB), 1987

West Germany, then, has moved in the opposite direction to the USA. Whereas the latter was transformed during this period from a net creditor into a net debtor nation, West Germany became a country rich in overseas assets.

West Germany as a financial centre

The strengthening of the West German economy's international role during the second half of the 1980s was not, however, brought about solely as a result of the country's productive, financial and speculative investment abroad. By pursuing an economic policy aimed at improving the international competitiveness of the West German money and financial markets, and despite intense international competition, West Germany's Conservative–Liberal Government has succeeded in establishing West Germany as one of the world's financial centres.

> West Germany has the advantage of having a monetary and financial system which is completely open to the outside world; a freely convertible currency and total freedom from restrictions on the movement of capital have long been a distinct merit of the German economic order. On the basis of West Germany's domestic stability, the deutschmark has been able to become a reserve and investment currency of international import. Of course, changes in the economic system world-wide, in particular the development of new financial levers, represent a constant challenge to the domestic financial markets. However, the principles of order by means of which stability and the market economy are preserved, and which West Germany observes so strictly, create the conditions which will enable her to maintain and extend her role in the international interplay of forces. (DBB), 1986

There are plenty of data to illustrate what is meant here. According to information from the Deutsche Bundesbank, in 1985 the deutschmark accounted for approximately 7% of all currency issued world-wide and 14.5% of the world's foreign currency reserves (after the American dollar), and continued to rank as the world's major international loan and reserve currency. During the first half of the 1980s, German bonds were taken up, to an increasing extent, by overseas investors, with the result that between 1982 and 1985 the value of 'trans-frontier long-term capital transactions' almost trebled:

> Between 1980 and 1984 West Germany, with 16%, ranked third among the big five industrialized nations in terms of the total value of trans-frontier portfolio movement, behind the United States and Japan (both with 30%) and ahead of Great Britain (14%) and France (8%).

The money assets created and lent abroad as a percentage of the total wealth created and loans raised domestically also rose from 8.4% in 1982 to an estimated 17.2% in 1985.

> In a world league which calculates the extent of each country's economic relations with the rest of the world, West Germany lay in second place behind Great Britain (18%). She was followed by France (12%) and at some distance by Japan (7%) and the USA (4%) — admittedly both countries with larger domestic markets for financial transactions.

So what do these figures reveal? They indicate that West Germany is participating actively in the extension of a speculative world economy. This economy is no longer concerned with improved investment opportunities in manufacturing sectors, but rather, and primarily, with the creation of competitive advantages in the contest for the money capital which is constantly moving around the world. It is an economy geared always towards short-term profit, in the form of interest or rent. The constant improvement in methods of communication, deregulation or liberalization of the financial and banking sectors in the major industrialized nations, the abolition of taxes on monetary transactions, and so on have led to an incredible increase in volume of (money) capital moving around the world. Taking advantage of such movements of capital, that is making use of them to strengthen domestic banking systems and capital markets, has become one of the basic tasks facing national monetary authorities. Figures show that West German investors and banks have not done at all badly at it over the last few years.

German banks and Third World debts

Increased competition on the world monetary market has naturally mitigated against both an ordered retreat by West German banks from credit dealings with the Third World and the realization of a policy designed to disencumber developing nations which are unable to pay their debts.

West German banks themselves and public institutions like to play down the proportion of the Third World's debts in which German banks have an interest. The DBB alludes at more or less regular intervals to the relatively small volume of debts owed to German banks by countries which are unable to repay. For example, an extract from its monthly report from January 1987 reads:

> A glance at the group of countries which are the major debtor nations reveals that at the end of 1985 German credit institutions had a 7% interest in the total borrowings . . . of this group of countries, i.e. considerably less than say the American banks and the Japanese banks, but also less than the British, French and Canadian banks. The largest of these five groups of banks (the American banks) accounted for almost two-fifths of the debts concerned. Of course, the German banks have increased somewhat their credit commitments to the major debtor nations as a group in recent years, but the 1985 increase was attributable predominantly to the effects of exchange-rate fluctuations, i.e. to the weakening of the US dollar against the deutschmark.

Like the DBB's earlier publications, this excerpt gives the impression that West German banks are less embroiled in the current international debt crisis than the banks of other industrialized nations and would therefore seem to contradict somewhat the DBB's critical comments on the huge increase in loans extended to the developing nations by the banks in the 1970s. Having said that, the DBB has never directed its criticism at the role of the West German banks in particular. If anything, their part in the formation of an international debtors' pyramid is always implicitly played down.

Table 5.2
Debts receivable by the German banks from the world's 15 most heavily indebted nations (US$ billion, year end)

Country	1984	1985	Country	1984	1985
Brazil	3.87	4.68	Philippines	0.40	0.46
Mexico	3.37	3.57	Ecuador	0.24	0.27
Argentina	2.04	2.54	Colombia	0.24	0.26
Venezuela	1.92	2.07	Peru	0.17	0.23
Nigeria	1.26	1.35	Morocco	0.19	0.21
Yugoslavia	1.17	1.16	Ivory Coast	0.08	0.10
Chile	0.82	0.97	Uruguay	0.09	0.10
			Bolivia	0.09	0.10

Source: DBB

Table 5.2 shows, however, that at the end of 1985 the German banks had debts receivable from the four major Latin American debtors alone of US$12.86 billion. Based on an average of the official exchange rates quoted on the Frankfurt foreign exchange market in 1985, these debts amounted to over DM37 billion. At first glance, this sum would appear not to be all that high, particularly when compared to debts receivable from the same debtors by the 16 largest US banks of over US$60 billion. If it were the case, however, that the bulk of the German loans had been extended by fewer banks, in particular West Germany's three big banks (the Deutsche Bank, the Dresdener Bank, and the Commerzbank), then total lendings of DM37 billion would be extraordinarily high in relation both to the banks' own capital funds and to their total profits.

Equally high is the risk that the countries of the Third World might call a total halt to interest and capital (re)payments. For some of the banks a suspension of interest payments could generate losses running into an estimated five times their balance-sheet profits. Since information is in short supply, we have of course been forced to make certain assumptions, the correctness of which will have to be tested when better statistical material is made available, but assuming, for the moment, an interest rate of 10%, then the West German banks would have had to bear revenue losses of DM3.7 billion had the four major Latin American debtors suspended interest payments once and for all in 1985. Some of the banks would probably have been unable to pay dividends, and that would have resulted in a fall in the prices quoted on the stock exchange for bank shares.

The suspension of interest payments by the heavily indebted developing nations would, however, also have more far-reaching consequences for the West German banks. In view of the high degree of international interconnection in the transnational banking system, the losses incurred by the US banks would undoubtedly also have an effect on the West German banks, since the latter are certainly among the major depositors of the former. If the major Latin American debtor nations were to suspend their interest payments and the big US banks were to incur losses accordingly, then their overseas depositors, including the West German banks, would not escape untouched.

In view of their interests in the situation, it is no accident that representatives of the West German banks have not felt compelled to criticize the recessive and anti-social adjustment policies of the IMF or to denounce their recessive effects on the debtor countries, despite the fact that they are also having a negative effect on West Germany's export industries. On the contrary, both the West German Government and the banks themselves stand wholeheartedly behind the IMF's 'crisis management' of the past few years.

Comments made by Werner Blessing, a member of the board of the Deutsche Bank, are a perfect illustration of their support. In his analysis of Latin America's present debt situation, Blessing disputes the assertion — made, among others, by the UN Economic Commission for Latin America (UNECLA) and the Inter-American Development Bank (IDB) — that Latin America is now being compelled to effect a massive transfer of resources in the form of interest payments. According to Blessing, and many others, this assertion is based on a misconception, since interest payments are the other side of previous transfers of capital to Latin America in former times. Accordingly, interest payments are not a transfer of resources, but rather the just remuneration of overseas capitalists for their provision of loans in days gone by. Consequently Blessing consistently condemns all attempts to evade or defer the economic policy measures which are necessary in the debtor countries if they are to meet interest payments under the prevailing world-market conditions. In conjunction with the West German Government, the German banks have therefore pleaded for compliance with the IMF's adjustment programmes, for the implementation of the Baker Plan and for drastic adjustment in the developing countries. Regardless of the economic and social distress which this causes in such countries, the transfer of capital from the poor to the rich nations should continue.

The West German banks' engagement in international credit dealings has assumed such dimensions that many of these banks are dependent, for better or for worse, on the preservation of existing international debtor–creditor relations. As such, they are dependent on the indebted nations effecting and completing a massive transfer of capital overseas in the form of interest payments and on the stability of the US banks. They are also dependent, for better or for worse, on the ability of the US banks, particularly those in New York, to function as international clearing-houses. As a result they have no alternative but to accept the economic policy conditions imposed by such banks on the IMF, the World Bank and, above all, their own governments.

Intensification of global conflict

World economic recession, rising or consistently high unemployment, falling investment rates, high international interest rates, reductions in the price of exports from the Third World, and a cut in the number of international loans extended by transnational banks to heavily indebted developing nations were as much the cause as an expression of the world economy's increased tendency to international crisis in 1982. The West German Government responded with economic policies designed to improve the international competitiveness of the West German economy.

In this respect, the government's policy of reducing the country's new borrowing had a dual function: it meant that the country's return on investment could be increased by means of an implicit redistribution in favour of business income; and it checked rises in the domestic price level and curbed domestic demand with the intended result that the country was able to realize a higher balance of trade surplus.

Naturally, the favourable international situation also played a part in this development:

> Import prices have fallen as a result of the decline in the dollar rate and falling petroleum prices over the last year of 19% (Schubert 1986). Around half of the increase in real income in West Germany in 1986 was due to a redistribution at the expense of the countries which supply her imports. Accordingly, the price stability of the past year has been caused primarily by lower import prices; as a consequence, there has been an increase in real terms in the level of private consumption, which was hitherto so low that it weakened the upturn. (Arbeitsgruppe Alternative Wirtschaftspolitik, 1987)

In addition, until 1985 increases in the value of the dollar had the effect of setting in motion a powerful export impetus, not only in West Germany but also in other EC countries which are important export markets for West Germany, and also enabled the DBB to realize huge exchange-rate gains which, when credited to the national budget, contributed to the success of the government's consolidation policies. Hence West Germany profited directly from the USA's high balance of trade deficits and from the depreciation of the dollar.

Had West Germany pursued a fiscal policy as expansive as the one pursued in the USA (her monetary policy was not contractive), then the favourable international conditions which existed at that time would probably not have precipitated such a pronounced balance of trade and current-account surplus. Under such circumstances exports would certainly have decreased and imports increased more than they did. Nor would the deutschmark have appreciated so markedly. In fact, it would not necessarily have improved the international competitiveness of West German banks and business, either at the time or in the future. Such a policy, would, however, have been appropriate, at least in the short term, from the point of view of the overall development of the world economy. Instead, the Conservative–Liberal Government preferred a policy of budget consolidation which was coupled with an obvious negative social balance.

The increase in the volume of goods and capital being exported by German firms and banks, which is now taking place in the midst of a global economic crisis in the Third World, and growing tendencies to crisis in the world economy do not merely draw attention to Germany's realization of a competitive edge over other industrialized nations. They also show that West German banks and businesses are preparing for a period of fierce competition, for a situation in which market shares are retained or, if possible, increased, during a period of stagnation or at best only slight expansion in world trade. West Germany is not only developing into one of the world's major creditors but is also making economic preparations to secure a not inconsiderable part of the upper classes' income through transfers of interest and profits from abroad.

Today not only West Germany but other industrialized nations also are under threat from the possibility that the USA might attempt to win back her lost competitive position through both a further decline in the dollar rate and by implementing protectionist measures. An international recession would be unavoidable. Unlike what happened during the crisis which led to world economic collapse between 1929 and 1931, an international struggle might well then develop at the highest level which would not be settled by currency devaluations but only by means of tougher consolidation policies, namely reductions in public spending.

This threat becomes even more pronounced when Europe declares her top economic policy priority to be the maintenance of international 'efficiency' (and when even the conservative Reagan Administration was advised not, for example, to restructure the national budget in favour of military spending but to reduce government spending overall). Closer international economic relations is cited by state economic policy-makers as the driving force behind their wish to establish a better climate for international competition on the assumption that this would also correct the huge structural incongruities in the world economy. Even ecological considerations and the low rate of population growth in West Germany are now being used as an excuse for postponing both the restructuring required and to some extent also the required increase in public expenditure.

The conflict is obvious. Greater public expenditure is only compatible with the maintenance of an adequate current-account surplus, i.e. with the preservation of West Germany's role as a financial centre and of the 'efficiency' of the export sector, if it is part of an internationally co-ordinated policy. This policy would have to recognize existing market shares in times of unabating economic recession and keep international competition for new market shares in check in times of growth in the world economy. In particular, the question arises as to how the USA's balance of trade deficit, which currently equals around 70% of West Germany's total exports, can be eliminated without some export markets being closed to surplus countries like West Germany. However, the prospect of political co-ordination has retreated well into the background. Conservative crisis strategies at international level no longer allow any political scope for international real and financial markets, with their incredible speculative features, to develop unhampered. As a consequence, conservative crisis policy will inevitably turn further inwards in order to implement and legitimize its economy measures and its redistribution of income and wealth. World-wide this can only be a bad sign as far as living conditions are concerned.

Recommended Reading

Arbeitsgruppe Alternative Wirtschaftspolitik (1987) *Memorandum '87*, Cologne.
Blessing, W. 'A Commercial Banker's View: Beyond the Debt Crisis — Latin-America: The Next Ten Years', *International Herald Tribune/Inter-American Development Bank*, Paris.
Deutsche Bundesbank (1986) *Geschäftsbericht für das Jahr 1985*, Frankfurt.
Deutsche Bundesbank (various issues) *Monatsbericht*.

6. A Shift in the Balance of Power from the Atlantic to the Pacific Basin

Ulrich Menzel

On the threshold of the Pacific Age

For more than 2,000 years, until the end of the fifteenth century, the Europeans regarded the area around the Mediterranean as the centre of the world, despite the political, cultural and economic diversity of its neighbouring states and peoples. The quality of the transport facilities in that region meant that it formed an ideal unit. The fact that other cultures existed in geographically remote parts of the world was either not known or contact was so slight and so time-consuming that knowledge of them was somewhat mythical in nature. The Silk Road, which linked Ch'ang-an, the former capital of the Chinese Empire, with Antakya on the eastern edge of the Mediterranean over a distance of 6,000km and for over a millennium and a half, provided the only contact of any note with cultural areas such as India and China.

None of this changed until the late-fifteenth century, when innovations in the fields of shipbuilding and navigation transformed the previously unnavigable Atlantic into a waterway. The Portuguese sailed along the African coast, rounded the Cape and reached, first, the legendary land of India then, soon after, China and even Japan. The Spaniards crossed the Atlantic and colonized the West Indies. Under the Treaty of Tordesillas (1493) Pope Alexander VI, acting as arbitrator, divided the New World between the Spaniards and the Portuguese. The Portuguese were followed by the Dutch, whose shipbuilding techniques were more advanced, and the Spaniards by the English and the French. First long-distance trade and then the establishment of plantations and colonies in the New World caused the centre of gravity of the Old World to shift gradually from the Mediterranean to western and northern Europe. Venice, Florence, Byzantium, Baghdad and Damascus were replaced as centres by towns which had formerly been on the periphery, such as Lisbon, Cádiz, Malaga, Bordeaux, Le Havre, Antwerp, Amsterdam and London. This shift in the centre of gravity, which had been triggered by trading capital and the formation of a series of rival bourgeois nation-states, intensified during the eighteenth century when the process of industrialization which had begun in England spread rapidly throughout north-west Europe. The massive exodus of settlers to the New World in the nineteenth century made it possible for that continent to be opened up; railway construction, steam-ship travel, and the invention of the freezing process created the technical preconditions for an international division of labour which extended for the first time not only to luxury items but also to mass-produced goods. The world economy and world politics were directed from the west coast of Europe, which after the end of the nineteenth century regarded the east coast of North America as an extension of itself. It was of no consequence as far as this concentration in the Atlantic was concerned whether the Portuguese and the Spaniards, the Dutch, French, English or the United States were the dominant powers. The rest of the world was colonized from there and incorporated through military force into the world market. The old highly advanced civilizations, the victims of this shift in the centre of gravity, either degenerated (the Mediterranean area and the Islamic world along the Silk Road), were destroyed by their colonizers (Latin America) or wasted away, and appeared to be incapable of anything more than delaying-actions of the sort mounted in South, Southeast and East Asia.

Since the beginning of the 1970s this 500-year-old world order has once again been placed in jeopardy. Of course, World War I and the October Revolution in Russia enabled new world powers to appear on the scene which, after World War II, reduced the status of the European heartlands irrevocably and whose conflicts have since assumed global significance. None of this, however, made any difference to the fact that the world's centre of gravity was in the Atlantic. But since the 1970s there have been growing signs that the centre of gravity is on the point of shifting to the Pacific, more precisely to the North Pacific–East Asian area. There are basically five factors which point to this:

- The revitalization of the old advanced civilizations of East Asia, which set in at the end of the nineteenth century. This revitalization began in Japan following the Meiji Restoration in 1868 and led, in an unparalleled *tour de force* and despite her disastrous defeat in the Pacific War, to Japan being promoted to the world's second-largest economic power. After some delay it reached China, which after several failed attempts at reform during her imperial and republican periods, has been able since the founding of the People's Republic to boast a remarkable degree of industrialization and which, since the Shanghai Communiqué of 1972, has become a force to be reckoned with in world politics. Since decolonization it has also reached the new nation-states in the region, which as NICs are about to follow Japan's lead.
- Both of the superpowers, the Soviet Union and the USA, are not merely Atlantic powers; they also border on the Pacific. For a long time the Pacific regions of both countries were regarded as being of secondary importance, and their principal functions were to feed European Russia and the American east coast respectively. But all that is changing. The new growth industries in the USA are in California, Oregon and Texas. The crisis in the old industries of the Midwest and on the east coast has provoked the suggestion that the economic and political centre of gravity of the USA is shifting to the West and that this is encouraging a new approach to foreign trade and policy. Projects designed to open up Siberia, Japanese

involvement there and, not least, militarization in the Far East have likewise enabled the Soviet Union, since the 1970s, to become a Pacific power, although Siberia is being opened up no longer exclusively towards Europe but also to the East.

- It is possible to perceive a radical reorientation of the economic and political relationships of the remaining countries in the region — Australia and New Zealand, and the Association of South-East Asian Nations (ASEAN) and Gulf states — away from their European mother countries and towards Japan and the NICs of East Asia. This is leading to the establishment of a regional division of labour whereby Japan tends to provide the top-quality technology, the NICs concentrate on established industries, Australia, the Persian Gulf and some of the ASEAN countries supply raw materials and foodstuffs, and the remaining labour-intensive industries are palmed off onto cheap-labour economies such as China and India. As part of this process of reorientation, the world infrastructure is also being reorganized, and its points of reference are no longer restricted to the Atlantic region. Here we should mention Japan's planned second Panama Canal which will be aimed at Brazil, the Baikal–Amu–Magistrale, which will open up Siberia to the east and even the supertankers built in East Asia(!) and the new ports and shipping routes, air connections and submarine cables which are being built in the Pacific region itself.

- Attempts are being made to unite the countries of the region in a Pacific Community, whether along the lines of the EC or in the form of a free-trade zone, by means of institutional links. Though the political opposition of those concerned appears to be almost insurmountable, the attempts have sprung from a marked trend towards closer economic relations which cannot be ignored. After all, the countries of the Mediterranean formed a unit despite their cultural differences.

- East Asia, primarily Japan, has become the world's major exporter of capital over the last few years thanks to its large trade surpluses. Since the USA is by far and away the major recipient of these capital exports, it is possible to conclude that Japan has also become the USA's largest creditor, ahead of Europe.

Here we must ask whether the world's future centres of gravity might not once again include old Ch'ang-an, as in the days of the Silk Road, as well perhaps as Tokyo, Peking, and Shanghai, Seoul, Hong Kong, Taipeh, Singapore and Kuala Lumpur, and whether it might not be these, along with Los Angeles and San Francisco, Melbourne and Vladivostok, which determine the world's destiny.

The economic ascent of the Pacific region

Although the above outline of a trend which has had a huge impact on world history has a certain plausibility, it will nevertheless remain unsatisfactory unless supported by hard facts. The following indicators and a comparison between them and the corresponding figures from the Atlantic countries are intended to back up the above thesis.

Table 6.1 is the result of a comparison between the rates at which the national product of the East and Southeast-Asian countries has grown over the last 25 years and the corresponding figures for the Atlantic heartlands.

Table 6.1
GDP of selected countries, 1960–84 (US$ billion)

	1960 GDP	1984 GDP	1984 GNP/head	Growth per annum 1960–70	1973–84
	US$ billion		US$	%	%
Japan	44.00	1,255.06	10,630	10.4	4.3
Singapore	0.70	18.22	7,260	8.8	8.2
Hong Kong	0.95	30.62	6,330	10.0	9.1
Taiwan	2.53	58.03	3,050	9.6	7.7
South Korea	3.81	83.99	2,110	8.6	7.2
China	42.77	281.25	310	5.2	6.6
Malaysia	2.29	29.28	1,980	6.5	7.3
Thailand	2.55	41.96	860	8.4	6.8
Philippines	6.96	32.84	660	5.1	4.8
Indonesia	8.67	80.59	540	3.9	6.8
USA	505.30	3,634.60	15,390	4.3	2.3
Canada	39.93	334.11	13,280	5.6	2.5
W. Germany	72.10	613.16	11,130	4.4	2.0
France	60.06	489.38	9,760	5.5	2.3
UK	71.44	425.37	8,570	2.9	1.0
Italy	37.19	348.38	6,420	5.5	2.1

Source: World Bank, *World Development Report*, 1983, 1986; *Taiwan Statistical Data Book*, 1985

During the 1960s, a period of world-wide expansion, the rate of growth in East Asia was roughly twice that in North America and Western Europe. During the last 15 years, when growth in the Atlantic region has, to a large extent, slowed down, it has actually been three times higher. This is true even of such Third World countries as the ASEAN states. The continuing recession in the Old as well as the New World has thus swept over East and Southeast Asia almost without trace. In absolute terms Japan achieved the rank of the world's second-largest economic power ahead of the Soviet Union in 1981, and the NICs have now reached the same position as the smaller European nations. If one were to take account of the problems caused by fluctuating exchange rates, which invariably arise when making comparisons on a dollar basis, then the 40% appreciation of the yen against the dollar since the autumn of 1985 would make it necessary for Japan's GDP for 1984 to be revalued upwards by almost US$480 billion, France's entire GNP for roughly the same period. On a per capita basis Japan, Singapore and Hong Kong have moved up into the leading group of industrialized nations, and Taiwan, South Korea and Malaysia are comparable at least with the Eastern European and wealthy Latin American nations. But more remarkable still than the absolute values are the changes which have taken place. During the 1950s every country in the region, with the exception of Japan, still belonged to the poorhouse of the world and, according to the World Bank's definition of 1987, counted as one of the world's least developed countries.

Table 6.2
Exports and shares of world trade, selected countries, 1960–85

	in US$ billion		*as % of world exports*	
	1960	*1985*	*1960*	*1985*
World	128.250	1,934.346	100.0	100.0
Japan	4.055	175.683	3.16	9.08
South Korea	0.033	30.283	0.03	1.57
Taiwan	0.164	30.723	0.13	1.59
Hong Kong	0.689	30.055	0.54	1.55
Singapore	1.136	23.756	0.89	1.23
China	1.860	26.478	1.45	1.37
6 countries	7.692	316.978	6.20	16.39
USA	20.412	213.146	15.92	11.02
W. Germany	11.415	183.406	8.90	9.48
France	6.862	97.726	5.35	5.05
UK	10.609	101.332	8.27	5.24
USSR	5.563	87.201	4.34	4.51
5 countries	54.861	682.881	42.78	35.30

Source: Calculated with reference to the *UN Yearbook of International Trade Statistics*, 1964; *UN Monthly Bulletin of Statistics*, 8/1986; *Taiwan Statistical Data Book*, 1986; *Statistical Yearbook of China*, 1981

The changes which have taken place are the result of an unparalleled expansion in foreign trade.

In 1960, before the onset of the export boom, the volume of East Asian foreign trade (again, with the exception of that for Japan) was still no more than marginal. By 1985 the exports of the six East Asian heartlands had increased in absolute terms 41-fold, and their share of world exports had grown from 6.2% to 16.4%. This compares with a relative decrease for the five big

Atlantic nations from 42.8% to 35.3%, although the volume of their exports increased appreciably in absolute terms during this period. If one also takes account of exchange-rate fluctuations, the picture looks even better for East Asia.

Although it is possible to argue that the supremacy of the Atlantic is still pronounced, this position does not take into account the fact that both the USA and Canada, but also the Soviet Union, also border on the Pacific and that, as such, to claim the total of their foreign trade for the Atlantic is inadmissible. Hence Table 6.3 endeavours to separate out intra-Pacific trade, at

Table 6.3
Foreign trade matrix for the Pacific region, 1960–83

	Exports to the region as a % of total exports		*Imports from the region as a % of total imports*	
	1960	*1983*	*1960*	*1983*
Japan	55.7	62.4	63.3	54.7
China	12.9	62.7	4.0	61.2
South Korea	85.9	61.5	74.0	63.6
Taiwan	77.0	74.4	80.4	61.2
Hong Kong	58.5	69.1	64.4	80.9
Macao*		52.7		89.7
Singapore	60.5	84.5	74.9	73.4
Malaysia	50.7	71.6	61.1	71.6
Indonesia	69.7	88.7	53.2	73.3
Philippines	77.4	75.8	80.6	65.6
Thailand	75.0	57.5	64.3	65.5
Brunei		96.6		76.7
Papua New Guinea*		58.5		89.0
USA	31.0	44.2	36.4	52.7
Canada	62.8	82.0	71.1	82.5
Australia	36.1	59.3	32.3	62.8
New Zealand	22.9	56.1	38.3	67.9
17 countries	41.0	61.5	48.4	59.7
Regional share of world trade	12.7	20.6	12.8	20.6
The 17 countries' total share of world trade	30.9	33.6	26.4	34.5

* Column headed '1983' refers, for these countries, to 1982.

Source: Calculated with reference to the *UN Yearbook of International Trade Statistics*, 1964; *UN 1983 International Trade Statistics Yearbook*; *Taiwan Statistical Data Book*, 1986; *Statistical Yearbook of China*, 1985; *Korea Statistical Yearbook*, 1984

least to the extent that this can be determined from statistics compiled by each of the region's trading partners.

'Pacific region' is defined here so as to cover North America, Oceania, East Asia and the ASEAN states, a total of 17 countries. The region's Latin American neighbours and the South Asian countries have not been taken into account, and the island nations, Indonesia, North Korea and the Soviet Union have not been included due to the absence of statistics. Despite these limitations, Table 6.3 gives a clear picture of the situation.

Between 1960 and 1983 the economic relations between almost all of the countries quoted became considerably closer, both in terms of exports and imports. China, still almost completely integrated into the Council for Mutual Assistance (COMECON) in 1960, Argentina, New Zealand, Canada and the USA, still clearly oriented towards Europe at that time, are spectacular cases and help to qualify the figures in Table 6.2. A relative increase in intra-Pacific trade as a percentage of total world trade from just under 13% to 21%, something approaching that for intra-Atlantic trade, is a further consequence of this development.

To sum up, it can be said that:

- since the beginning of the 1960s, East and Southeast Asia have become the real growth centres of the world;
- this growth has been determined to a large extent by a disproportionately high increase in foreign trade; and
- foreign trade increasingly means intra-regional trade and has caused the region's major neighbours to shift their attention away from the Atlantic to the Pacific region.

The long-term orientation of the US economy towards the Pacific

The shift of the economic centre of gravity within the USA to the Sun Belt and to the Pacific coast is a post-war phenomenon, covered in detail in current literature in this field. Less well known is the fact that the westward shift in foreign trade began much earlier and has advanced much further.

Figure 6.1 demonstrates the percentage distribution of US foreign trade over Europe, and Asia and the Pacific, from 1821 to 1986, that is since statistics of this kind were first compiled. It confirms the statement made at the beginning of this chapter that throughout the nineteenth century the USA was an unmistakably Atlantic economy, with around 75–80% of her exports going to, and around 60% of her imports coming from, Europe. The Asian–Pacific region was no more than a minor trading partner. It was, at any rate, less important than Latin America and Canada.

Since the turn of the century this pattern of distribution has been changing. Although there has been a great deal of fluctuation as a result of two world wars, exports to Europe have fallen steadily throughout the twentieth century to well under 30%, whilst the Asian–Pacific region has been gaining ground

Figure 6.1
The USA's foreign trade by region, 1830–1986
(%)

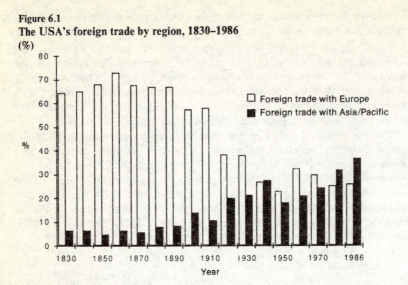

since the 1920s — since the major advance in Japanese industrialization — and replaced Europe as the major recipient of the USA's exports a couple of years ago. On the import side the trend is even more marked. The Asian–Pacific region replaced Europe as the USA's major supplier as far back as the 1930s or 1940s, although the trend was reversed for 15–20 years after World War II. During the mid-1970s the region once again became the USA's major supplier, and with 43% of the market at present sells almost twice as much as Europe and has even vastly exceeded its own 1940's peak value. Analysis of the composition of the USA's trade-flows provides the following explanation: a substantial part of the USA's basket of export commodities is, and has been in the past, foodstuffs, agricultural produce and mineral substances. During the nineteenth century these goods were sold in Europe and were responsible for unleashing the Great Depression.

European protectionism, nowadays invoked by the EC, and surplus production have resulted in a reduction in the USA's European sales, and the industrialized and NICs of East Asia, which are, without exception, conspicuous for food shortages and a serious dearth of raw materials, have proved an obvious alternative outlet. Conversely, industrialization in East Asia, which in the 1920s and 1930s was restricted, in the export industries at least, to light industry, has provided that region with a major market in the USA and has already resulted in European goods being driven out. As Japan's industrialization has advanced and new export industries have grown up in the NICs, the region's range of exports has expanded to include consumer durables, semi-finished products and investment goods, with the result that European exporters have also had to tolerate declining market shares for these goods in the USA. It has been argued, however, and not without some justification, that overseas investment has been replacing the trade in goods ever since the 1920s, and that if that is the case then trade-flows alone do not give a true picture of a country's foreign-trade orientation. Since US direct investment is undertaken mainly in Europe, and overseas investment in the USA comes primarily from Europe, actual economic relations are probably closer than trade-flows alone suggest.

In fact, US direct investment did not increase enormously merely in absolute terms between 1950 and 1980; Europe's share of that investment also rose, to around 45% by 1980. It was this trend which provided the setting for the American challenge, which hit the headlines in Europe particularly in the 1960s. Since 1980 the trend has altered in two respects: the value of US direct investment has stagnated in absolute terms, and Europe's share has remained constant. What has increased is the proportion of the USA's direct investment which has been allocated to the East Asian–Pacific region. Though the ratio of direct investment in this region to direct investment in Europe is still 1:3 (instead of 1:4), we should not forget that, unlike with trade, we are talking here not about the value of new investment but about the value of total existing investment, and that changes in the ratios are therefore effected only over a long period. In the last five years alone the East Asian–Pacific region has become the USA's major investment zone.

A similar tendency is apparent also in the origin of overseas direct investment in the USA. Although at two-thirds Europe's share, it is still larger than that of the East Asian–Pacific region, it has been declining since the early 1970s. During the same period Japanese direct investment in the USA has risen from zero to over 10% and may well have received another boost in 1986, with the result that Japan is now the USA's major overseas supplier of new direct investment. Although the overseas investment of the other East Asian countries is still limited, it is increasing and is also concentrated in the USA.

As we have seen in Figure 6.1, statistics relating to the partner concentration of US trade confirm the move towards East Asia. Although the USA's overall economic relations with Europe may still predominate, it would appear that based on the trend of the last eight years Europe has also lost ground, and fallen to second place, as regards the partner concentration of US overseas investment. Clearly, the claim that a Pacific centre is emerging is supported not only by East Asia's growth rate but also by the US economy's reversal of polarity in the matter of foreign trade. This reversal began as far back as the 1920s, and the process of erosion of the Atlantic economy thus set in very much earlier than is generally imagined. How, then, is this affecting the balance of power between Japan and the USA?

Japan provides the USA with resources

The USA's twin deficit (1985 budget deficit = US$212.3 billion and 1986 trade deficit = US$125.4 billion) is at the moment the most easily quantifiable expression of the American supremacy crisis. Both deficits are, to a considerable extent, the result of developments whose causes can be traced back to the Pacific region. The USA consequently feels that it is facing a double challenge:

- A military challenge from the Soviet Union, whose militarization in the Pacific (the expansion of its fleet of submarine and surface vessels at bases in Vladivostok and Petropavlovsk-Kamchatskiy and its stationing of SS20s in Siberia, where they are within range of US bases in Japan, Guam and the Philippines) poses a threat to the USA's traditional military superiority in the North Pacific. This is one of the reasons behind the USA's attempts to win back her military supremacy since the end of the 1970s by means of radical increases in the defence budget from US$116.3 billion (1979) to US$252.7 billion (1985). These increases in the defence budget are largely responsible for the country's budget deficit.
- An economic challenge with long-term and probably serious consequences both from Japan and increasingly also from the NICs of East Asia. These countries' greater competitiveness both in the traditional industries, and also increasingly in the sphere of new technology, is the major cause of the USA's current-account deficit, which has increased equally radically since the late 1970s.

However, both deficits have to be financed. Since the balance of payments always balances on principle, the gaping hole in the USA's current account always has to be offset by an equivalent influx on her capital account. This influx is also desirable because of its positive effects on the budget deficit, which can no longer be made up on the domestic capital market due to its size and the low rate of saving in the USA. But although a budget deficit has the effect of pushing up interest rates, and thus of attracting capital imports, it also damages the USA's competitive position by dint of its high capital costs and high dollar rate (until the autumn of 1985) as a result of the huge amounts of capital then being imported. All this in turn increases the current-account deficit even more. The whole process reveals a major contradiction in US policy: the Department of Defense is prepared to put up with deficits in order to restore the USA's threatened military supremacy, whereas the Department of Commerce wants to restore competitiveness and must therefore have an interest in reducing both deficits. So far the Pentagon is proving the stronger of the two.

Who, then, finances the USA's twin deficit? When the OPEC countries dropped out of exporting capital after the fall in the price of oil only the countries with large balances on their current accounts were left. Just a glance at Japan's balance of payments over the last few years reveals clearly that, after West Germany, Japan is the leading candidate.

The Japanese trend towards growing surpluses set in first in 1971, but was interrupted by the rise in oil prices during the 1970s, only to take an even more passionate hold when the price of oil finally fell again. Between 1980 and 1986 Japan's current-account balance was transformed from a deficit of US$10.7 billion into a surplus of US$86 billion. In order to restore equilibrium to the balance of payments, the surplus had to be matched by an increase in capital

Table 6.4
Japan's balance of payments 1968–86 (US$ billion)

	Current balance	Trade balance	Balance of services	Capital balance
1968	1.048	2.529	– 1.306	– 0.239
1969	2.119	3.699	– 1.399	– 0.155
1970	1.970	3.963	– 1.785	– 1.591
1971	5.797	7.787	– 1.738	– 1.082
1972	6.624	8.971	– 1.883	– 4.487
1973	– 0.136	3.688	– 3.510	– 9.750
1974	– 4.693	1.436	– 5.842	– 3.881
1975	– 0.682	5.028	– 5.354	– 0.272
1976	3.680	9.887	– 5.867	– 0.984
1977	10.918	17.311	– 6.004	– 3.184
1978	16.534	24.596	– 7.387	– 12.389
1979	– 8.754	1.845	– 9.472	– 12.976
1980	–10.746	2.125	–11.343	– 2.324
1981	4.774	19.967	–13.573	– 9.672
1982	6.850	18.079	– 9.848	– 14.969
1983	20.799	31.454	– 9.106	– 17.700
1984	35.003	44.257	– 7.747	– 49.651
1985	49.169	55.986	– 5.165	– 64.542
1986 (p)	85.966	92.659	– 4.633	–131.814

+ = net influx   – = net outflow   p = provisional

Source: Bank of Japan, *Balance of Payments Monthly*, December 1986; Bank of Japan, *Economic Statistics Annual*; 1985

exports, as the last column of Table 6.4 demonstrates. In fact, during that same period Japan transformed itself from a net importer of capital to the value of US$2.3 billion into a net exporter of capital to the value of US$131.8 billion.

A glance at the bilateral balance of payments between Japan and the USA reveals that in 1985 more than half (US$33.2 billion) of Japan's US$64.5 billion surplus went to the USA. Conversely, 35% of the USA's net capital imports came from Japan. In 1986 both of these trends may well have strengthened considerably. Of the remaining 65% of the USA's net capital imports, around half came from Western Europe (primarily West Germany). The other half were illegal imports which show up in the US's balance of payments as a 'statistical discrepancy'. Violent shifts of this kind in the bilateral balance of trade naturally have consequences for each of the country's international positions as debtors and creditors. It is not the annual value of the flows, but the accumulated value over several years which is meant here. It is generally acknowledged that throughout the nineteenth century the USA was a net importer of capital and that she did not become a net exporter of capital until

Figure 6.2
Japan: overseas assets and liabilities, 1978–*86*

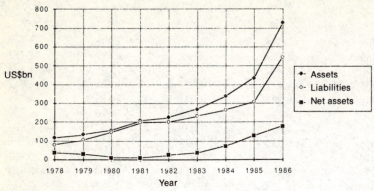

Source: Bank of Japan

Figure 6.3
USA: Overseas assets and liabilities, 1978–86

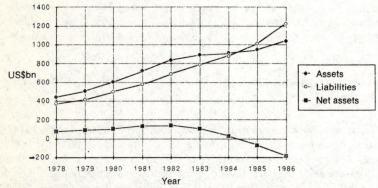

Source: Survey of Current Bussiness

1914. This change indicated, among other things, her promotion to the rank of leading economic power and over the next 70 years led to her being transformed into the major creditor nation on earth. The last five years have been sufficient, however, to radically reverse that transformation, with the USA becoming one of the world economy's net debtors and Japan one of its net creditors.

In 1982 the USA still had at her disposal net overseas assets worth US$147 billion, that is overseas assets exceeded overseas liabilities by this amount. By 1984 these assets had already melted away to US$28.2 billion and by 1985 had been transformed into net liabilities of US$66.4 billion, an amount which then trebled by 1986 to US$179.9 billion. On the other hand, between 1981 and 1986 Japan's net overseas assets increased from US$11 billion to US$262 billion.

Finally, the depreciation, now amounting to more than 40%, of the dollar against the yen since the autumn of 1985 provides an interesting footnote. On the surface it would appear to herald an improvement in the bilateral trade balance since the depreciation of the dollar should correct the two countries' bilateral competitive positions. But, so far, it has had no effect on the trade in goods but has merely encouraged Japanese direct investment in the USA. It has, though, had an effect on Japan's long-term capital investment (and that of other countries) in the USA. At the end of 1984 this stood at around US$30 billion and at the end of 1985 at around US$66 billion. Since this investment was undertaken almost exclusively in dollars, Japanese investors may well have sustained losses estimated crudely at US$19–20 billion when the investments are converted into yen. A real crisis contribution.

The shift of the world economy's growth centres to the Pacific Basin does have political causes and consequences: not only has the USA become a debtor nation, she has become the world's major debtor (within the space of two years), whilst Japan has taken her place as the world's major creditor nation. As a result, the USA can no longer finance the cost of her leading role in world politics alone and is increasingly forced to rely not only on her European allies but also, and in particular, on Japan. This, together with Japan's ever greater transfer of arms-related technology and the new strategic role which she has been given in the North Pacific regarding the Soviet Union, is a sure sign that the USA's alliance with Japan has become the second supporting pillar of that nation's global strategy after NATO.

Recommended Reading

Calder, K. E. (1985) 'The Making of a Trans-Pacific Economy', *World Policy Journal* 2 (4).

Katz, J., Friedman–Lichtschein, K. and Tilly, C. (eds) (1985) *Japan's New World Role*, Boulder.

Menzel, U. (1985) *In der Nachfolge Europas. Autozentrierte Entwicklung in den ostasiatischen Schwellenländern Südkorea und Taiwan*, Munich.

——— (1987) 'Japanische Außenpolitik und Amerikanische Hegemoniekrise', *PROKLA* 1, Berlin.

Nukazawa, K. (1983) 'Political Arithmetic of Yen for Dollar', *The World Economy* 6 (3).

7. The Developing Nations and the International Division of Labour

Folker Fröbel/Jürgen Heinrichs/Otto Kreye

From Bretton Woods to the dollar crisis

The accumulation model which served as the framework for capitalist development during the first few decades after World War II was characterized by a unique combination of freedom of entrepreneurial activity world-wide and social partnership and Fordism (see pp. 000–00) in the industrialized nations of the West. At the centre of the capitalist world a balanced expansion in output and mass consumption, consistently strong economic growth and something approaching full employment provided capital with both a guarantee of economic primacy and a degree of social acceptability.

In international relations, the USA, by virtue simply of her overwhelming economic importance and the dollar's position as a world currency, acted as a regulatory authority, a function which in a politically disunited world economy can only be performed effectively by a supreme power. As a result, armed intervention became almost completely unnecessary as a means of guaranteeing the prerequisites for international capitalist production. The friendly neutrality which the USA exhibited towards pro-Western independence movements in the colonies arose out of her interest in opening up the old colonial empires to international, primarily US capital.

As far as the relationship between capital and nature was concerned, the new model merely strengthened the old established mechanism whereby the costs of private-sector production within a competitive economy were externalized as much as possible. Among other things, this meant both the unrestrained plundering of natural resources and the exploitation for profit of regenerative deposits.

A policy of 'containment' and of preventive revolution (which could cover measures as severe as military intervention) also afforded the new model protection from East–West antagonisms, that is from the challenge posed by non-capitalist social orders.

Despite all of the decolonization which had taken place there, this extremely Western-industrialized-nation-centred accumulation model assigned to the South a peripheral role in the capitalist world, just as previous models had done; for the most part the developing nations were integrated into the world economy as exporters of raw materials, as outlets for industrial goods and through relatively modest direct investment. When necessary they also served on the periphery as suppliers of cheap migrant labour.

At any rate, the developing nations' share of the total GDP created by the world's market economies (both those in the industrialized and those in the developing world) fell between 1948 and 1970 from approximately 17.5% to around 15.5%; during the same period their share of world exports and imports each fell from 30% to around 18%.

In many parts of Latin America (with its long history of political independence) and Africa and Asia (where political independence movements have been successful in the post-war period) national bourgeoisies pursued a policy of integration in the world market which took the form of import substitution. This was an attempt to stimulate the development of domestic industrial capitalism through the implementation of import restrictions of all kinds and to lay the foundations for an independent and self-financing process of industrialization. The attempt recognized totally the principle of world-wide freedom of entrepreneurial activity, the very basis of the *Pax Americana*, and was therefore receptive to, and at the same time limited by, the interests of transnational concerns and their direct investment in developing nations with all of its widely recognized consequences of dependence on overseas supplies, foreign management and foreign technology.

Logically, such policies should have been based around (bourgeois) agrarian reforms. In most of the countries concerned, however, things were prevented from going that far by a coalition of domestic (for example, big land-owning) and overseas (for example, multinational) interests (cf. Simon). (Remarkably and for very specific reasons Taiwan and South Korea were both exceptions.) Because of this structural hurdle to a dynamic improvement in the (domestic) purchasing power of the masses, the vast majority of the countries concerned quickly reached the limits of this peripheral development model. Towards the end of the 1960s there were signs, confirmed by uprisings and *coups*, that many local bourgeoisies had begun to change direction. Their motives for doing so, the form which that change of direction took and its timing only become clear when one considers the contradictory logic inherent in the post-war model with its centre of gravity in the industrialized world. Before we turn to this, let us first glance at the progress of the developing nations during the first few decades of the post-war period and evaluate the prospects for a dynamic development in the future.

Of course, in retrospect it is obvious that the policies pursued at this time by the national bourgeoisies in the countries of the South were largely unsuccessful, at least when measured against the declared aim of bringing about independent, self-financing, domestically oriented industrialization and of raising the general standard of living. Seemingly paradoxically, these policies nevertheless contributed greatly in countries as different as Brazil and Mexico, Taiwan and South Korea, the developing nations in the Mediterranean and the Caribbean to the creation, or perhaps the non-prevention, of the prerequisites for a subsequent period of world-market-oriented capitalist (partial) industrialization. They created both an industrial reserve army of disciplined and cheap labour and elements of an administrative and industrial infrastructure. The negative aspects of this success were: years of stagnation or even deterioration as regards the already atrocious living conditions of the majority of the population of the Third World; and, as a result of economic dependence on international capital, an erosion of the scope for selective participation in the international division of labour of the kind which would take into account the need of the nation concerned for a process of indigenous industrialization.

As far as the prospects for a non-capitalist development in the future are concerned, it has to be said that the global balance of power between the world's various social systems has certainly not altered during this period in favour of socialist formations (this statement refers only to the countries of the geographical South, a term used by the United Naitons to define the developing nations). In fact, the opposite is true and, naturally, preventive counter-revolutions and military intervention directed from abroad, and in particular from the USA, have played a considerable part in this. Cuba is virtually the only example of a country which has succeeded in eradicating a capitalist social order, thanks above all to the enormous support which it received from the Soviet Union and China. Nevertheless, it should not be forgotten that in a world-wide context the socialist (or, to be less controversial, the non-capitalist) camp has been consolidated during this period. In particular China, which is widely known to regard herself as a Third World nation, has so far proved capable of resisting the undesirable tyranny of world-wide accumulation, despite all of the pressure placed on her to do so, but without being forced to refute the assertion that selective participation in the international division of labour can be advantageous.

From the dollar crisis to the debt crisis

During the late 1960s and early 1970s, after several decades of prosperity in the Western industrialized nations, the post-war model of capitalist development was plunged into crisis. It was, admittedly, not until a momentous world-wide reorganization of economy and society, accentuated by the first oil shock and a severe recession in the mid-1970s, became perceptible that there was any widespread reaction in the industrialized world. Only then did it become impossible to ignore the most serious depression since the world economic crisis of the 1930s.

In technical terms, our explanation of the crisis consists of evidence that it was inevitable that the mechanisms inherent in the system would, however paradoxical it may appear, sooner or later undermine the social primacy of capital, its profitability and the ability of the post-war model to regulate itself without crisis to the same degree as the successful functioning of the social-partnership and social-state model. Despite the delaying action of the workers, the business world met (and is meeting) this challenge with the help of appropriate business strategies: by exercising restraint when it comes to productive investment, by giving priority to financial investment and speculative transactions instead of to investment designed to encourage expansion, by speeding up investment designed to increase efficiency, through geographical shifts in production ('world-wide sourcing') and through new forms of transnational business co-operation.

Mass unemployment in the industrialized world, combined with appropriate government assistance (the abandonment of services provided by the social state, the deregulation of the labour market) has made it possible for firms to reduce their costs, to deploy their workforces more flexibly and to enhance the conditions for the speedy introduction of new technology in order, eventually, to replace the post-war model of capitalist development, which has been plunged irrevocably into crisis, possibly with a new model which is equally capable of making social compromises and equally efficient economically.

What does it all mean for the Third World?

Since the early 1970s, after decades of stagnation, industrial production for the world market has increased considerably in the group of countries known as the Third World nations. This important change in the structure of the international division of labour (new international division of labour) came about as a result of two conceptually different, but in reality closely related developments:

- First, the essentials for industrial world-market-oriented production were created in many parts of the world around this time; this gave firms the opportunity (and, through the competitive mechanism, soon also compelled them) to take advantage of the locational advantages in the developing world. In addition to a virtually unlimited reserve army of cheap labour, manufacturing technology was available which made it possible to subdivide even complex manufacturing processes and to assign the part processes, in suitable combinations, to different locations; efficient means of transport and communication permitted the rapid, reliable, and relatively inexpensive transportation of goods and information, and the continuous direction and supervision of production at any location, however far away. Equally, firms were able to take advantage of a multitude of benefits derived from the infrastructure, loans and subsidies. They also enjoyed government support in disciplining their workforces. Thus the opportunities which existed for profitable world-market-oriented production in the Third World cannot in any way be attributed exclusively to the availability of cheap labour.
- Firms, especially those from the industrialized world, were under increased pressure to find a new way of combining all available options for the purposes of reducing costs and increasing the flexibility with which the workforce could be deployed and thereby initiating a world-wide reorganization of purchasing, manufacturing and marketing (that is, world-wide sourcing).

This concurrence of circumstances explains why the industrial production of manufactured goods for export, as well as the export-led production of agricultural and mining raw materials and of services (such as tourism), was now immediately proclaimed by the apologists for, or beneficiaries of, the system as a new 'developmental model'. Many Third World countries began to develop the infrastructure which would be required for all this, often under the influence of international 'development aid' organizations and programmes. Soon there was a surplus of suitably equipped locations; in the course of the contest which this triggered many developing nations felt compelled to offer multinationals increasingly favourable local conditions, such as more investment aid, higher export bounties, higher tax relief, lower wages and worse working conditions for the workers.

As a result, the developing nations' share of world exports of manufactured goods rose dramatically from around 4.5% in the 1950s and 1960s to around 13% in 1984 (see Table 7.1); in 1985 a fall to 12% was recorded. East and South East Asia, which accounted for three quarters of the exports, were by far and away the most successful regions; overall, exports from the Third World were highly concentrated in a small group of about ten Asian and Latin American countries.

This structural change in the international division of labour, which has been perceptible since around 1970 and continued at least into the mid-1980s (most recent figures available), was largely the result of the inclusion of new manufacturing locations by the multinationals, whether through overseas direct investment and formal participation in the developing nations, through production under licence or through other methods of utilizing productive capacity in the developing nations without formal capital participation on the part of the transnational company. As a consequence, however, the developing nations are increasingly coming up against the commercial strategies of international capital, which they find increasingly difficult to influence and which are characterized by high mobility, relocation, further relocation and re-relocation, by the introduction and allocation of part-production and by the many forms of co-operation which exist between firms.

If, in view of all this, one were to enquire into the chances of national policies being successful in the 1990s, one might expect the answer that on balance and with infinitely few exceptions the chances could only be described, as they were in the 1970s, as slight. The conditions under which the majority of the population lives have not improved on average at all; in many places they have deteriorated. In absolute terms poverty has increased in virtually every capitalist developing nation, and in many regions the consequences of the continuing predatory exploitation of nature and the destructive treatment meted out to the natural phenomena which guarantee life have shown themselves to be far more devastating than they were previously. For example, the number of droughts and floods recorded has doubled in comparison to the previous decade, and new forms of capital-intensive export-oriented farming methods are laying claim to and destroying more and more new acreage.

Increasing dependence on exports goes hand in hand with increasing

Table 7.1
The developing nations* share of world exports of selected groups of goods (%)

	1928	1937	1950	1960	1965	1970	1975	1980	1984	1985
All groups of goods	25.5	27.4	31.3	21.4	19.6	17.6	24.0	27.9	24.6	23.3
Primary products	38.0	41.6	—	36.6	35.5	34.5	44.3	48.6	40.9	40.6
Foodstuffs	40.3	44.1	—	37.0	34.0	31.8	28.9	28.5	31.2	32.5
Raw materials	—	—	48.0	34.8	32.1	30.5	27.7	28.1	26.0	26.4
Mineral fuels	36.3	40.2	63.9	60.5	63.1	63.5	73.8	72.3	57.3	56.5
Iron, steel, non-ferrous metals	—	—	—	12.3	12.9	14.3	9.1	12.1	15.4	14.8
Finished goods	6.5	5.1	—	4.2	4.6	5.2	6.7	9.4	13.2	12.0
Chemical prod.	—	—	8.4	4.0	4.2	4.6	5.9	6.3	7.8	7.4
Machinery & electrical goods	—	—	—	—	0.9	1.8	3.1	5.9	9.9	9.0
Passenger cars	—	—	1.1	0.7	0.7	0.5	1.4	1.7	2.0	1.9
Textiles	—	—	—	—	16.3	15.4	17.5	22.1	27.2	23.4
Clothing	—	—	—	—	—	21.1	32.0	36.5	47.7	50.4
Other manuf. goods	—	—	—	—	—	7.6	9.1	11.9	16.8	14.5

* Developing nations: 1928, 1937 — Africa excluding southern Africa; Latin America; Asia excluding Japan + Korea + Formosa Island, excluding the Soviet Union; 1950ff — Africa excluding South Africa; the Caribbean, Central and South America; Asia excluding Japan and excluding centrally planned economies; Oceania excluding New Zealand.

Sources: League of Nations, *The Network of World Trade* (for 1928 and 1937); United Nations, *Statistical Yearbook 1965* (for 1950); UNCTAD, *Handbook of International Trade and Development Statistics, 1972* (for 1955 and 1960); United Nations, *Monthly Bulletin of Statistics, 3/1971 and 5/1971* (for 1965), *5/1982* (for 1975), *5/1985* (for 1970), *5/1987* (for 1980, 1984 and 1985); GATT, *Networks of World Trade by Areas and Commodity Classes, 1955–76* (for 1955); and own calculations.

dependence on imports. For one thing, products suitable for the world market cannot be manufactured without materials and other primary products from abroad, for another, the neglect and displacement of production designed to meet domestic requirements also leads to the importation of consumer goods. The number of countries which is dependent on ever larger quantities of imported basic foodstuffs and which at the same time is increasing exports of agricultural (non-traditional) produce rose sharply during the 1970s.

In many of the countries on the periphery the expansion which has taken place in the field of export-oriented agriculture and in industry has displaced what were the still viable remains of subsistence economies or of subsistence production, as well as other small-scale agricultural and industrial businesses, without offering the families robbed of their living as a result of this expansion adequate compensation in the form of new job opportunities. Small- and medium-scale industries, some of which were built up in the course of the previous period of import substitution, have either disappeared again or have been reduced frequently to acting as ancillary suppliers for world-market-oriented production controlled from abroad. A great many jobs have disappeared in this sector, whereas in the vast majority of cases the total number of new jobs created in the field of export production has remained small in comparison to the large number of unemployed or underemployed. Moreover, any new jobs created are invariably unstable, dependent on fluctuations in demand and very selectively filled.

During the 1970s many developing nations, among them, surprisingly, a number of countries which had embarked upon what were, for a time, particularly rapid programmes of world-market-oriented (part) industrialization, ran up massive external debts. There is clearly a link between the international indebtedness of these countries and the fact that their industrialization processes were export-oriented:

- to a large extent the governments in these countries financed both the creation and expansion of infrastructure for, and investment in, world-market-oriented production itself by raising loans abroad;
- investment loans raised abroad were largely used for purposes other than the declared purpose (such as consumption or as flight-capital);
- for the most part foreign currency earnings from export production were and are used either to finance the repatriation of profits or as flight-capital; and
- when indebtedness reached the level at which debts could no longer be serviced out of current export surpluses, it became necessary for governments to raise new loans and therefore to increase their indebtedness.

As a consequence of the burden of their debt, the economies of the countries concerned are still, perversely, devoted exclusively, whatever the cost and without taking into account any possible effects on human lives and nature, to forced export-production. The sole purpose of this is to raise enough money to service the country's debts.

The post-war accumulation model has been plunged irrevocably into crisis: persistently poor growth, rising mass unemployment, the effective abandonment by firms in the industrialized world of the social partnership, ominously high imbalances in foreign trade, the debt crisis in the Third World and the equally ominous extent of the USA's growing (internal and external) indebtedness. The way in which social democratic governments managed the crisis during the 1970s was predictably not a recipe for countering either the poor growth caused by structural factors or mass unemployment or for transforming the 'social' into an 'economic and social market economy'. In the short and medium terms individual firms were able to influence development much more effectively through an extensive world-wide reorganization of their purchasing, manufacturing and marketing strategies.

Despite the peripheral role which it ascribed the developing nations, the post-war model had nevertheless kept its promise of development through a specific form of world-market integration (domestic-market-oriented industrialization stimulated by import-substitution policies and overseas investment). After the general failure of this development policy in the 1970s, a period of export-led growth induced a minor drive for export-oriented industrialization and thorough capitalization in a few of the countries of the Third World (in particular those which had previously undergone successful bourgeois agrarian reform); but simply because of the world market's extremely limited buoyancy during a period of virtual stagnation this could, of course, only happen in a very few countries. The best that many of the other developing nations could hope for was a minimal, but hardly permanent, increase in exports in a few unrelated sectors where part production was possible. (Note here the decline in the developing nations' share of world exports of manufactured goods between 1984 and 1985 which, should it continue in the coming years, will signal the definite end of that period of export-led growth in the Third World as a whole!) At worst, they risked unforeseen entanglement in debt bondage. With this in mind, what would the consequent implementation of the new accumulation model envisaged by conservative policy-makers mean for the Third World as a whole?

The eradication of underdevelopment would require systematic cultivation of domestic markets, an improvement in the living conditions of the mass of the population and democratization in the developing nations. Yet there is no place for all that in this model. The development of economy and society will be controlled for the unforeseeable future by each country's obligation to service its debts. Only those who have large incomes and the few more or less successful NICs continue to be of interest as outlets for consumer and investment goods. The rest, however, are finding that the ability to take decisions relating to economic activity, the use of resources and the distribution of output is now fast being taken out of their own hands. The opening up of markets, upon which the IMF has been able to insist by dint of its power to either extend or refuse further loans, leaves the developing nations at the mercy of the concentrated might of the multinationals. The outflow of economic resources, which has now increased to proportions which are considered alarming even in banking and financial circles in the North, continues. It is vital that this trend be checked.

Recommended Reading

Fröbel, Folker, Heinrichs, Jürgen and Kreye, Otto (1986) *Umbruch in der Weltwirtschaft*, Reinbek.

8. Mineral Substances on the World Market

Dorothea Mezger

During the 1980s the mineral-substance markets were plagued with rock-bottom prices, a glut of raw materials and surplus capacity in the mining and metal-working industries. A considerable part of this surplus capacity had been planned during the 1970s, which had been characterized by relatively high prices and a rather short supply of raw materials. The countries of the Third World are endowed with around a third (36%) of the world's mineral substances (after the Western industrialized nations and the state-trading countries), and those of them which obtain a considerable part of their foreign earnings by exporting mineral substances (countries such as Chile, Peru, Bolivia, Zambia, Zaire, Zimbabwe, Botswana, Namibia, Mauritania, Liberia, Indonesia, Malaysia, Papua New Guinea amongst others) were particularly badly hit by this price-surplus trend. The future economic prospects for these exporters must be viewed even more pessimistically in the medium term if growth in the industrialized world is not to stagnate. The major reason for this is that new technology is having the effect of modifying demand for mineral substances in the industrialized world.

Since the beginning of the 1970s the countries of the Third World have been able to increase their share of world mineral-substance consumption considerably, from 11.2% in 1961 to almost 30% in 1984. However, the increase continues to be restricted to certain regions, in particular East Asia, whilst African consumption, for example, has come to a standstill at the old level.

Price trends and indebtedness

More than ten years after the raw materials boom, raw materials prices, in particular those of mineral substances, have fallen a great deal. In 1987 they reached their lowest point since World War II. In 1985 real (= adjusted for inflation) raw materials prices were generally:

- 27% lower than the average for the 1950s
- 13% lower than the 1960s' level
- 23% lower than the 1970s' level
- 10% lower than the 1980–85 level, which itself was already low.

Since the beginning of the 1980s the prices of mineral substances have been moving along at a particularly low level. According to UNCTAD, the terms of trade for mineral substances have worsened markedly and at the beginning of 1985 were worth only 65% of their early 1980s' value. UNCTAD's Integrated Raw Materials Programme, a comprehensive blueprint for stabilizing raw materials prices, now exists only on paper. Many of the raw-materials-exporting countries have been forced into debt by the negative trend in price and output, the worsening terms of trade and the increased demand for foreign currency, which have come about as a result of successful development strategies along the lines of industrialization through import substitution. Almost all African and Latin American raw-materials-exporting economies, including those of Chile, Peru, Bolivia, Zambia, Zaire and Mauritania, are heavily in debt. The same is true of the economies of Brazil and Mexico, which are also major exporters of raw materials but which produce a broader range of exports and not merely mineral substances.

Of course, the negative trend in prices and output has not affected all mineral subtances to the same extent. Some of those raw materials vital to the defence sector (strategic raw materials) have bucked the trend, among them chrome, cobalt, tungsten and platinum.

Figure 8.1
World raw materials price index, 1891—*1986*

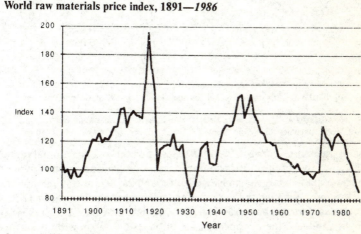

Source: *Le Monde Diplomatique*

Structural changes in metal consumption: the effects of post-industrial society

Iron ore, aluminium, copper, lead, zinc, tin and nickel account for more than three-quarters of all ores and metals traded on the world market. During the early 1980s they and manganese ore yielded 53% of all foreign earnings from non-fuel mineral subtances. Despite stronger growth in the industrialized nations since 1983, the increase in demand for mineral substances has remained lower than the general increase in demand.

Metal consumption varies greatly from one region to another and with the level of that region's industrial development. Overall, though, it is possible to discern a trend according to which consumption of mineral substances falls in relation to GNP world-wide.

Conventional models cite demand rigidity and the contest for every price into which the heavily indebted nations in particular are forced, as well as the high standing of the dollar (until 1985) and high interest rates, as the reasons that mineral substances prices are so low. At least as important as these supply factors, however, is the demand side. Table 8.1 shows the long-term trend in the relative fall in demand for various metals.

Table 8.1
Trend in the falling consumption of the major mineral substances (average of annual rates of growth in consumption 1951–83 (%)

Metal	1951–61	1964–74	1974–79	1979–83	1981–85
Iron ore	6.2	4.5	0.1	–1.2	1.0[a]
Aluminium	9.2	8.4	3.0	–1.1	3.0
Copper	4.7	2.9	3.5	–1.9	0.2
Lead	4.1	2.8	4.4	–1.9	0.7
Zinc	4.9	3.8	1.1	–0.8	1.7
Tin	1.0	1.2	–0.8	–2.0	1.1
Nickel	6.2	5.7	1.9	–2.3	4.3[b]

Notes: [a] Only boom years 1984/85.
   [b] In 1985 the western world's nickel consumption fell by 5% on the previous year.

Sources: *Metallstatistik, Metallgesellschaft*, various years; *World Metal Statistics*, World Bureau of Metal Statistics; Gonzales-Vigil, F. (1985); *Mining, Annual Review*, 1986

Even in the boom years of 1984 and 1985, when the average annual rate of growth in the GNP of the OECD countries was 3.7%, consumption of mineral substances remained largely unchanged, although the light metal, aluminium, fared considerably better than, say, copper. Whereas the European OECD countries plus Portugal had a GNP growth rate of a little over 2.3% (1984/5), they slightly reduced their copper consumption, as did Japan with its average GNP growth rate of 4.8% (1984/5). Nor did the consumption of iron ore correspond to the growth in the world's GNP, and in 1985 the Western world's nickel consumption fell by 5% on the previous year, though it was still higher than it had been during the years of recession. An examination of a longer period reveals an enduring trend towards reductions in the consumption of mineral substances.

The relative fall in demand cited above has a specific regional breakdown which correlates with the level of industrialization. Whereas world steel consumption, for example, rose by almost 1% (annual average) during the period 1970–80 (in the first half of the 1970s the increase was actually over 5%), it fell by almost 3.4% in the USA and by 1.7% in the EC. During the recession of 1980–82/3 world steel consumption fell by 8.8%, US steel consumption by 14.6% and EC consumption by 4.9%. These trends, which were not fundamentally revised, but rather confirmed, by the relatively small quantitative increase in the consumption of mineral substances during the boom years after 1983, served to corroborate the prognosis of a smaller increase in metal consumption in the future.

The major cause of this fall in consumption is the fact that the pattern of consumption in the industrialized nations has been changing as these nations move towards the post-industrial or service society. Both the income level which an economy reaches and the industrialization model which it chooses are crucial to the way in which its consumption changes. When an economy reaches a high national-income level metal consumption falls, and this is what has happened in the industrialized nations. The high-tech sectors of industrial society are material-intensive rather than metal-intensive, a fact which is demonstrated by the development and use of new kinds of materials. Polymeric materials, plastics and high-stress-bearing fine ceramic materials, as well as new kinds of alloys, are now competing with the older, metalline substances. The restructuring and modernization of the production process is resulting in the development of new technologies which permit greater flexibility in production and save energy, mineral substances and labour. Here reductions in weight and the miniaturization of products and machinery are of particular significance. The purpose of this process of modernization and restructuring is to reduce costs and thereby improve productivity and profitability. Technical changes designed to achieve greater productivity and profitability may be regarded, therefore, as the real driving-force behind lower mineral prices. The mineral resources of the exporting countries of the Third World are particularly affected by such developments, since these create new technological needs which magnify old-established differences. In general, relatively more mineral substances are used during the early stages of industrial development, but this higher level of consumption can be reduced in today's NICs and other developing nations if modern technological processes are adopted there.

Vertical and horizontal integration in the raw materials sector

In addition to these long-term, technological determinants of demand, there are further technical developments taking place in the fields of exploration, mining and metal-working which increase the technological needs and the dependence of the mineral-exporting economies of the Third World. One such new technology in the field of exploration, for example, is a new computer software package (known as an 'expert system') which instead of collecting new data permits the extraction of new information by better combining and evaluating existing data, and makes it possible for multidisciplinary data to be networked automatically. Improved geological models based on improved software and better multispectral satellite identification are yet more examples. There have been comparable technical developments in the field of mining, for example new computer-controlled technologies which ensure an optimal choice of routes inside rock.

With the exception of countries such as Chile, Brazil, Mexico, and a few Southeast Asian exporters of raw materials, the Third World countries have barely adequate engineering expertise to get even a general idea of or to assess the new developments. They therefore remain particularly dependent on the expertise of the mining companies. This dependence is part of the structure of the international mineral-substances sector, which is characterized by vertically and horizontally integrated, transnational raw materials companies. In the mining sector vertical integration means that the mines, the refinement of ores, smelting, semi-finishing, transportation, marketing and financing may all be in the hands of one company. Vertical co-operation covers the ways in which companies associate with each other, by segmenting the market or through market agreements and old boys' networks, all of which limit competition between them. Large consumers of mineral substances, such as West Germany's metal corporation, are integrated into this horizontal and vertical division of the raw-materials world and participate in the financing of large projects. Third World exporters of raw materials, on the other hand, do not enjoy the benefits of operating world-wide but are restricted to their own territories. They have control only over their own resource base and are rarely vertically integrated to any great extent. Basically, they remain tied into the strategies of the large companies through joint ventures, technology, management contracts, distribution networks and financial agreements, and often have little room for manoeuvre. The major exceptions have already been mentioned. Through vertical integration the large companies are able to secure benefits for themselves which range from special tax arrangements (profit switching) in third countries, through transfer prices and legal transfers of their operating profits, privileges which are not available to Third World countries. (One exception is the *Companhia Vale do Rio Doce*, a Brazilian company which is in the process of transnationalizing.)

Competition and adjustment on the world markets

Low prices do not merely affect the Third World countries but also, for example, the mining companies. The latter, however, generally have a better chance of coping, for instance by closing mines or introducing new technology, and with the help of the benefits of vertical and horizontal integration. These companies close mines far more often than Third World exporters. There have, for instance, been many copper mines closed in the USA during the 1980s, and other branches of the mineral-substances industry have also been affected. Closures of this kind are incomparably more difficult for those countries of the Third World which are dependent on exports. Since the large-scale closure of unprofitable working mines virtually breaks the economic back of economies based on mineral exports, the World Bank and the EC grant rehabilitation loans even when this makes general market adjustment more difficult. As a rule, however, these rehabilitation loans are linked to the IMF's and World Bank's normal structural adjustment programmes, which are primarily pursued at the expense of the poor and the poorest sections of the population and which sometimes jeopardize their physical survival.

Adjustments in supply must be made, for failure to do so can lead to markets collapsing, as did the tin market in 1986. The tin market operated on the basis of the only agreement which existed for raw materials (for mineral substances) and which was supervised by the International Tin Council. The signatories were the six exporting countries (Malaysia, Indonesia, Thailand, Australia, Zaire and Nigeria) which shared 61% of the market. Under the agreement, the signatories supported the price of tin, and the market was directed by means of export quotas. Over the last ten years Brazil, which is not a member of the International Tin Council, has been particularly successful in dramatically expanding tin production in the Amazonas region. She took advantage of the high prices by continuing to toss her produce on to the world market, until that market collapsed. The collapse of the market led to the collapse of the entire Bolivian mining industry (see pp. 000–00).

There are many forms of competition which producers can use to force their competitors out of the market. One particularly obvious example is that used by the world's largest ore pit, the iron-ore pit *Grande Carajas* in the Amazonas region of Brazil, whose customers include the big steel companies in West Germany and steel companies in Japan and Korea. Older producers, such as Mauritania and Liberia, are being driven from the market place by *Grande Carajas* and are now virtually unable to find buyers for their ores.

Mineral substances and the 'development' myth: Bolivia and Zambia

'It is said that even the horseshoes in Potosi [Bolivia] were silver' (Eduardo Galeano). But that was in the seventeenth century. Since then not only Bolivia's silver reserves but her tin reserves also have been largely exhausted. For years the state has been subsidizing the tin produced by the state-run company, COMIBOL, because its production costs are far higher than the world-market price. In 1985 an IMF austerity programme was announced which provided for the abolition of subsidies on foodstuffs, the lifting of controls on the peso, the removal of import restrictions and the denationalization and decentralization of state-run companies, conditions imposed by the IMF during fresh restructuring negotiations which took place when the country became incapable of paying its debts in 1984. Some 42,000 workers lost their jobs as a result, COMIBOL dismissed 5,000 workers after the collapse of the tin market in 1986 and a further 14,000 are still to be dismissed. At the end of 1986 the miners and their families began a hunger strike in an attempt to force through a claim for higher compensation for the loss of their jobs. After that miners began leaving the mining areas because they could no longer find food there.

The informal sector, run primarily by the wives of the unemployed, grew tremendously. In the future mining is to be an economic activity like any other and no more. Bolivia's mineral reserves are largely exhausted.

The history of the Zambian mining industry, unlike that of Bolivia, which dates back 500 years, goes back only 65 years, to the time when the country first began to exploit its copper reserves during the colonial age under the auspices of what is now the world's biggest mining company, the Anglo-American Corporation (South Africa), and its other major shareholder, American Metal Climax (AMAX, USA). Over the last 20 years Zambia has obtained 90–95% of its foreign earnings from copper. In 1964, when the country won its independence, Zambia, still under the direction of its foreign advisors, decided on an ambitious programme of industrialization through import substitution. After 1978/9, transfers to her part-nationalized shareholders, a reduction in foreign earnings and the worsening terms of trade, as well as the systematic neglect of the agricultural sector, a neglect which continued beyond the colonial age, and increased demands on the foreign-currency budget caused by the development strategy which it had chosen forced the country more and more heavily into debt and finally into economic collapse. As a result of deficient capital expenditure on replacement and a shortage of spare parts, the mining industry itself was so badly hit by the economic crisis that spontaneous restrictions on output were introduced and mine closures announced. Accordingly, Zambia was forced to cut production from around 650,000 tonnes (1978) to only 436,000 tonnes (1986). Since the mines will have been largely exhausted by the year 2000, the World Bank, the EC and the national authorities are preparing the country for its post-copper phase. Zambia is now only able to exist on the basis of her creditors' restructuring programmes. Her remaining mineral resources already belong to the banks. Since 1978, IMF missions have been flying in and out of the country and, with the help of the World Bank, implementing structural adjustment programmes which are intended to transform Zambia into an exporter of agricultural produce and which, at the end of 1986, led to uprisings which left some of her citizens dead.

Bolivia and Zambia demonstrate, one in slow and one in quick motion, the consequences of a world-market-oriented 'development strategy' based on exports of mineral substances. The destruction without compensation of the non-renewable resource system, in other words, the undermining of these two and comparable Third World economies, is based on an old myth related originally by Agricola (1494–1555), the first modern mining theorist. Agricola argued that the money which would be earned from mining would more than compensate for the loss of fish, game, birds and forests. Fish and birds aplenty could be imported into mining regions. In Zambia, Bolivia and other mineral-substance exporting economies this myth has produced hunger.

The capitalist world economy's *destruction without compensation* of mineral substances means that non-renewable resources are being treated like infinitely reproducible commodities. The world-market price does not contain any element of compensation for the progressive and irreversible exhaustion of these raw materials. Although such an economic approach may be profitable from the point of view of the industrialized nations in the medium term, that is only the case for as long as their own, direct economic interests are all that is at stake; when a raw material in one country is exhausted, that is can no longer be profitably exploited, then it is imported from another country. The industrialized nations even regard the ecologically destructive mining of the oceans and the ecologically no less-devastating mineral exploitation of Antarctica, against which a Greenpeace expedition recently tried to warn the world public, as possible sources of their raw materials. However, when the mineral-substance base of an exporting nation in the Third World is destroyed, a form of economic plunder which generally accompanies permanent ecological predatory exploitation, then only indebtedness and poverty are left working at the face. The form of development which enables backward nations to catch up with the industrialized world, a form of industrialization which is socially tolerable, has never yet been achieved in the Third World using this method.

Recommended Reading

Gonzales-Vigil, F. (1985) 'New Technologies, Industrial Restructuring and Changing Patterns of Metal Consumption', *Raw Materials Report* 3 (3).

Leontief, W., Koo, J. C. M., Nasar, S. and Sohn, J. (1983) *The Future of Nonfuel Minerals in the US and the World Economy*, Lexington (and elsewhere).

Mezger, D. (1987) *Economics as if Matter Mattered. Nature Resources, Development and the Death of Nature*, London.

Mining (annual review) various issues.

Vorfelder, J. (1987) *Rettet die Antarktis*, Greenpeace Report 3, Reinbek.

9. Agricultural Raw Materials on the World Market

Gerd Junne

For many developing nations agricultural raw materials are practically the only source of foreign currency and the international debt crisis is ensuring that this remains the case, for in order to tap other sources of income the countries concerned would require financial resources, particularly loans, from abroad, yet they are seldom credit-worthy.

For 12 developing nations agricultural produce accounts for over 80% of total exports. Eleven of these countries are in Africa. In a further 18 countries agricultural exports account for 60–80% of all exports. The foreign earnings of at least 30 developing nations are thus predominantly dependent on the exportation of agricultural produce. Their position is particularly precarious. In the mid-1980s raw materials prices fell dramatically, and apart from those for oil reached their lowest since World War II. The worst affected have been agricultural products. Their price currently stands at only one-third of its all-time high, which was reached in 1973.

Figure 9.1
Index of real world-market prices for agricultural produce
(1980=100)

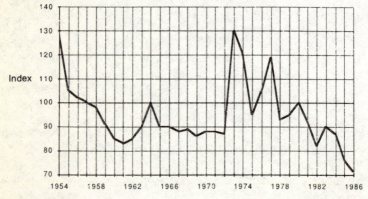

Source: UNCTAD.

IMF policies have undoubtedly contributed to this malaise. Many countries have been forced to adopt savings programmes which have required them to devalue their currencies. The immediate effect of a devaluation is that the exporter receives more of the domestic currency for his goods than before. This has tended to signal to farmers that they should increase their output for exportation, and the resulting glut has helped to bring about the fall in the world-market price. The export orientation forced upon the debtor nations under IMF rehabilitation programmes has had much the same effect.

Which factors have contributed to the fall in the world-market price for agricultural produce and is there any prospect of these prices making a good recovery in the future? For that is the only thing which can prevent those developing nations which are dependent on the export of agricultural raw materials from sinking deeper into debt.

Causes of the fall in price of agricultural produce

There are four reasons for the fall in price: increased productivity; the replacement of agricultural raw materials by industrial products; the agricultural policies of the industrialized nations; and the increasing self-sufficiency of many developing nations.

Increased productivity   Since World War II agricultural sectors world-wide have been undergoing a continual process of modernization. By employing modern technology and chemical fertilizers, farmers in the developing and industrialized nations have been able to increase their yields per hectare considerably, and this increase in productivity has contributed greatly to the fall in producers' prices.

Replacement by industrial products   Many agricultural products are being replaced more and more by industrial products. This is the case, for example, for natural rubber, which now has to share the world market with synthetic rubber. Wool and cotton have also been replaced to a considerable degree by synthetic fibres. Although changing patterns of consumption in the industrialized world have weakened the trend towards synthetic fibres in the clothing industry, the industrial fibres jute and sisal have been almost completely superseded by synthetics. In fact, in the early 1980s world consumption of jute was less than half its 1960s level. Over the same period consumption of sisal dwindled to less than a quarter. The consumption of wool and cotton also fell, although less dramatically. Even foodstuffs (and food additives, such as flavourings) are beginning to be replaced by industrial products. For instance, new sweeteners have been developed with the aid of biotechnology, small quantities of which are sufficient to produce the same sweetness as much larger quantities of sugar. They are used primarily in low-calorie products (e.g. Coca-Colalight), for which there is growing demand in the industrialized world. In the future, synthetic protein, which can be extracted with the help of bacteria from crude oil, natural gas and various waste products, will go some way towards replacing vegetable protein (such as soya). Furthest advanced is the industrial production of certain 'agricultural' produce, small quantities of which already fetch a high price. These include flavourings, fragrances, essences and plant-based medicines, whose active ingredients come increasingly from industry. The result of all this is that imports from the developing nations are becoming surplus to requirements.

The agricultural policies of the industrialized nations   There is virtually nowhere in the world where the prices of agricultural produce are left to the free interplay of supply and demand. Particularly ingenious and costly forms of intervention have been developed in the EC countries and in the USA. Between them these countries spend US$70 billion each year in subsidies in order to guarantee their farmers an income which can keep pace with that of the rest of the population. These subsidies have led to surplus production which has had to be sold on the world market and has therefore forced down price levels. One striking example of this is the world sugar market. The EC, once a net importer of sugar, is now by far the major exporter of sugar on the world market.

Price wars between the USA and Europe in respect of grain have been responsible for a further fall in prices. Of course, we are talking here primarily of foodstuffs and not of agricultural raw materials in the narrower sense. Around two-thirds of the world's exports of foodstuffs come from the industrialized nations (above all the USA and the EC). On the other hand, approximately two-thirds of the world's agricultural raw materials come from the developing nations.

The increasing self-sufficiency of many developing nations   It is not only the industrialized nations which are supplying themselves to an increasing extent with foodstuffs and agricultural raw materials. A growing number of developing nations are also reducing their dependence on imported foodstuffs. This is especially true of a number of Asian countries. Between 1971 and 1984 some of these countries (Indonesia, South Korea, the Philippines and Pakistan) achieved average annual growth rates for grain production of 4–5%. They are thus on the point of ceasing to be net importers and becoming exporters, with the result that supply on the world market is increasing whilst demand is falling off. The leading importer of vegetable oils and fats, India, is expanding its own production constantly in order to be able to limit imports. The majority of the importing nations is forced into such policies by a shortage of foreign currency.

The four points mentioned above are the reasons that world-market prices for agricultural produce have reached an all-time low. But what will the future bring? Is the current situation really no more than a cyclical decline which will be followed by a new upturn, or has there been a structural change in the price structure which will lead to permanently low agricultural prices?

Influences on future price trends

Let us now look again at the factors already cited in order to assess their probable influence in the future.

Future increases in productivity
There is nothing to suggest that agricultural productivity will rise less quickly in the future than in the past. On the contrary, the development of biotechnology is speeding up the cultivation of new high-yielding plant varieties and helping to ensure that progress in the sphere of productivity will be greater rather than less in the future. Productivity increases are nevertheless spread in a remarkably unequal manner over the various countries (and inside these countries). The more advanced developing nations, such as Brazil and Malaysia, are able to initiate improvements much more quickly than say the majority of the African countries. As we can see if we look at current exports of palm oil and cocoa, this means that the more developed nations can probably win a higher proportion of the world's agricultural exports. In Malaysia and Brazil production of these two commodities is increasing fast and driving the traditional exporters from the market-place, whilst exports from the African countries are stagnating or declining. It is, however, these very countries, the poorer African countries, which depend primarily on the export of agricultural produce. On pp. 000 reference was made to the fact that of the 12 developing nations for which agricultural produce accounts for more than 80% of total exports, eleven are African countries. The unequal development of productivity is causing the structure of world-trade flows to change to the disadvantage of the very countries which are already in the most difficulty.

Replacement by industrial products
Developments in the field of biotechnology are making it increasingly possible for foodstuffs and other goods hitherto produced in the agricultural sector to be manufactured using industrial processes. The fact that this is technically possible does not, however, in any way mean that it is also profitable or that it will catch on. A more likely scenario is that biotechnology will move in the opposite direction in the future: products which have hitherto been manufactured from a crude-oil base can increasingly be produced from renewable agricultural raw materials. One major example of this is the production of fuel for cars from sugar. In Brazil more than a million cars already run on ethanol made from sugar instead of on petrol.

In principle, the same end-products, for example plastic, can be extracted from a wide variety of agricultural raw materials, such as potatoes, straw, milk, sugar or maize. From this we can see that different agricultural raw materials are becoming more and more interchangeable. Sweeteners are no longer extracted from sugar-cane and sugar-beet alone. Nowadays maize or potato starch can also be transformed into sweeteners (fructose) with the aid of enzymes. In the USA this is happening on a large scale, and that country now consumes more sweeteners which have been extracted from maize than sugar.

Accordingly, the USA has cut sugar imports. This reduction in imports from the developing nations has contributed more than any other factor to the fall in the world-market price for that commodity. In a whole series of countries (in the Caribbean and the Philippines) sugar production has virtually collapsed as a result of this development, and this has left several million agricultural workers unemployed there.

A comparable trend can be discerned in the cultivation of cocoa as a raw material for the chocolate industry. Until recently cocoa butter was the major ingredient of chocolate and ensured the correct melting point ('in your mouth, not in your hand'). With the help of biotechnology other (cheaper) fats can now be modified to such an extent that they have the same property. Cocoa imports will therefore be replaced in the future to a large extent by imports of other oils and fats, for example, palm and soya oil.

The increasing interchangeability of different agricultural raw materials will have a huge effect on the foreign earnings of the countries which produce raw materials, for in future processors will be constantly on the look-out for the cheapest raw materials, and the producers will increasingly be played off against each other. This is likely to exert constant pressure for lower prices. The existence of substitutes will also make it increasingly difficult for international raw-materials agreements to be concluded which guarantee producers a minimum price for individual products, such as cocoa or sugar. Already the price of sugar cannot be regulated independently of the price of maize (and other primary products from which starch can be extracted), and the price of cocoa is likely to be influenced in the future by changes in the price of palm oil. As a result, producers of raw materials are likely to be deprived of the opportunity to stabilize their earnings from exports through raw-materials agreements.

The agricultural policies of the industrialized nations
In the past surplus production in the industrialized world has contributed greatly to low world-market prices for agricultural produce. It is questionable, however, whether this situation will last. Surplus production has placed a great deal of strain on national budgets, and these are bound to go even further into the red as world-market prices fall. Opposition to the agricultural policies which have led to such enormous surpluses is therefore growing. Numerous measures have been proposed which it is hoped will help to reduce the surpluses. These measures include reallocating acreage on which grain has previously been produced for export to alternative crops which can make a contribution towards reducing each country's imports. The EC, for example, is encouraging increased cultivation of flax and oleiferous plants (such as rape and sunflowers). Production of such plants would cut down on imports of other natural fibres and of palm and soya oil. So whilst it may well be the case that the surplus production of the industrialized nations will be less of a strain on the world market in the future, a fall in exports caused by a switch to other cultivated plants would also result in a reduction in imports. The world-wide surplus would not be reduced, but merely moved — from the industrialized nations to the developing nations. The stabilization of prices for the products in

which the USA and the EC dominate would then lead to strain being placed on the price of agricultural commodities which come primarily from the developing nations.

Increasing self-sufficiency of the developing nations

A shortage of foreign currency will also make it necessary in the future for developing nations to reduce their reliance on imported agricultural products as much as possible. In the long run biotechnology will help them to realize this objective through its contribution towards the development of new plant varieties which are less reliant on irrigation, chemical fertilizers, pesticides and other costly ancillary supplies and which can grow in ground of a worse quality (with a high salt or acid content). Many developing nations which have until now been importers on the world market for agricultural products today have the potential to become surplus countries. This could lead to the world-market-oriented production of agricultural *bulk goods*, which no longer fetch attractive prices, becoming increasingly concentrated on the developing nations whilst the agricultural sectors in the highly developed nations switch to commodities with a higher net product.

This would not mean any enduring improvement in the revenue position of the developing nations. The poorer developing nations would, after all, not be able to share in the development, and export opportunities would only open up for the advanced developing nations where low price levels were no longer stimulating production in the industrialized nations. Accordingly, a large increase in foreign-currency revenue could not be expected.

An examination of the factors which have led to low prices on the world market for agricultural produce reveals that these factors may also have an effect in the future. A permanent price rise is therefore not likely. Naturally, bad harvests, wars and other circumstances may cause the price of individual agricultural products to rise temporarily, but a general and more or less enduring rise in the price level cannot be expected.

What this does mean, however, is that those developing nations whose foreign-currency revenue is derived essentially from the export of agricultural produce will be forced to take out more and more loans unless they are able to break away from their concentration on agricultural products for export. There is therefore no good reason for the developing nations to specialize in the production of agricultural raw materials as some countries have been urged to do by the IMF.

10. The Debate on Development Policy

Wolfgang Hein/Theo Mutter

Going back on the pledge to modernize

Anyone wishing to understand the 1980s' debate on development policy cannot avoid looking at modernization theory. The problems currently being experienced by the developing nations, from the marginalization of large sections of the population to the debt crisis, are largely the result of the modernization-led policies of the 1950s and 1960s. Moreover, every 1970s' or 1980s' paradigm of development theory or policy has ended up as a theory of modernization, from the basic needs strategy as a modification of the modernization strategy, through the *Dependencia* School, to the Neo-Liberals. Yet the historical circumstances which lead to the predominance of a particular development strategy are by no means identical to the circumstances of its success. Over the last few years the term Fordism has been used increasingly to describe the world-wide capitalist accumulation model of the post-war era. Modernization strategy has proved useful as a way of propagating Fordist structures in Third World countries; but at the same time these structures have done more to prevent than to facilitate the intended wholesale modernization of society.

Many aspects of the theories summarized briefly above require explanation. The theory of modernization works on the assumption that development is identical to the transformation of a traditional society into a modern society, with particular reference to those social and political changes which are both the prerequisites for and the consequences of industrialization within a society. Different authors and different disciplines have stressed different aspects of modernization. For example, Walt W. Rostow's economic theory of modernization emphasizes the scientification of production, a positive attitude towards economic advance (for which read growth), the emergence of a dynamic enterprise culture, the establishment of a 'powerful, centrally governed nation-state' and the creation of institutions which promote growth and permanent social change. Accordingly, a modernization strategy is one which purposefully promotes just such a process of transformation: by propagating ideas, modes of behaviour, patterns of consumption and institutional forms from the industrialized nations, (the 'modern' societies) in non-industrial traditional societies; and by the state carrying out this modernization inside the country concerned despite both possible opposition from the traditional élite and the fact that modes of behaviour adopted by the poor are not conducive to modernization. In the past the idea of state intervention in the purposeful promotion of development linked in with many industrialized nations' experiences of the form of development which allows underdeveloped countries to catch up, particularly in the second half of the nineteenth century; although carried out under fundamentally different circumstances, the success of the Marshall Plan in Western Europe appeared also to confirm the supposition that a rapid process of modernization can be induced with relatively insignificant injections of capital.

Against this background and allowing for previous attempts at spontaneous import substitution, but also with the aim of weakening the economic and political dominance of the traditional agrarian oligarchies, a package of economic policy measures such as the one below was implemented in almost every country in Latin America:

- The state apparatus itself took an active part in promoting modernization, among other things by encouraging the expansion of the material and social infrastructure, by making available subsidized loans and by setting up state-owned concerns.
- The national currency was systematically overvalued, making imports cheaper but exports more expensive on the world market and offering few incentives (relatively low revenue in the national currency) for the production of raw materials with fixed world-market prices to be increased.
- In order that national industrial output could be built up, even when the currency was overvalued, high customs duties were required on products manufactured in the country itself. This protected such lines of production from foreign competition, but still permitted the cheap importation of primary products.
- A strategy of this kind leads to deficits, both in internal financing and in foreign-trading relations (balance of payments). Thus the primary function of co-operation in the field of development was to finance those deficits, the assumption being that modernization would bring with it rapid improvements in the efficiency of the national economy and that repaying the loans would therefore not pose a problem.

The effects of strategies of this kind are well-known:

- Almost every country where such a strategy was implemented experienced fairly long periods of industrial growth, although the forms of industry which emerged were considerably different in character, ranging as they did from a simple job-contract processing to diversified industrial structures (such as those in India and Brazil) with considerable national technological expertise.
- However, modernization processes of this kind were by no means completely successful everywhere in the Third World; their usual

characteristics are: structural heterogeneity, both between what are mostly rather small modern sectors and between expanded social sectors which are still basically traditional in form but which have lost their characteristic dynamism; large regional discrepancies; an extremely unequal distribution of income and wealth; and the marginalization of large sections of the population.

- The industries which emerge as a result of such modernization are characterized by a high degree of technological dependence, since the import of primary products is encouraged through the overvaluation of the national currency, whilst on the other hand the great protection afforded finished goods guarantees a steady domestic market.

- The deficitary nature of this type of development ensures structural dependence on overseas finance and leads, should this finance be placed in jeopardy either for political reasons or as a result of a world economic crisis, to the swift collapse of the whole strategy.

Ultimately, the whole debate on development policy over the last 15 years centres on the question of how this kind of development should be interpreted: whereas the exponents of the *Dependencia* School regard it as a specific historical form of development which merely perpetuates those antagonisms between the metropole and the periphery which have characterized capitalism from its earliest beginnings, the Neo-Liberals see the distortion of the competitive mechanism through state intervention and the accompanying loss of efficiency as the root of all evil.

Most interesting of all, however, are the strategic conclusions which can be drawn from the various ways in which underdevelopment is explained. There are three basic lines:

- If underdevelopment is viewed as the result of a country being incorporated into the capitalist world system in such a way that it becomes dependent upon that system, then it can in practice only be overcome by some form of release or dissociation from the world system. Depending on their political orientation, authors go on to talk either in terms of state-interventionist measures such as protective tariffs and greater intervention in foreign trade (foreign-exchange controls, controls over transnational concerns etc.) or of revolution aimed at overthrowing the capitalist mode of production inside the society in question (here Cuba is regarded as the model, and the Chile of the *Unidad Popular* as an attempt at achieving the same result by parliamentary means).

- In the 1970s the works of authors who had not fundamentally given up on the prospect of modernization and who blamed the process of 'deformed modernization' on internal factors (the power of national oligarchies, the historical strength of traditional structures etc.) produced specific new variations on modernization-oriented state intervention. These were characterized by the catchphrases 'redistribution' and 'the meeting of basic needs'. The basis of these development-strategy proposals was that the historical process of development which the industrialized nations had undergone could not simply be reconstructed elsewhere, but that specific development-policy measures were necessary if modernization was to be achieved on a large scale.

- Neo-Liberal approaches, on the other hand, completely ignore the material structure of national modernization processes; national economies are regarded as abstract units which function according to universal economic laws. From such a point of view it must be possible to ascertain the differences between the 'real inefficiency' of a state-interventionist strategy and the theoretical efficiency of an economy regulated entirely through the market economy; indeed it is hardly surprising that almost every attempt to date to achieve this theoretical efficiency in reality has failed. Be that as it may, the considerations which underlie the World Bank's structural adjustment programmes are purely economic: where the basic economy features of a society have previously been distorted by state intervention then these should be improved through the freeing of market mechanisms (the reduction of customs tariffs, subsidies and trade restrictions; the elimination of imbalances of the kind previously maintained by political mechanisms, such as chronic national budget and balance of payments deficits).

The Fordist approach to development

Let us look behind the arguments advanced above and in particular at the transnational and global power structures and reproductive structures which were dominant when the processes of modernization were being carried out. Since then a great many works have been published which incorporate one or other of the above approaches to development, and in particular those analyses which arise out of the concept of Fordism. This concept claims to cover the reproductive forms most prevalent in the industrialized nations in the post-war period. During the mid-1980s it was used successfully to explain partial modernization processes in the Third World. The concept of Fordism is based on the characteristic structures of semi-automated assembly-line production as introduced by Henry Ford and which quickly spread throughout the entire automobile industry and other branches of industry. This form of production brought a huge increase in worker productivity, making it possible for consumer durables to be mass-produced relatively cheaply for the first time ever. Its first success was the famous Model T Ford. Increases in productivity were linked to the fact that a broad stratum of buyers was beginning to gain access to goods which had hitherto been regarded as luxury articles. This stratum of buyers even included large sections of the working classes, and it was this which created the conditions under which markets could be found for the goods produced. In terms of society as a whole, the Fordist model is made up of the following component parts: increases in real wages for large sections of the population, social-welfare mechanisms, and state-sanctioned institutions for the settlement of class conflicts and disputes over distribution.

If one examines the content of the modernization strategies of the past few decades from this standpoint, it is clear that they served above all to transfer to the nascent Third World the economic and socio-cultural model of development known as the Fordist accumulation model. The transfer was bound to fail, of course, since the preconditions for a sweeping process of Fordist modernization — the industrial base, the social and material infrastructure and a growth in agricultural productivity such as that which occurred in Europe in the lead-up to the industrial revolution — did not exist in the Third World. Nevertheless, in some countries the rapidly increasing income of the upper middle classes, which contrasted with the falling real income of the lower classes in the towns and on the land, created the basis for a 'peripheral-Fordist' accumulation model: the very classes which accounted for the bulk of effective demand were able to increase their incomes, whilst those whose low incomes did not permit them to demand luxury goods or consumer durables to any great extent sustained losses. Thus the private automobiles, household electrical appliances, and other products individually consumed by the middle classes in the Third World were able to score a success, albeit a limited one. Although the results of the process — increasing social and regional polarization and the pauperization of large sections of the population — were not quite what the modernization-ideologues had expected, they were nevertheless in no way inconsistent with the interests of those leading forces within society (transnational concerns, the bureaucracies, the middle classes and the bourgeoisies in the countries of the Third World) which supported the modernization strategy. The propagation of the 'American way of life', the interests of transnational concerns in expanding the markets for the standardized products which they had developed for the mass consumer-goods market in the industrialized world, and social conditions in the somewhat more advanced countries of Latin America all came together in the process of internationalization of domestic markets.

A New World Economic Order?

The oil crisis of 1973–6 marks the most obvious crisis of Fordism to date. The precipitous rise in oil prices brought in huge extra profits for the oil-producing countries and concerns. Immediately after the crisis attempts were made to recycle the idle Petrodollar, but since productive investment opportunities were limited, available funds flooded into the international credit system. During this period most developing nations were therefore able to raise loans easily and, to begin with, on relatively easy terms. It was during these years that the foundation stone was laid for the present debt crisis.

Subsequent calls for a New World Economic Order are regarded by some as the political outcome of the oil crisis. The scarcity and simultaneous rise in price of essential raw materials strengthened the hand of the Third World, which at the 6th Special General Meeting of the UN in 1974 won support for an extensive catalogue of demands relating to the reorganization of international economic relations. The industrialized nations, at the time in a rather weakened position, put forward no suggestions of their own, but instead retreated defensively behind a blocking strategy.

The Third World's catalogue of demands was distinguished at first glance by its apparently radical tone. Yet it was actually more concerned with winning fairer treatment for the developing nations through the steady improvement of the existing world economic order. For example, certain weaknesses in the prevailing modernization strategy had to be overcome: in an attempt to increase exports, transfers of technology were to be made easier and access to the industrialized world's markets for manufactured goods freer. In the meantime, however, the industrialized nations' defensive strategy had paid off. The intensification of the international economic crisis made it more than obvious that the developing nations' increased strength had been temporary. From one UNCTAD session to the next the developing nations softened their demands and were eventually forced totally onto the defensive; heavily in debt, they had their backs to the wall.

Studies on Africa carried out by the World Bank show that even constant growth and other favourable basic conditions will not be capable of solving the problems of the developing nations. It is difficult to imagine a clearer acknowledgement of the failure of approaches based on modernization theory and of *desarrollist* (see Glossary) approaches. Yet the structural adjustment programmes which the World Bank and the IMF are currently imposing on the developing nations are no different in essence to these earlier strategies: the organization of free world trade according to Western notions must remain at all costs; any reform of the system must be limited to measures which can help it out of the present crisis.

To some extent even Neo-Liberal concepts of development are now falling in with such development strategies. They have adopted the theory of comparative cost in its statistically simplified form as a justification for the consolidation of the 'old international division of labour'. The objective is not the modernization or development of the various economies or societies of the Third World; all analyses and political projects are geared towards the operation of the capitalist world economy and world trade and credit.

Using the changed world-market conditions and the fundamental short-comings of existing strategies as their starting point, the exponents of *desarrollismo* have developed a broader concept which has become known as Neo-CEPALism and which, although it is in many respects a rehash of old ideas, also endeavours to systematically examine the changed international situation and pay more regard to the domestic sphere. Nevertheless, this too has proved to be a highly economically oriented model which is hardly concerned with modifying the balance of power within society at all. One of its major characteristics is that the strategy has two strands. At international level the scope of funding has to be extended in order to make structural reform possible and financeable. The uncertainty presently aroused by the short-term restructuring of debts rules out any long-term process of transformation. In addition to a generous programme of debt restructuring and reduction, the conditions placed upon access to the markets in the industrialized world should be eased so that countries do not have to remain indefinitely on the intravenous drip of the international financial system. This would appear to be all the more important owing to the fact that the technological development of the last few years has deprived the Third World of at least some of its competitive advantages. Geographical shifts in production due to labour-cost differentials are now less important. Instead, productivity differentials have increased further.

The UN Economic Commission for Latin America (ECLA) therefore regards the development of the domestic market and co-operation between the countries of the Third World as being just as important a prop for creative policies of stabilization and reform. Since the construction of national and complete apparati of production is neither wise nor possible because of technological development, the narrowness of the markets and the lack of financial power, the concept explicitly incorporates regional co-operation. The planned economic development must not, however, merely encourage the construction of modern industry; the taking into account of ecological factors, the adoption of simple technology and the concerted promotion of small-scale industries and medium-sized industrial concerns as particularly flexible and dynamic agencies of economic development are all part of the strategy. To this extent, concepts such as the basic needs approach or those which advocate switching over to non-state-run organizations are thoroughly appropriate to such programmes of reform.

It would, therefore, be rash to dismiss the programmes and conditions of international organizations as nothing more than interference in the affairs of the developing nations. For one thing, the construction of huge bureaucracies and inefficient apparati of state should not be regarded as totally negative as a matter of principle, particularly since the disproportionately large machinery of repression, which is the functional equivalent in a liberal economic system since it is vital to that system's protection, is highly cost-intensive. For another thing, reforms initiated abroad are welcomed by some factions inside the countries which can derive benefit from the process of change; it is not always clear whether dynamic forces of this kind have an exclusively negative effect on power relations within the societies concerned.

Even US interests which push their way so forcefully into the structural programmes of the IMF and the World Bank are not as homogeneous as it is often thought. Several authors question whether the foreign policy known as immobilization strategy on the one hand and the pursuance of economic interests on the other are actually complementary. Instead, a clear contradiction can be seen here. If implemented consistently, harsh economic programmes would have an incendiary effect on the domestic political scene. They are therefore toned down politically through the granting of trade concessions and special loans and the negotiation of special agreements. There is then political scope within the countries themselves, for, say, neo-CEPAList attempts at reform.

Alternative approaches

Which of the possible alternatives is anything more than a theoretical Utopia? In its conception the Nicaraguan mixed economy policy is one feasible alternative. Though the state is striving for supremacy and control over the entire economy in Nicaragua, this means the government taking on a central control function and the role of an aid planner rather than that of a participant. In most sectors the means of production are being permitted to, and should, remain in private hands. Nevertheless, the private sector too is being made to recognise the country's new objective, the *logica de las mayorias*: appropriate economic policy measures are being taken to ensure that the interests of the majority and the satisfaction of their needs are given priority over the pursuit of private profit.

The state itself is an employer only in those areas which have some strategic importance or in which the private sector shows no interest. In the present climate lack of interest, as well as general uncertainty and reticence, are widespread in such circles, as is general opposition to the government. The state is being forced to use its own meagre funds to fill investment gaps all over the place.

The crucial problem with this model, however, is that the bourgeoisie, despite numerous economic concessions, does not appear to be willing to allow itself to be restricted to an economic role, and to give up its political power. The additional problems which confront the Sandinista Government have so far rendered a general evaluation of the strategy impossible. The unwieldiness of the central bureaucracy and the shortage of trained cadres, combined with the war forced on to Nicaragua from abroad which is tying up considerable resources, are a hindrance to systematic politico-economic structural change. Even the many kinds of subsidies on luxury consumption, which are intended to move the bourgeoisie to co-operate, limit the government's room for manoeuvre.

So far, of course, Nicaragua's political crisis and the military aggression of the USA have brought the Sandinistas nothing but stability on the domestic front. Understandably though, the situation has prevented them from taking any more concrete steps towards a mixed economy. Despite all of its shortcomings, the Nicaraguan approach is of great interest as a process of economic and social change inasmuch as it is not intent on forcing a radical break with old established structures or adopting unrealistic strategies of dissociation which regard such a break as a prerequisite for independent development.

Micaela von Freyhold, on the other hand, has put up for discussion a number of ideas which are fundamentally different from those which we have discussed so far. From the failure of all other developmental models, and from her conviction that the existing world economic order cannot actually be reformed for the benefit of the poor peoples of the world, she concludes that what is required is a complete departure from the economic approach. She takes as her starting point human rights, in particular political and individual human rights. Although she does not mention basic economic rights explicitly, the political order which she envisages allows for the establishment of a 'moral economy' which does not adversely affect either the dignity of humans or the prerequisites for their survival. Whereas the schemes which we have examined so far are all intended to develop the economy, the major objective of this approach, and the one from which all other objectives are derived, is the development of the individual. What is envisaged, then, is a new economic ethic; the starting point for any alternative development policy is the strengthening of movements and groups from below in order that they are able to demand their rights and achieve political self-determination.

From the point of view of the radical left-wing positions of the last two decades, perhaps it sounds defeatist when the introduction of bourgeois democracy is the major objective. What this underlines, however, is that it is not always possible to establish new Utopias. In fact, the same course has been steered by many other progressive movements in Latin America as the first step towards ridding themselves of dictatorships. Once this room for manoeuvre has been fought for then other changes can be born out of it.

  All in all, the debate on development policy has clearly been marking time. Either one attempts to effect old schemes, or a noticeably defeatist element gains the upper hand whilst one is grappling with the chances of political success. Amid all this upheaval there is a general feeling of helplessness within the various theoretical schools of thought. Perhaps this very helplessness denotes the seriousness of the crisis; for who knew, for example, during the 1930s how things would turn out?

Recommended Reading

UNECLA (ed.) (1985) *Crisis y desarrollo: Presente y futuro de America Latina y el Caribe*, Vols I, II, II, Santiago de Chile.

Hein, W. (1981) 'Fachübersicht: Zur Theorie der Unterentwicklung und ihrer überwindung', *PERIPHERIE* 5 and 6.

Hurtienne, Th. (1986) 'Fordismus, Entwicklungstheorie und Dritte Welt', *PERIPHERIE* 22 and 23.

Menzel, U./Senghaas, D. (1986) *Europas Entwicklung und die Dritte Welt — eine Bestandsaufnahme*, Frankfurt.

v. Freyhold, M. (1986) 'Gibt es eine grüne Entwicklungspolitik — kan es sie geben?', *PERIPHERIE* 25 and 26, 1986.

11. Is There a Way Out of the Crisis for the Indebted Capitalist World?

Thomas Hurtienne

In 1987 the future looked gloomier than ever before for the heavily indebted nations of the Third World. In Latin America and in the 15 most heavily indebted nations debt service, which after a great deal of negotiated restructuring was made up almost entirely of interest, absorbed almost 40% of export revenues and total debts accounted for almost 40% of each country's GDP. While it was mainly these countries which stood at the centre of international debate because of their huge absolute debts, the debts of the Black African nations rose to 50% of their GDP, those of the countries in the Near East to 68%, and those of the countries hit particularly hard by the fall in raw-materials prices, such as Zambia, Tanzania, Chile, Bolivia and Costa Rica, to way over 100%. Despite huge efforts to increase exports; drastic restrictions on imports and government spending, often at the expense of growth; and extensive anti-inflation programmes even the few countries which had hitherto been able to service their interest payments through large balance of trade surpluses, apparently without a great deal of difficulty, became increasingly incapable of paying. In February 1987 Brazil, the most heavily indebted nation of all, temporarily and unilaterally suspended interest payments as a result of the failure of the unorthodox stabilization programme which she had been following and which had aimed to combine the fight against inflation with high growth rates and a better distribution of income. Whereas Argentina had been rewarded for doing the same by being allowed, sooner than expected, to take advantage of the long-term restructuring on special terms which had been designed expecially for Mexico, the villainous Brazil was to be ostentatiously punished for its unilateral moratorium with international isolation and the untimely writing-off of the interest which it owed to the US big banks. Despite the fact that Peru had been declared credit-unworthy for sticking rigidly to its upper limit of 10% of export earnings for interest payments and, as a result, servicing its IMF and World Bank loans in part only, at the beginning of May 1987 Zambia became the first African country to follow her lead. Whereas the once moderate regime in Zambia thus accepted a speculative break with the IMF, the more left-wing regime in Ghana, the IMF's star pupil, continued to stick to the Fund's rehabilitation targets.

These transgressions, whereby individual debtor nations unilaterally restricted debt service payments, can be accounted for in terms of the hardship caused by an economic and social crisis which was becoming extremely grave. Although such moves were greeted with numerous declarations of sympathy from the other debtor nations, these nations did not join together to form a united front or even regional blocks, despite the fact that their own problems were often equally drastic. When all is said and done, the majority of the debtor nations apparently prefer at present to accept the case-by-case philosophy of the IMF and the structural adjustment programmes of the World Bank as necessary evils rather than to elevate the need for unilaterally imposed restrictions on debt service, so loudly articulated not so long ago, to the rank of a political concept. This highlights one of the major problems of the present phase of the debt crisis, a problem which cannot be explained by reference to the corrupt nature of the various political élites alone. First, both the fear of economic countermeasures being taken in the event of payments being unilaterally suspended and understanding of the devastating consequences for the financial and economic systems of the debtor nations of banks collapsing appear to have increased markedly. In this respect the Brazilian Government's redirection of oil tankers and alleged moves to put part of her remaining currency reserves into safe keeping out of the reach of the USA were more than symbolic acts. Second, the somewhat flexible attitude adopted by the IMF, the World Bank, the Paris Club, and the US big banks had precisely the effect intended, namely that individual debtor nations would see in this case-by-case approach an opportunity to have their debts restructured on a long-term basis and on easy terms such as those negotiated for Mexico in 1986 and would therefore avoid all collective measures which might hinder the achievement of this goal. Third, some sections of the political élites in the debtor nations no longer attributed the debt crisis exclusively to external factors, but also to the malformation of national post-war economic development models.

In some of the debtor nations (including, at the moment, Bolivia, Costa Rica and Ghana) this has meant largely uncritical acceptance of the positions taken up by the IMF and the World Bank. But even among those countries and political élites which have vehemently endeavoured to resist external interference from the IMF, the problem areas identified by that body have long been a component part of the intensive debate on alternative economic and social policies and on which corrective economic policy measures would be the most suitable. Accordingly, the problems (such as national budget deficits and subsidies, currency overvaluations and export discrimination, insufficient capital markets and defective control systems) associated with the domestic-economy-oriented model of industrialization used by the most heavily indebted developing nations are no longer being ignored in the debate on the crisis as a whole, as they were during the initial phase of the debt crisis, because the IMF and the World Bank have long since ideologically occupied these areas.

However, both the non-orthodox economic debates which have taken place first and foremost in Argentina, Brazil, Peru and even Zambia, and the corrective economic policy measures adopted by these countries as a result, are now facing the same old dilemma: on the one hand, long-term measures designed to breathe new life into the domestic market and to correct the worst social abuses require a marked reduction in the burden of debt service and a certain amount of success in checking inflation; on the other hand, these objectives can only be pursued in conjunction with moves towards financeable structural reform.

Domestic-market-oriented industrialization — a blind alley

Undoubtedly this real-life drama, the debt crisis, is attributable primarily to radical changes in the basis of the world economy since the end of the 1970s. Yet this should not obstruct our view of its deeper-seated origins in the unstable industrialization models adopted by almost every developing nation which it has affected. In recognition of their differing development needs and depending on the point at which they gained political independence, different countries have adopted domestic-market-oriented models of industrialization intended to enable them to catch up with the industrialized world which differ from each other in several important respects: in India and (in particular) in the large and medium-sized (in terms of surface area) countries of Latin America, all of whose single-use consumer-goods industries had undergone complete industrialization before World War II, industrialization models concentrated on setting up consumer-durables industries, including some primary-products industries, and on the modernization of the traditional consumer-goods industries. In the majority of the remaining developing nations, which had undergone industrialization and urbanization on only a minor scale by 1950, emphasis was placed on the establishment of single-use consumer goods industries and on increasing the number of industries which assembled imported components for the production of consumer durables.

Despite huge differences in levels of industrialization, in the dynamics of domestic markets and in the part played by the exportation of primary goods in the various countries using such models, the various forms of domestic-market-oriented industrialization intended to enable the developing nations to catch up were all characterized by similar deficits and imbalances: oligopolistic industries emerged behind high-tariff walls to supply the upper and middle classes with consumer goods, industries which, despite having low labour costs, had extremely high total costs as a result both of their not being able to benefit from economies of scale and of the low level of integration of industry in general. Although the high domestic-price levels, especially for consumer durables, which resulted, guaranteed foreign and domestic concerns high returns, they also impeded the exportation of such goods and made them more unattainable for large sections of the urban population. Prices in Latin America were up to three times higher than world-market prices.

The establishment in isolation of expensive consumer-goods industries to meet the demand of the urban upper and middle classes proved to be an utterly inefficient and socially unjust development model and one which mobilized insufficient national resources. This form of modernization might perhaps be described as imitative modernization: individual and collective learning processes were superseded to a large extent by the passive acceptance of prefabricated technology packages, patterns of consumption and thought patterns. Thus at the same time as it industrialized, import substitution also eradicated creativity and independent learning processes. In doing so, it prevented nations from embarking upon an arduous but highly educational journey which would give them the ability to change independently, and concentrated instead on showing them an easy path to industrialization which was based on the finishing of consumer goods. To use an image: the form of industrialization intended to enable developing nations to catch up began by building the roof and the luxury apartments rather than with the construction of solid, strong foundations in the form of networked infrastructure, development-oriented agricultural and social structures and the kind of educational systems which stimulate independent learning.

The shortcomings in terms of development policy of imitative industrialization of this kind were thus largely home-made in the sense that in the majority of the developing nations they were the result of false decisions on development policy taken by the political élites. The fact that even the nationalist post-colonial élites in Africa which were insistent on independent third ways somewhere between capitalism and socialism (such as those grouped around Nkrumah in Ghana, Kaunda in Zambia and Nasser in Egypt) and the populist development-oriented regimes in Latin America (such as those of Peron in Argentina and Vargas in Brazil) continued to be influenced by imitative technological patterns and patterns of consumption must be food for thought.

The vicious circle of debt crisis and structural crisis

The ideas expressed below are based on three points. The first is that the form of development intended to enable developing nations to catch up has so far been nothing more than an indiscriminate transfer to the developing nations of the patterns of consumption and accumulation of the industrialized world, although at far lower per capita income levels. This transfer has largely failed to satisfy basic needs in the developing nations, has not adequately created the social structures which are a prerequisite for development, has left these nations with neglected agricultural sectors and extremely high rates of population growth and has ended up in a structural impasse which external loans can no longer help the developing nations to traverse. Second, it follows that the structural crisis produced by the domestic-market-oriented model of industrialization will certainly not disappear automatically, even allowing for the availability of more fresh money from the banks and, or in the form of, development aid. Naturally, the solution of the debt crisis through a massive debt reduction is a vital prerequisite for any significant structural reform. Yet even a radical remission of Third World debts of the kind hardly conceivable, bearing in mind the hands in which power is currently concentrated, without a far-reaching world economic crisis, would be a vital, but by no means the only precondition for the necessary rectification of the development model mentioned above. The shift in the internal balance of power to a new reforming coalition, the change in the composition of the political élite and the (at least) partial withdrawal of the privileges enjoyed by the economic élites which this would require represents just as great a challenge. Third, one is thus forced to venture the undoubtedly provocative theory that it was the debt crisis which made the pressure for structural change inevitable: with the drying up of the sweet poison of unchecked net influxes of credit, the sudden disappearance of the accruing 'overseas savings' in the form of high current-account deficits, and the net transfer of capital inevitably linked with this, the burden of debt has created a problem which may well prevent governments, parties and various groups within society, at least in democratic regimes, from denying the existence of developmental deficiencies and force them to place more emphasis on their own, unharnessed development potential.

Although structural crises can increase the political scope for processes of structural change, the accompanying narrowing of the financial scope increases the risk of authoritarian and monetarist responses to the crises. The dilemma inherent in the heavily indebted developing nations' present situation lies in the dangerous vicious circle of mutually causative and therefore mutually obstructive stabilization policies, initial moves towards necessary structural reforms and a gradual defusing of the debt problem.

The Brazilian experience

I should like to present a rather untypical example of how overseas indebtedness in the 1970s was able to induce improvements in national industrial structures through periods (in the case of Brazil, a third period) of import substitution for capital goods, semi-finished products, raw materials and fuel. In countries where this occurred — Brazil is the most striking example — it is more than likely that debt-induced industrialization will also have positive long-term effects. Higher levels of industrial integration meant that some of the structural shortcomings of domestic-market-oriented industrialization could be eliminated. The costs of producing consumer durables and capital goods fell continuously throughout the 1970s until, at the beginning of the 1980s, they reached a level comparable with that on the world market. This level only became distorted as a result of the overvaluation of the currency and thus had to be adjusted through export subsidies. Unlike almost every other Latin American country, the efficiency levels and international competitiveness of Brazilian industry increased to such an extent that since the beginning of the 1980s Brazil has exported far more industrial goods than she has imported. Although this was, of course, partly the result of the 1981–3 economic crisis as intensified by the debt crisis, the trend also continued after the subsequent sharp economic upturn which led in 1986 to the production levels of the pre-crisis period being reached once again. Not until the currency reform failed at the end of 1986 and the extent to which the currency was overvalued increased dramatically as a result did it fall off. The huge increase in Brazil's exports of industrial goods which occurred despite both growing protectionism, especially on the part of the USA, and the poor demand for imports in the developing nations was accompanied by a drastic reduction in imports of industrial goods. Though this was partly attributable to the poor investment dynamics of the government sector, the sector which had been hit hardest by the debt crisis, Brazilian industry's greater self-sufficiency and the reduction in imports of unnecessary capital goods which had only been purchased because large external loans for government projects were conditional on such action also played a part. At the same time, however, crude-oil imports also fell to half their 1981 value, since the rapid expansion in the nation's crude-oil production, which was financed with the help of external loans, was increasingly able to cover the nation's consumption.

There were two reasons why industrial growth was strong in Brazil even though interest payments of 5% of her GDP were absorbing her balance of trade surplus: the multiplier effect of a large export surplus combined with less than fully utilized productive capacity which, because of the integrated structure of industry, led to a revitalization of demand for primary products in Brazil and not to an increase in imports; and the marked increase in industrial wages, exemption from tax of those on low incomes and an expansive financial and fiscal policy which deviated in the extreme from IMF conditions, all of which were linked to Brazil's transition to the semi-democratic *nova republica* in 1985. The other side of this accelerated growth policy was, of course, that inflation went up and could be checked only temporarily by the rigid price controls introduced as part of the currency reform of 1986. Since at the same time the minimum wage and industrial wages were rising dramatically, Brazil experienced an enormous consumer boom which reached almost every social stratum and affected not only high-class consumer durables but also and especially single-use consumer goods.

Due to the fact that there was no broad adjustment of prices, however, the consequences of this democratization of consumption were that suppliers boycotted the products whose prices had been frozen at too low a level, such as meat, dairy produce and cars, there was an increase in hidden surcharges and, at stable exchange rates, a decline in the competitiveness of Brazilian exports. The left-wing Keynesian attempt, backed up by structural reforms, to combine price controls with high growth rates, a redistribution of income and a drying out of the financial sector, whilst at the same time financing interest payments to the banks from large balance of trade surpluses thus had the opposite effect to that which had been intended: the fact that inflation, interest rates and rents rose faster after the end of 1986 than they had done before the currency reform meant that both real wages and investment, which had increased slightly, both fell dramatically once again, and because exports were falling whilst the volume of imports remained steady Brazil's monthly balance of trade surplus disappeared. The result was that interest payments had to be suspended.

The failure of this economic policy experiment, known as the *Plano Cruzado*, shows that there is no easy way, even with a reasonably favourable industrial structure such as that which existed in Brazil, to check inflation and obtain improvements in income for the masses whilst at the same time keeping up large interest payments.

Unorthodox stabilization programmes: Peru and Zambia

When, however, even large highly industrialized countries find that structural factors prevent them from combining unorthodox stabilization policies with a fundamental restructuring of a socially unjust development model then it is easy to assess the immensity of the problems which the vast majority of the developing nations face: non-integrated industrial structures, an extremely high degree of dependence on the export of industrial goods, rather undynamic primary-products export industries and extremely limited production of basic foodstuffs.

At first the debt crisis and the fact that countries such as Peru and Zambia were forced to turn to the IMF and to implement the adjustment programmes imposed upon them by the Fund corrected those countries' defective developments in a way which is hardly compatible with the IMF's and the World Bank's concept of modernization: instead one is ominously reminded of the failed Neo-Liberal experiments carried out in the more highly industrialized nations of Latin America, where the currency devaluations, import liberalization and elimination of subsidies which the IMF demanded led not only to a drastic fall in the price of exported primary goods but also to a crisis in the consumer-goods industries, which were highly dependent on large volumes of imported primary goods. Instead of making the domestic industries more efficient by increasing the external pressure for them to be competitive, currency devaluations and foreign-exchange rationing increased production costs so radically that the domestic industries could withstand neither the competition which they faced from the liberalization of imports of consumer goods nor that from the nascent small-scale businesses with their simple, adjusted productive processes, their use of primary products available on the domestic market and their early capitalist forms of exploitation. Whereas imports of consumer durables from the NICs of East Asia and from Japan soared, growth in many of the single-use consumer-goods industries and the simple work-tools industries became concentrated in the informal sector, on concerns operated out of backyards and shacks. A huge process of de-industrialization and massive reductions in formal employment and real-wage levels were all related to an upturn in the goods-producing informal sector, which on the one hand offered a guarantee of survival during the crisis, but on the other exposed the defective development of the heavily importing industrial sector through the use of adjusted technology and local primary products and suggested that in future industrial policy would have to be directed to a greater extent towards the use of national resources.

At the same time as this rather spontaneous and only temporary restructuring of industrial production was taking place, the pressure of the foreign-currency crisis also forced a change in the attitude of state planners to the production of foodstuffs by small farms, against which they had previously discriminated. In order to cut down on imports of foodstuffs, Zambia first raised agricultural prices to a level which would encourage small farmers to produce more for urban outlets. However, in December 1986 the rise in agricultural prices, which was actually rather overdue in terms of development policy, and the reduction in subsidies on urban food prices also demanded by the IMF, led to an increase of roughly 120% in the price of cornmeal; this and falling wages brought explosive urban unrest which left 15 dead and the domestic political scene in turmoil. As a result, President Kaunda's regime, which regarded itself as humanist–socialist, felt compelled to put the IMF adjustment programme on ice, to postpone the planned exchange-rate devaluation, to reintroduce the subsidies on foodstuffs and to follow Peru's lead by reducing debt-service payments to 10% of Zambia's annual net foreign-currency revenue.

After both the disaster of the IMF adjustment policies implemented in Peru under Belaúnde (1980–85), which were intended to fight both the excess demand supposedly responsible for her high rates of inflation and her huge national budget deficit by means of an austerity programme and in doing so achieved instead the opposite (a flight to the dollar as the only recognized currency), and the 1985 electoral success of the new populist–reformist president, Alan García, Peru postponed her planned currency devaluation and implementation of austerity policies, unilaterally reduced debt-service payments and initiated a democratic 'revolution in production and redistribution' which was designed to encourage both a more strongly networked economic structure oriented towards mass consumption and an increase in the domestic demand of the masses (through the government's policies on wages and employment). Whether this combination of unorthodox attempts at stabilization, rises in real income and strong growth in the mass consumer-goods industries on the one hand and extreme overvaluation of the currency and increased importation of foodstuffs on the other is capable of stimulating anything more than a sham boom must be extremely doubtful in the light of the Brazilian experience. Since the country's balance of trade surplus had fallen to US$5 million and despite interest payments having been substantially reduced to US$820 million, payments could only be financed by reducing the country's currency reserves by US$600 million and from the country's dollar revenue of US$400 million from the illegal cocaine trade. As it had done in Brazil, the rapid expansion in demand for consumer goods even continued during periods in which wages rose only slightly and when investment was insufficient. However, policies determined by demand alone, such as this one, are neither capable of preventing inflation from rising again once productive capacity has been fully occupied as a result of a lack of investment nor of contributing to the solution of the structural crisis. As was also the case in Brazil, it is clear that even new, reform-oriented political élites prefer, for obvious reasons related to the question of mass poverty and democratic legitimation, to find popular short-term sham solutions than to set out on the more troublesome and risky path of structural reform. In addition, the Peruvian experience shows that even an extremely large reduction in debt service, the foregoing of new loans and direct investment, and a reformist policy of redistribution do not amount to a new, indefinitely strong development model.

The interests of the political élites

Strategies aimed at solving the debt and structural crises must both be implemented in the correct order and made up of the correct combination of stabilization policies and structural reforms. That order and combination have still to be discovered. It will be a difficult process. The solutions so far proposed and elaborated by the debtor nations must be viewed against the backdrop of this not voluntaristically surmountable dilemma of mutually causative, but at the same time mutually obstructive corrective economic policy measures.

In evaluating the debt problem the greatest amount of common ground is to be found at international conferences, which for the most part are supportive of the demands put forward in *Quito* and *Cartagena* in 1984: that the industrialized and developing nations should accept joint responsibility for the debt problem, that debt service should be restricted to a reasonable proportion of export revenues and should not under any circumstances absorb more than 25–30% of foreign-currency proceeds, that repayment periods should be extended to 20 years for refinanced debts and exorbitant rates of interest reduced to a 'fair' level, that terms of trade should be fairer and that a fundamental reform of the world monetary system must submit even industrialized nations with large current-account surpluses to the disciplinary controls of a reformed IMF, as proposed in the old Keynes plan. The problem with this declaration is the question of how, by whom and when these demands should be met. Whilst Fidel Castro still swears by a common debtors' front, which he regards as the only way of solving the present crisis, other national governments, regardless of their political orientation, hope instead to get the best for their countries through the correct combination of good conduct and threatening gestures. It is important to remember here that a great many national élites have themselves profited, and are still profiting, either directly or indirectly, from the debt crisis.

The large amount of capital which has flowed into external and internal unproductive, but high-yielding and above all secure, financial investments is an indicator of the extent to which political élites have profited. As a result of overvalued currencies, high rates of inflation, low profit-expectations and the resulting shakiness of economic policies, a large part of the Third World's external debts have flowed back into the industrialized nations in the form of the private flight-capital of the wealthy and of businesses, primarily through the over-factoring of imports and the under-factoring of exports. Foreign-currency investments there have been judged to be more secure and more profitable. The amount of capital which left the 18 most heavily indebted nations between 1976 and the end of 1985 has been estimated by the Morgan Guarantee Trust Company at a minimum of US$200 billion (two-fifths of their debt) and that which left Latin America alone at US$120–130 billion (a third of its debt). The trend in these figures has been confirmed in other studies. Moreover, at the end of 1985 the amount of capital flowing out of some of the indebted nations was extremely large when measured against their foreign debts: 139% for Venezuela, 98% for Argentina, 88% for Mexico, 80% for Malaysia and 63% for Nigeria. With economic and political élites growing extremely rich through this external and internal flight of capital, it is not surprising that their pursuance of their own interests has resulted in the failure of fundamental financial reforms. It has proved impossible to eliminate the resulting budget deficits, despite pressure from the IMF, and unless accompanied by debt reform every injection of fresh money has encouraged more private plundering of the state's coffers. In view of this precarious situation (which has meant the masses footing the bill for the structural and debt crises, whilst national élites have continued to profit from them) any proposal aimed at diffusing the debt problem which ignores this private expropriation of public external debts plays instead into the hands of the national élites. It would certainly suit the latter perfectly if debts were to be cancelled on a large scale and new loans extended for the resumption of their hitherto abortive development strategies. Unfortunately, certain sections of the left-wing debate on indebtedness have not adequately recognized the situation. Even if it is considered unavoidable on economic or moral grounds for debts to be reduced or even cancelled, it is vital that the national élites of the semi-industrialized, most heavily indebted nations, which should not be confused with the neo-colonial puppet regimes of Africa or Central America, are not released from the proportion of the debt crisis for which they are responsible.

Though large sections of the left-wing intelligentsia in the industrialized nations have made little progress in the same direction, in the debtor nations themselves an initial phase characterized by similarly simplistic views has been succeeded by one characterized by a more sophisticated and more realistic approach. Hence the former trade-union leader and chairman of the Labour Party in Brazil, the legendary Lula, who until recently still appeared to believe in the ability of debt moratoriums to perform miracles, criticized the moratorium announced by the Brazilian Government in February 1987 as a sham solution and a diversion from the much more important question of fighting inflation at home.

The new CEPALism

At present the intensive debate being conducted in the UN Economic Commission for Latin America (ECLA/CEPAL) and which has been mirrored in numerous policy documents is playing a leading and trail-blazing part in evolving innovative development strategies. In view of the future development prospects of the capitalist industrialized nations and the large extent to which these will regulate the world economy, ECLA's assumptions for the next ten years are that growth rates for industry and world trade will be far lower than the average for the 1950s and 1960s, although higher than the average for 1980–85. Poor growth will be combined with rapid technological changes in the industrial, economic and social structure of the industrialized world as well as constantly higher levels of, or even rising, mass unemployment. The massive deployment of state inducements, the large-scale absorption of the finance available world-wide and the concentration of direct investment on the industrialized nations will fuel the struggle for the restructuring of the international system of comparative advantages, whilst preventing interest rates from falling to any great extent. Rapid technological change in the key post-war industries will lead to an even greater reduction in the use of raw materials in each unit of production and therefore a reduction in demand for primary products and further falls in relative prices. In large sections of the previously rather high-wage consumer-goods industry flexible automation will bring about a cost-induced geographical shift in production back to the industrialized nations. The fact that this will increase the level of industrial self-sufficiency of the industrialized nations as a group will lead to a growing inability on the part of the majority of the developing nations to export to the rest of the world. At the same time international interest rates will, despite a slight decrease as compared with 1980–85, rise to a level higher than that of the average for 1950–80, and the industrialized nations will become increasingly protectionist as a result of the structural crisis and high unemployment connected with the technological change.

On account of these gloomy development prospects for the majority of the developing nations, it will no longer be possible to alleviate the debt crisis by means of processes originating within the market. Instead, this will have to be done by means of a politically negotiated devaluation of debts to the level already being signalled by the international financial markets. By the time that such a compromise solution becomes generally accepted during the next world economic crisis, the US big banks will have written off the majority of their bad debts through the gradual creation of provisions. Although the devaluation of the debt will thus hit individual banks, it will no longer lead to the banking crisis still widely feared since 1982. The other side of this conceivable, but by no means certain, scenario would, of course, be a marked cutback on new loans. These would rarely be extended by international big banks, but instead by public development agencies with accumulated stocks of capital funds of their own and by counterpart funds financed out of debt repayments in national currencies. Whether this relatively optimistic scenario will actually take place during the next world economic crisis is uncertain.

Regardless of what the future may bring, however, the heavily indebted semi-industrialized nations are now facing a crucial and complex challenge: over the next few years they must attempt simultaneously to gain control over rising inflation by means of short-term stabilization programmes, to extend slowly the scope for productive investment by reforming the public and financial sectors, and to take the first steps towards carrying out endogenous creative modernization of both the industrial-core sector and two hitherto neglected sectors — those dealing with the production of basic foodstuffs and with the social infrastructure.

This scenario, according to which the present structural crisis is actually viewed as a development opportunity, works on the assumption that both the political pressure and actual scope for social innovation, already extended by new production technology, have increased, whether despite or because of the extremely limited economic and financial freedom of governments to take action. The political élites in the large and medium-sized nations in Latin America can therefore no longer react to the dual challenge of structural crisis at home and technological revolution in the industrialized nations with passive imitation of existing technological models and patterns of consumption. Of course, this in no way means that trends in development of this kind will be met with even quasi-automatic acceptance in every country during the difficult transitional phase over the next few years. The threat of an authoritarian solution to the crisis cannot be ruled out! All the same, ECLA insists on providing the self-democratizing regimes of Latin America with a concrete, long-term target for the future: a tangible Utopia. Its key terms are efficiency, creativity, equality and democratization. The new ECLA strategy is modelled on the NICs of East Asia although not, of course, on the authoritarian reductions in wage-levels and levels of consumption made there for the purpose of both increasing internal rates of saving and accumulation and improving international competitiveness. Despite these high social costs, ECLA still regards this path of development as a successful attempt at avoiding the defective alternatives offered by the debate on development policy. It is no longer a question of domestic market or export, tariff protection or free trade, state or power, industry or agriculture, and the import versus independent development of technology. Instead, the strategy is based on a selective and flexible combination of instruments of control and on targeting development policy. Compared with the balanced 'policy-mix' of the East Asian countries, ECLA today sees (its own old model of) domestic-market-oriented industrialization and the liberal export-oriented path of development (advocated by the IMF and World Bank) as nothing more than the two extreme examples of unbalanced, one-sided prioritization.

In the first case, that is under old CEPALism, inefficient consumer-goods industries with high price levels which curbed both exports and domestic-market demand were established behind high non-selective protective tariffs by overseas subsidiaries; a country's passively imitative importation of technology prevented it from developing independent technological capabilities. The lifting of protective tariffs under Neo-Liberal free trade policies, on the other hand, led to shock increases in the pressure of competition. This resulted in inefficient industrial production being replaced by cheap imports from East Asia, paid for out of external loans, and to growth becoming concentrated on the export-oriented agricultural sector, which was alleged to have comparative advantages. Thus neither strategy (in particular the second) vigorously encouraged the developing nations to pursue technological capabilities of their own. This could, in fact, have been done in the first case (excess-protectionism and passively imitative importation of technology) by understraining the developing nations' own concerns and in the second (excess-protectionism and huge volumes of cheap imports) by overstraining them. Whereas in the first case external loans were needed to fill the gaps created by dismembered, inefficient industrialization, in the second they were used instead to finance cheap imports and a huge exodus of capital.

A tangible Utopia for Latin American development

Since the old domestic-market-oriented model of industrialization can no longer be used because of the faults in its design and because Neo-Liberal attempts at correction have proved to be an even bigger blind alley, Latin America's future development strategy should, to ECLA's way of thinking, combine a number of different development policy targets:

- The high and 'frivolous' tariff protection afforded the consumer-durables and modern non-durable consumer-goods industries run by foreign concerns must gradually be reduced in order to move such concerns, by means of increased competitive pressure, to speed up modernization-oriented investment, including in the smaller sectors, which are not yet geared to exporting. The capital goods required for this can already be produced domestically in the larger Latin American countries, so that in order to avoid unnecessary imports in this field the hitherto rather minor tariff protection afforded such products must be increased and, as in Brazil, market reserve policies must be extended to cover information technology for industry. Reducing the price of such high-quality consumer goods, long regarded, even down to the car, as a component part of the urban wage-earner's inevitable reproduction costs, could intensify the conflict which has hitherto existed between their acquisition and the meeting of basic needs.
- The importation to date of technology for the simple consumer-goods industries, most of which are controlled by domestic concerns and which still account for the bulk of industrial output, must be replaced by a policy which actively promotes indigenous technology and exports. On the one hand, this should help Latin America to acquire a technological capability of its own and, on the other, should encourage domestic production of capital goods previously imported often because markets were too small to justify domestic production — by employing new computer-based manufacturing methods which allow greater flexibility and minimum effects and which can increasingly also be produced in the larger countries within the framework of market reserve policies or through joint ventures. The selective modernization of traditional mass consumer-goods industries with capital goods produced in the country concerned is a major precondition for raising the level of reliance on domestic products and therefore of improving efficiency. If competitiveness is promoted and exports increased then this

might also lead not to yet more increases in the profits earned by oligopolies, but to falling consumer prices.

- Selective modernization of the mass consumer-goods industries must be combined with a massive campaign to encourage small farmers to produce foodstuffs and to some extent also agricultural raw materials. For only if what has previously been rather sluggish productivity per unit of area can successfully be improved with the help of intensive agricultural advice, favourable terms of credit and in the long term also through the use of biotechnologically improved varieties adapted for the area concerned will it prove possible to reverse the unfortunate situation whereby the foodstuffs industry's demand is concentrated on a few medium-sized and large modernized concerns so that lower middle-class sectors can also benefit from increased production of mass consumer goods without the country in question having to carry out fundamental agrarian reform, which is difficult to achieve.

- The social (education, health) and material (mass transport systems, housing) infrastructures, which limp along way behind the general level of development, must be tackled by governments as a matter of priority through their investment policies, since in the long run they will form the basis of any learning-intensive qualitative growth and as a way of eliminating the worst social abuses in the short and medium terms. According to ECLA, when financial resources are in short supply a marked improvement in the efficiency of the health service and education system can best be achieved by pairing these off with the new electronics industries. Attention should therefore be focused less on the manufacture of individually used consumer goods and aimed instead at public and investment goods which will rapidly and cheaply improve the efficiency of the health service and the education and mass communications systems. As a result of glaring underprovision and inefficiency in these areas in the past, ECLA sees a unique opportunity, especially for those large countries with protected national information-technology industries, for low-cost modernization of the social infrastructure to be combined with the expansion of national and regional markets for this new industrial sector through specialization in the mass production of relatively simple and inexpensive systems. The deployment of electronic systems on a massive scale will be made easier by the favourable age structure of the population (half of which is under the age of 15), which represents a supply of learning potential and creativity of which little use has so far been made.

- The energy policies pursued should be revised fundamentally and attention focused separately on the dramatic ecological problems in town and country. Instead of dubious large-scale projects which require a great many imports and a great deal of finance from abroad, the emphasis should be shifted to decentralized power supplies such as smaller hydro-electric power stations, thermal power-coupling systems and various forms of solar power, and the programmes which already exist to promote the more rational use of energy and energy-saving should be intensified.

- It is imperative both that the financial sector, overexpanded as a result of overseas indebtedness, should adapt to the new circumstances and that a far-reaching reform of the tax system should take place in order to raise the domestic rate of saving and increase tax revenue and thereby gradually broaden the range of finance available for industrial investment and government infrastructure projects. In view of the heavy burden placed upon the public sector by overseas indebtedness, this will require a rigidly controlled spending policy which eschews pompous large-scale projects, abolishes unduly high subsidization of large-scale enterprises, attempts to combat the sinecure economy in the state sector and instead backs more decentralized projects at a community level.
- In order to provide against the failure of the transition during the 1990s, democratic institutions must be strengthened at all levels, including that of the hitherto rather weak local authorities and the intermediary organizations which are so vital to the elimination of major social tensions: political parties, trade associations, trades unions, co-operatives and others which represent the interests of the poor population. ECLA hopes that in this way large sections of the population will be mobilized, particularly at community level, that democratic attitudes towards compromise will be strengthened and that the potential for innovation within society, which has hitherto not been harnessed, will be released, above all in local government, co-operatives and self-help organizations.
- Democratization and structural change require external protection. This need is to be met by various forms of regional integration within Latin America ranging from joint research projects in the fields of biotechnology and microelectronics to an increase in intra-regional trade flows and the elaboration of joint proposals aimed at diffusing the debt crisis.

A plea for democratic reform

Many of the structural changes proposed by ECLA are not new in every detail and have been the subject of debate in numerous Latin American countries for a long time: in the programme of reform, entitled 'Hope and Change', advocated in Brazil in 1982 by the then opposition party and present party of government, the *Partido Movimento Democratico Brasileiro* (PMDB); in the Jaguaribe Plan, 'Brazil 2000'; in Peru in the García Government's graduated plan; and in Argentina in the plans for reform drafted by President Alfonsín's industrial policy advisors. What is new about neo-CEPALism is instead its great emphasis on combining efficiency, equality, creativity and political decentralization. On the one hand, a clearly increasing micro- and macroeconomic level of productivity and efficiency is viewed as a vital prerequisite for the gradual eradication of serious economic and social inequalities, since growth in worker productivity in all sectors of the economy can, if accompanied by sufficiently strong competitive pressure, lead to falling consumer prices and greater scope for non-inflationary wage increases. On the other hand, the increase in the general level of efficiency necessary for the elimination of inequalities and imbalances can only be achieved where there is a high degree of technological and social-learning potential. Creativity can only develop, however, when the basic economic, social and political conditions are characterized by sufficiently strong competitive pressure, a flexible government policy of support, a good deal of decentralization in political decision-making and a functioning democratic system of checks and balances, of power and organized opposing power. In this respect, ECLA regards recent attempts at New Democracy as an innovative potential capable of co-determining future economic development to a large extent. Today ECLA places more value on the taking of innovative action within the economy, society and politics than it does on the speedy implementation, advocated by the structuralists of the 1950s and 1960s and currently being demanded by the radical Left in Latin America, of fundamental structural reforms. Besides, such reforms, especially agrarian reforms, would clearly place too great a strain on the present power relations.

ECLA's scepticism towards the feasibility, but also the desirability, of radical structural reform has a great deal to do with its redefinition of the role of the state in the development process. Whilst the old ECLA strategy saw governmental planning in the field of development as being of central importance and the Left in Latin America today still regards the power of the state as the major force for change, ECLA now regards the omnipotence of a centralized state apparatus which stifles the potential for social innovation at local level, props up an inefficient and socially unjust sinecure economy, and tends towards a wasteful love of all things big, as the major obstacle to an economic, social and political renewal based on learning. Democratic transparence and control of the state apparatus, state-owned concerns and the political élite must therefore be combined with considerable decentralization in the field of political decision-making and a revaluation of the market control system along the lines of the social democratic maxim: 'as much state as necessary, as much market as possible'.

The advantage, but also the disadvantage, of this pragmatic strategy for reform probably lies in the development of a general framework within which gradual, mutually causative and strengthening processes of reform take place at a level below the politically sensitive level of radical structural reform. Yet even the political feasibility of this moderate reform policy remains highly doubtful in the present circumstances. In Argentina and Brazil, for example, the Democratic Gap is currently characterized by a revival of popular authoritarian policies rather than by the actual establishment of democratic structures at all levels. Similarly, the present economic situation is characterized more by a desperate manoeuvring back and forth between orthodox and non-orthodox stabilization programmes, between draft reforms and the bitter opposition of the old-established élites, between bravado in the face of the creditor banks and apologetic submission on the debt front, and between radical rhetoric and actual powerlessness than by the purposeful introduction of sweeping reform packages. Even the intermediary social organizations are characterized by the weakness to which they have been reduced by the crisis, by an increasing lack of perspective and by their adoption of the ideological positions and fighting of the ideological battles of the past, rather than by a high degree of innovativeness.

This rather gloomy overall picture of the Latin American nations may cause many observers, and in particular the victims of the crisis, to regard ECLA's cautiously optimistic vision of a future Utopia as sugar-coating. But the picture can be seen in another light. For the simple reasons that old solutions are always less effective and end up more quickly in a blind alley and that the existing political power relations rule out radical structural reform, those old élites under pressure as a result of the increasingly chaotic crisis have been able to check the development of radical popular movements by resorting to a few specific elements of the ECLA reform strategy.

In search of new paths

With the danger growing that political élites in the debtor nations might react to the debt crisis with rash authoritarian monetarist measures, it is becoming crucial that a solution to the crisis be found, that the essential external prerequisites for internal structural reform be created. The Baker Plan and the toughness with which some of the debtor nations had conducted negotiations, as well as the fear that debtors might form cartels, had already led to the IMF and the World Bank agreeing to a proportion of the debt relief demanded by the Cartagena Group since 1984. A new round of debt-poker was ushered in by Brazil's unilateral moratorium in March 1987; the US banks armed themselves against further concessions by making extensive capital provisions. On the one hand, the banks which made such capital provisions visibly strengthened their hand for future restructuring negotiations since this gave them almost total immunity from extortion; on the other hand, their action strikingly demonstrated the fragility of the crisis management so far, and in particular the policy of deferring the interest on *de facto* bad debts by converting it into new loans without getting any closer to a long-term solution. As a result, however, the pressure exerted by the smaller banks, Congress and the US Treasury Department increased. In view of the fact that they believed a world economic recession to be imminent, they demanded that the debt crisis be solved through a combination of interest concessions on old debts and the partial remission of those debts.

In the light of all this, support increased for the suggestion — put forward by various protagonists, including churches and unions, the Cartagena Group and ECLA, the Peruvian and Brazilian Governments, and above all Fidel Castro and Raul Alfonsín — that a distinction should be drawn between 'legitimate' debts, which were to be repaid and should be restructured, and 'non-legitimate' debts, which were not repayable and should therefore be annulled. Non-legitimate debts were defined as those which had been caused by the drastic decline in the terms of trade, rises in interest rates above the historic values of the 1950s and 1960s, and the protectionism of the industrialized nations, all matters for which the debtor nations bore no responsibility. In 1982 these would have accounted for around half of Brazil's external debt. In addition, the churches, the unions, some of the opposition parties, Fidel Castro and Alfonsín designated as non-legitimate all external loans raised by military regimes which had not been democratically elected. For Brazil and Argentina this would have covered almost the entire external debt. Of course, this broadening of the definition of non-legitimate debts raised the almost insoluble question of how loans taken out by semi-democratic governments (Mexico, Venezuela, Costa Rica), used largely for the same type of prestige projects and to finance both the import of consumer goods for the middle classes and a large exodus of capital, should be treated. Since the rather indefinable hard core of the debts which even the World Bank has admitted were caused by external shocks corresponds approximately to the reductions already granted on the international financial markets under debt restructuring agreements, a partial debt remission, if it should ever materialize, would in fact relate to this part of the non-legitimate debt.

Some experts from ECLA and the Cartagena Group have put forward another argument for a partial debt reduction. It is, they say, precisely those countries which have used their huge foreign debts unproductively, that is to finance the import of large volumes of consumer goods in particular, but also of capital goods for prestige projects, which have helped to improve markedly the industrialized nations' export prospects since 1974. If all of the debtor nations had, like South Korea, used their external loans to expand radically their industrial-export opportunities, as the World Bank and the IMF recommended, the social costs to the industrialized nations of such a policy would have been far higher. Some of these debts should thus actually be treated as export-promotion loans at preferential interest rates and as structural crisis alleviation loans with a high gift element.

In addition, many left-wing unions stress, as does the Central Labour Union (*CUT*) in Brazil, that the interest paid to the banks in the past amounts to a great deal more than the total of the debts and that logically all debts should be annulled. The weakness of such sweeping demands is obvious: they ignore the fundamental premises on which capitalist market economies and the existing balance of political power are based. Equally controversial, however, is the question of what form a partial debt remission might take. Whilst the political élites in Latin America want nothing to do with it, the left-wing opposition parties, various sections within the churches and the left-wing trades unions rightly insist that it would have to be combined with an improvement in the living and working conditions of the majority of the population and should under no circumstances be allowed simply to release these élites from their debts and their political responsibility. The question arises as to how this could be managed, since in most of the major debtor nations the bulk of the burden is, in any case, already being borne by the public sector. One by no means completely unrealistic idea, which is being discussed more and more in Latin America, is that it should be done through the counterpart fund of a new

Marshall Plan. According to such a plan, debts remitted would have to be paid, including by state-owned concerns, in the national currency into a fund which could be used, according to strictly defined criteria, to finance investment of relevance to development. In this way the increase in internal savings for long-term investment called for by the World Bank and the IMF, but also considered imperative by ECLA, could be given repeated boosts. The major problem with such a fund would, of course, be the question of who should and could control it. Representatives from the industrialized nations, but also some from the debtor nations, consider it vital that it should be controlled, to a limited extent, by a reformed World Bank, whether for the purposes of co-operating with the creditors or for the purpose of taking the wind out of the sails of initiatives (such as the Bradley Plan) from the US Congress which require a high degree of external direction (the opening up of markets, a favourable climate for direct investment and the abolition of market reserve policies).

The suggestion that the World Bank should have limited control over the debtor nations' reform and development programmes encountered massive opposition at first, both from sections of the political élites, which did not wish to have to comply with its policies on the extension of credit, and by a large section of the Left, which still regards the Bank as an agent of international capitalism which would necessarily implement policies harmful to the masses. Opposition has, however, mellowed to a certain extent, since some of the World Bank's and IMF's demands are identical in some respects to both the structural changes advocated by ECLA and to Left–bourgeois national reform programmes. The crucial difference concerns the way in which they should be implemented (suddenly or gradually) and whether, as the forces of reform insist, they should be combined with programmes designed to improve the living and working conditions of the majority of the population. Contrary to the conspiracy theories expounded by many left-wingers, the World Bank and the IMF have recently shown, at least in Africa, that they are more than able to tolerate a flexible combination of market-economy structural changes on the one hand with social programmes of a completely different kind, and wage increases, on the other (as they did with the left-wing regime in Ghana), without immediately brandishing the capitalist club. Under present power relations the World Bank and the IMF have been assigned a central control function over the big banks. This should not be relinquished lightly, as Neo-Liberals such as Friedman and also large sections of the Left would prefer, but should instead be reformed into a channel for co-ordinating government decisions, as demanded by Fidel Castro. The dimensions of the current debt and structural crises in the developing nations of Latin America, and also in Africa, require new solutions which can only be found if old ideological stereotypes are abandoned. It is precisely because such reorientation cannot be expected from the victims of the crisis and the abortive rehabilitation programmes promoted by the IMF and the World Bank that the still better-off left-wing intelligentsia is duty-bound not to insist on outmoded solutions such as the nationalization of the banks and key industries. The structural deficits of the majority of the developing nations cannot be successfully overcome only with anger and fury at indefensible conditions. That anger and fury must be accompanied by the large measure of creativity which these emotions fire.

Recommended Reading

CEPAL/ECLA (1985) 'Crisis and Development in Latin America and the Caribbean', *CEPAL Review* 26, August.
Esser, K. (1987) 'Lateinamerika in der Krise. Neostrukturalismus als wirtschaftspolitische Reaktion', *Vierteljahreshefte der Friedrich-Ebert-Stiftung* 107, March.
Fajnzylber, F. (1983) *La industrializacion trunca de America Latina*, Mexico.
Hurtienne, Thomas (1985) 'Wirtschaftskrise internationale Verschuldung und Entwicklungspotentiale in Lateinamerika', *PROKLA* 59, Berlin.
O'Donnell, G. (1985) 'External Debt. Why Don't our Governments Do the Obvious?', *CEPAL Review* 27, December.
PREALC (1985) *Beyond the Crisis*, Geneva.

Part II
From Argentina to Zaire.
Case Studies of the Debtor Nations

12. Argentina: The Bitter Legacy of the 'Sweet Money'

Gabriela Simon

Indebtedness and the exodus of capital

In March 1976, when the Argentinian military seized power in a *coup d'état* and, a little later, forced a recessive economic programme on to the country, no one could ever have imagined that this regime would one day go down in Argentinian history as the country's biggest-ever contractor of debts. At the time, the order of the day was to 'shrink (the economy) to a healthy size', to adjust to the world market and to put an end to Argentina's financial chaos, the blame for which was laid at the door of the previous, Peronist, government. In the event, the Argentinian economy shrank substantially during the period of military rule. Only a few found the experience health-giving, for the only section of the population which was able to profit from the generals' economic policies was the *patria financiera* or financial bourgeoisie, a small part of the Argentinian bourgeoisie which made ample use of previously undreamed-of opportunities to increase its wealth through speculation.

When Raul Alfonsín took up his post as president at the head of a democratically elected government in December 1983, he had a number of major promises to his electors to keep. The new government was expected to be relentless in its efforts to shake off the past. As well as rectifying the violations of human rights committed during the dictatorship, an enquiry was to be conducted into the economic offences of the same period, for the generals left the Argentinians not only with traumatic memories of years of gratuitous state terrorism, but with an oppressive external debt. At the end of their reign Argentina's mountain of debt ran to more than US$50 billion. In 1976, before the military dictatorship had taken power, it had been US$7 billion. Servicing this debt soon became an almost intolerable burden for Argentina's democratic new beginning. Between 1984 and 1986 the country had to pay US$15 billion in interest alone to overseas creditors, an amount equal to almost a quarter of Argentina's GNP.

What made this mountain of debt interesting in political terms was not so much its size but, above all, its origin, for a large part of Argentina's external debt had resulted from the flow of capital, sometimes illegal, out of the country (capital flight). Argentinian citizens were estimated to have overseas assets of US$30–35 billion, around two-thirds of the country's entire debt. Between 1976 and 1981 the external loans which had poured into the country in such abundance had been used time and again to finance lucrative speculative transactions. *Plata dulce*, or 'sweet', speedily acquired money, had come to embody this new blueprint for gain, and at the end of a series of successful speculative transactions the speculator invariably had an overflowing account in an overseas bank. The public debate which began at the end of 1983 on the illegitimacy of part of the country's external debt was connected with the hope that through this it might be possible for Argentina to politicize her debt negotiations with her creditors. The creditor nations' solidarity with the 'new democracy' in Argentina would, or so it was hoped, be translated into huge concessions when it came to the question of debt. It was, however, a vain hope.

The creditors reacted to the new democratic government with unflinching severity. By doing so, they stopped the development of new economic policies oriented towards a revitalization of the country's productive forces in its tracks. The enquiry into earlier economic offences was wound up after a short time, for giving details of these illegal dealings might have provoked conflicts not only with the still-powerful *patria financiera* but also with foreign bankers, upon whose goodwill Argentina had become more dependent than ever before. Just three years after the end of the military dictatorship the government was finally forced to grant an amnesty to tax evaders and those who had exported capital in order to get some idea at least of the value of the 'illicit' funds which existed at home and abroad. The democratic government had yielded to the demands of the international financial sector, and by accepting the end result of the unrestrained enrichment which had taken place during the dictatorship had also accepted the price which had to be paid for it.

De-industrialization and debt

The process by which Argentina acquired her debts was fundamentally different to that by which other heavily indebted Third World nations acquired theirs. Until the outbreak of the debt crisis in 1982 the majority of the debtor nations were able to achieve relatively high rates of growth. From the very beginning, however, Argentina's indebtedness was a component part of an economic plan for recession and de-industrialization. Argentina's external debt was acquired during a period when the old oligarchic classes were once again taking the destiny of the country into their own hands and reshaping its economic policies in their own interests. Ever since the process of industrialization first began in Argentina towards the end of the nineteenth century, the country's history has been marked by violent and cyclical fluctuations between the traditional poles of society: the agricultural and financial oligarchy, on the one hand, and the industrialization-oriented classes, the (relatively weak) industrial bourgeoisie and the working classes, on the other.

The oligarchy, whose power was rooted in Argentina's highly concentrated land-ownership, was traditionally characterized by a pronounced lack of interest in the technical development of the apparatus of production. Its wealth lay in the fertile lands in the pampas, where it was possible to earn huge profits with a minimum of capital expenditure and where for many decades speculation yielded more than any kind of productive investment as a result of rising real-estate prices. The fast-money mentality has been characteristic of this class since time immemorial. In the face of this, attempts at developing a viable industrial base repeatedly came up against relatively large obstacles. Despite a history of industrialization stretching back over more than a hundred years, Argentina's industrial structure remained fragmentary and dependent on the import of the vast majority of the investment goods which the country required. As long as this dependence on imports remained intact, so too would the power of the farmers, who had become Argentina's natural producers of exports because of the great fertility of Argentina's soil. Industrialization continued to be linked to the export capacity of the agricultural sector, and since investment in agriculture was virtually non-existent and the agricultural sector therefore stagnant, despite extremely favourable conditions, this sector consistently represented the major barrier to industrial development. Periods of accelerated industrial accumulation regularly ended in balance of payments crises, since rapid expansions in the value of investment goods imported were accompanied by stagnation or even slight reductions in the volume of goods exported. A balance of payments deficit invariably led, via the processes of devaluation and inflation which followed, to serious recession in the industrial sector.

Political power shifted in step with the cycles of crisis which these structural characteristics caused. A shortage of foreign exchange not only marked the beginning of a recession, but invariably also ushered in a new government oriented towards protecting the interests of the agrarian and financial oligarchy and whose political creed was economic liberalism. Devaluation of the Argentinian peso and the abolition of subsidies were then the order of the day. In this way, the government was able both to restore financial soundness to the balance of payments and top up the state coffers, and the resulting funds could be redistributed firmly in favour of the big farmers. Periods of currency erosion, falling wages and mass unemployment were always periods of prosperity for the agrarian oligarchy, for devaluation meant that farmers' dollar-earnings from the export trade increased dramatically.

At first, the military *coup* of 1976 proceeded according to this same pattern. During the Peronist Government's final year in power inflation had been running at more than 400% per annum, and the government had left a huge national deficit and a balance of payments deficit of US$3 billion. The military reacted in the usual way. Immediately after taking up his post, its first minister for economic affairs, José Martínez de Hoz, laid the foundation stones for his new market-oriented economic policies: the Argentinian peso was devalued by 80%, the budget deficit cut drastically, real wages rigorously reduced by a third and price controls eased. These levers should have been sufficient to sweeten the export trade for the agrarians, to stifle not only industrial and consumer demand but also imports, and in this way to take into account both the profit interests of the oligarchy and equilibrium in the balance of payments.

However, in the 1970s the world market underwent a crucial change. A sudden expansion in the international financial markets and a massive increase in the money capital available provided the Argentinian oligarchy with opportunities which it had hitherto never dreamed possible. In 1977 Martínez de Hoz adopted a strategy of accelerated external indebtedness. Unlike the debt policies pursued in other Latin American countries, Argentina's external loans were not used to finance a breathing-space which would allow an increase in the pace of industrial development before the economy was forced to succumb to the pressure to adjust which was being brought to bear by the world market. Argentina's indebtedness was part and parcel of a policy designed to open up the economy, to integrate the Argentinian economy into the international markets. This policy involved not only the abolition of protective tariffs but also the almost complete liberalization of regulations governing the transnational movement of capital and the freeing-up of interest rates on the national credit markets. As a result, international-trading and money capital was able to flood the Argentinian markets virtually unhindered.

For the industrial sector the consequences of this strategy, which took its bearings from the doctrine of Neo-Liberalism, were devastating. Industrial production suffered not only from the now relentless competition from abroad, for which it was no match after a traditional history of development both oriented towards the domestic markets and shielded from foreign imports, but also from the fact that unexpected astronomical rises in interest rates made profitable production completely impossible. Argentina was the perfect example of a country ruthlessly pursuing a strategy of de-industrialization. Between 1975 and 1982 industrial output fell by 20%, employment in the industrial sector by 40%. Crisis and mass unemployment made it possible for wages to fall from 49–32.5% of national income. The economic decline left Argentina with a hopelessly ruined industrial structure whose technological underdevelopment had intensified in the face of international competition.

Speculation as a blueprint for gain

Nevertheless, there were a number of national firms which not only managed to make ends meet during this period of economic decline, but were even able to expand vigorously. These firms all had sufficient liquid capital, good relations with the government and a measure of good luck in their financial dealings. In fact, whilst industrial output fell and many concerns sank ever more deeply into debt, business was booming in the financial sector. The liberalization of the financial markets, high and greatly fluctuating interest rates and the unregulated influx of money capital from abroad had created an ideal climate for speculative financial dealings. Within the shortest possible time, the financial sector expanded dramatically. An absolute frenzy of speculation broke out which completely supplanted industrial activities and transformed the Argentinian financial market into a positive inferno of speculation.

Other than the traditionally speculative agrarian oligarchy, the group which profited most from all this was that section of the industrial bourgeoisie which had access to the international markets and could juggle with sufficiently large amounts of money capital to enable it to offset possible speculative losses. Whilst the industrial bourgeoisie increasingly lost interest in the national market, a newly constituted ruling class emerged which was drawn from the country's powerful financial groups — the *patria financiera* (financial bourgeoisie). Its destiny was bound up with the speculative expansion of the nation's financial sector and Argentina's integration into the international financial markets.

The influx of money capital from abroad played a key role in this process. Initially it was a prerequisite for the unchecked expansion of the Argentinian financial sector and later a vital means of restoring equilibrium to the balance of trade, which slid further and further into the red after the abolition of protective tariffs. In order to guarantee the constant influx of foreign exchange, Martínez de Hoz pushed ahead, as part of his economic policy, with a two-pronged debt strategy: a simultaneous increase in public and private indebtedness. The first burst of public borrowing was of huge benefit to the military: between 1976 and 1982 it helped itself to around US$10 billion-worth of armaments paid for by the national debt. In addition, the Argentinian Government systematically increased its debts to a level in excess of its actual need for foreign exchange, and also used public concerns to procure international loans on a scale which far exceeded their demand for foreign currency. These loans enabled the government to top up its foreign-currency reserves and in this way to guarantee that capital would be used speculatively in the financial sector.

On the basis of its foreign currency reserves the government was able to offer an exchange-rate guarantee for the money capital flowing into the country as part of its programme of increasing private indebtedness, and this guarantee almost completely relieved those who speculated in foreign exchange of any currency risk. In this way it was possible to ensure that huge amounts of capital continued to flow into the country in the short term despite the country's rapidly worsening balance of trade. The exchange-rate guarantee operated on the basis of a fixed cycle of devaluation. This was divided into small steps (*tabilita*) which were taken even if the rate of inflation far exceeded the rate of devaluation. The difference between the rates of inflation and devaluation made speculation in foreign exchange a dream business: someone who changed the dollars which he had acquired on the international markets into financial assets denominated in Argentinian pesos and which, because of the high inflation rates, offered a nominal interest rate of more than 100%, and who then changed them (only slightly devalued) back into dollars, could increase his money many times over within a very short period. These dreamlike speculative dealings spouted the *plata dulce* (sweet money) with which the financial bourgeoisie lined its pockets during these years at the expense of the rest of society — for the bill for all this would have to be paid later by others, by those who had already had to bear the costs of de-industrialization and the large-scale destruction of jobs at the height of the speculation.

However marvellously the speculation and the influx of external loans may have functioned over the years, it was clear that one day this speculative utilization model would collapse. Huge balance of trade deficits and the collapse of several banks which were no longer able to cope with the turbulence of the speculative trade finally gave the starting signal for a huge wave of capital flight. The government honoured its exchange-back guarantee and at first financed the exodus of capital from its accumulated foreign-currency reserves, then later by raising even more loans on the international markets. Nevertheless, the Argentinian financial system collapsed under the weight of the now uncontrollable wave of capital flight. The Argentinian peso had to be devalued several times in quick succession, each time by 30%. The exodus of capital and galloping inflation plunged the country once again into a serious crisis.

Just under eight years of military dictatorship had landed the Argentinian population with the longest and most profound crisis in its history. In a country which had always been able to boast a standard of living above the average for the Latin American continent, and which could be more readily compared to that in Europe, large pockets of poverty had emerged for the first time ever. Argentina's external debt had increased five-fold, whilst at the same time industrial output had fallen by more than 20%. During the wave of capital flight in 1980/81 alone, Argentina acquired debts amounting to US$23.2 billion, 30% of the country's entire national product. By the end of 1983 Argentina's debt service commitments had risen to 250% of her total income from exports. Eight years of monetarist economic policies and integration in the international financial markets had fundamentally altered the face of Argentinian politics for decades to come. Argentina's dependence on the international banks and on the IMF may well prove a serious obstacle to the development of a new economic policy which is not oriented towards the interests of the financial and agrarian bourgeoisies.

A new beginning and capitulation to the creditors

The democratic government of the *Unión Cívica Radical* (UCR), which took office in December 1983, was under pressure from the very beginning from two sides: not only Argentina's creditors, but also her population now began to make demands. Having suffered a 40% fall in wages since 1976, the many hopes of Argentina's workers rested on the new government. The UCR's election slogan had been '100 years of peace, affluence and democracy', and one of the first measures which it took, even before the end of December 1983, was to increase the minimum wage by 70%. The increase was acompanied by a promise that real wages would rise annually by 6–8%. This kind of economic policy was, of course, not compatible with the recessive conditions which accompanied IMF stand-by credits. When Alfonsín finally declared that he intended to meet only those 'obligations arising from the legitimate external debt', which would have excluded some of the debts resulting from fictitious transactions and pure speculation in foreign exchange, Argentina was set for conflict with the international banks.

To begin with, the first UCR minister for economic affairs, Grinspun, attempted to conduct debt-refinancing negotiations directly with the banks and the Paris Club, but to no avail. The banks consistently refused to refinance even a dollar's worth of the debt without an IMF agreement. However, the Alfonsín Government was totally unable to service Argentina's debt. The military had left foreign-currency reserves of just US$100 million and arrears amounting to US$3.2 billion. Moreover, since the government had placed Argentina's entire private debt under its own control, servicing the debt would have devoured the bulk of the national budget and destroyed any scope for redistribution. In December 1983 an unofficial, but *de facto*, unilateral moratorium therefore came into force, and as a result Argentina's conflict with the banks intensified dramatically. In December 1984, after an almost ten-month-long tug-of-war during the course of which the banks stuck rigidly to their demand for an IMF agreement and threatened to cancel all commercial credit, Minister for Economic Affairs Grinspun finally yielded in a letter of intent to the IMF.

This, however, was only one of the banks' many conditions for the conclusion of a debt-refinancing agreement. First they wanted to satisfy themselves that the government was really politically capable of meeting the conditions set out in the IMF programme. It has to be said that the banks never treated the military regime which, as we now know, was responsible for ruining the country, with the same harshness and suspicion. Anyway, the IMF was given the task of testing the success of the government's economic policies every three months. Try as the administration under Grinspun might, inflation could not be fought successfully with the orthodox economic levers prescribed by the IMF (positive real rates of interest, devaluation, increases in the prices charged for government services), for its causes were more profound and structural. In fact, the IMF's prescription had precisely the opposite effect: it increased production costs and thus fuelled inflation further. Instead of leading Argentina to economic stability, the IMF programme ended in financial chaos; by the beginning of 1985 the economic situation was characterized by hyperinflation and a disastrous decline in the value of the currency. In February 1985, Minister for Economic Affairs Grinspun resigned, for inflation had veered completely out of control. The IMF cynically suspended its aid package shortly afterwards on the grounds that the Argentinian Government had clearly not succeeded in reducing the rate of inflation. Argentina had still not received a single dollar from the banks. In the financial chaos, the country as a whole edged towards crisis. Argentina was once again in danger of being swallowed up in a serious recession.

In June 1985, when the rate of inflation was approaching the dizzy heights of the 1000% mark, the government and the new minister for economic affairs, Sourrouille, dared to undertake an unusual experiment. On 14 June, Alfonsín announced a course of shock therapy for the economy which included not only a currency reform, but also a whole string of draconian anti-inflationary measures. The Austral Plan, named after the new currency, was described by Alfonsín as an anti-inflationary 'battle plan', and there was a great deal of talk about a war economy. The Austral Plan did indeed take the bull by its horns in terms of economic policy: it was an attempt to meet the IMF's criteria by unorthodox means. The central elements of the plan were a wages and prices freeze, although the wages freeze was tantamount to a cut in wages, since the monthly wage adjustment was to be limited to 90% of the adjustment for inflation. In addition to drastic cuts in government spending and the raising of taxation rates and government charges, the Austral Plan provided for regulated interest rates of 4–6% per month, which, on the basis of an exchange rate guaranteed by the state, was intended to provide lucrative investment opportunities in the Argentinian financial sector, especially for overseas capital.

Despite the fact that a number of the measures, such as the wages freeze, contained in this rigorous stabilization programme were authoritarian and that it would inevitably hasten the impending recession, implementation of the Austral Plan was, at first, widely acceptable to the population. The fight against inflation was seen as a national challenge, the Austral Plan — since it had been elaborated independently of the IMF — as a defence of national sovereignty. In spite of the fact that foreign loans were now flowing again — although, of course, these were only sufficient to finance part of Argentina's debt service — the Austral Plan triggered a serious recession. In 1985 industrial output fell by more than 10%, real wages, according to official figures, by more than 15%. Although the government was quickly able, as a result of the rigorous prices freeze, to get inflation down to a monthly rate of less than 2%, the situation remained potentially inflationary. Amongst firms the pressure on costs had increased as a result of the high level of real interest rates and the burden which rises in taxation and government charges placed upon them, and, because of the burden which debt service placed on the country, the government was unable to stick for long to its original aim of limiting the size of the national deficit to the value of overseas loans flowing into the country.

The Austral Plan was to have been implemented in two phases. After the first, recessive phase, in which inflation was to be vanquished, the plan was scheduled to enter its second phase, in which controlled growth stimulated by the government would be accompanied by a restructuring of the Argentinian economy. The second phase was never implemented. Inflation was not vanquished, but merely strangled administratively by the prices freeze. Every loosening of the reins on prices and every increase in government spending, both of which were vital if Argentina was to go over to an expansive development, sent the rate of inflation rocketing skywards again. Plans to switch Argentina on to a growth path proved incompatible with both the government's anti-inflation policies and the burden of debt service.

The ultimate failure of the Austral Plan was, however, caused by external factors. It was the rapid decline in earnings from exports which finally undermined the stability of the Austral. After years of uninterrupted erosion, by 1986 the price of Argentina's major exports (grain, beef) had fallen so far that it proved impossible to compensate for the loss in income, even though the volume of exports had increased. In that year, Argentina's balance of trade surplus slumped to US$2.9 billion, around half of the target for 1985. Whereas in 1985 foreign earnings had still been just about sufficient to pay 85% of the interest due, in 1986 this figure fell to 49%. Faced with this dramatic worsening of the foreign-trade situation and growing speculation against the Austral, the Argentinian Government had no option but to resort to the instrument typically used to boost exports: devaluation. But devaluations and the rising prices of imports meant that it was no longer possible to stop inflation rising. At the beginning of 1987 inflation once again stood at 7% per month and was exhibiting positively upward tendencies.

One of the most absurd aspects of all this was that the countries which had forced these recessive economic policies on to Argentina and had stubbornly insisted on the payment of Argentina's debt service were the very same ones which prevented her from realizing the balance of trade surpluses which she required in order to meet their demands. The slump in Argentina's earnings from exports was caused more than anything by the agricultural protectionism of the EC and the USA and the stiff price competition forced on to the international agricultural-commodities markets by the EC. In order to be able to raise the foreign currency required for debt service, Argentina had continuously increased the volume of her exports, whilst at the same time reducing her imports, in 1986 to less than 40% of their 1980 value. During the same period the terms of trade had worsened by 25%. In the previous year alone grain prices had fallen by an average of 20%. Despite her enormous efforts to submit to the dictates of the balance of payments, Argentina's debt figures worsened: between 1985 and 1986 her debt ratio (the ratio of total debts to exports) rose from 481% to over 600%, and in 1986 her debt service ratio (the ratio of debt service to exports) stood at 76%.

In view of the disastrous state of the international agricultural-commodities markets, Argentina's only ray of hope would now appear to be for her to boost her exports of manufactured goods, but here too the situation is more confused today than ever before. The industrial decline which took place in Argentina during her period of military rule left the country with a completely outmoded and fragmentary industrial sector, for even the traditionally weak industrial bourgeoisie shifted its attention to the financial sector when speculation was at its height, and interest in developing the apparatus of production has been largely lost. The reason for this is that cyclical periods of economic boom encourage not primarily investment in the industrial sector but speculation in the financial sphere. The years of experimenting with different stabilization programmes have not led to an improvement in the unstable condition of the Argentinian economy. On the contrary. Restrictive monetary policies, including high real interest rates which make productive investment more difficult but financial investment lucrative, and the ultimately unavoidable erosion of the country's currency have once again increased the ever-present danger of Argentina's lapsing back into speculation.

More than anything else, Argentina's attempts at meeting the demands of her creditors through various kinds of stabilization programmes have resulted in the recurrence of her old problems: the fast-money mentality, which, along with recessive monetary policies, is undeniably scoring victories; the tendency to speculation, which is stimulated by high real interest rates and financial instability; a growing external debt; an increase in the amount of capital flowing out of the country and, of course, in unemployment; cuts in real wages; and increasing poverty in those sections of the population for which such stabilization programmes were definitely not designed. Argentina's creditors have succeeded in preventing the elaboration of a new set of economic policies oriented towards revitalizing the nation's productive resources and which could, on the basis of this, tackle fundamental structural reforms. It is as though Argentina's financial and agrarian oligarchy, which ruined the country during the period of military rule, were continuing to govern the country in the guise of the international banks and the IMF. Under pressure from her international creditors, Argentina's attempts at a democratic new beginning and her promise that economic policies would be geared towards the country's development needs, have turned into a clumsy juggling act with the old-established structures.

Recommended Reading

Barrera, Carlos (1985) 'Del Gradualismo al Shock. Es válido el Plan Alfonsín para América Latina?', *Neuva Sociedad* 79.

Branford, S. and Kucinski, B. (1988) *The Debt Squads: The US, the Banks and Latin America*, Zed Books.

Ehrke, Michael (1984) 'Spekulation und Auslandsverschuldung: Die Fälle Mexiko und Argentinien', Ehrke, M. et al. (ed.), *Lateinamerika, Analysen und Berichte 8*, Hamburg.

Jozami, Eduardo (1986) 'Lo interno de la deuda externa. El caso argentino', *Neuva Sociedad* 85.

Kosacoff, Bernard P. (1986) 'Industrialización y monetarismo en Argentina', CIDE: *Economía de América Latina* 12, Mexico.

Kürzinger, Edith (1985) *Argentinien. De-Industrialisierung und Ansätze zu ihrer überwindung, Schriften des Deutschen Instituts für Entwicklungspolitik* (DIE) 83, Berlin.

Schatan, Jacobo (1986) *World Debt: Who is to Pay?* Zed Books.

13. Brazil: The Giant's Debts

Elmar Altvater

Every 50 years . . .

From a historical point of view, Brazil's external debt during the 1980s was just as unexceptional as her moratorium on interest and loan-capital (re)payments. For example, Brazil was unable to pay the interest and amortizations on her external debt around the turn of the century (1898), with the result that the government was forced to ask the country's international lenders to grant a moratorium. The banks did not agree to this request unconditionally. It was arranged that the interest due should be capitalized, that is added to the amount of the loan, for three years and that loan-capital repayments should not be resumed until 1911; in fact, this proved unrealistic as early as 1914, since the sums payable exceeded Brazil's capabilities. In return for their modifying the terms of Brazil's debt, her creditors demanded consolidation, (that is that their loans be secured), public assets (from the railways to the shipbuilding industry) were pledged as part of the consolidation process, and the income which they generated used to secure Brazil's debt-service commitments. In addition, the creditors introduced austerity policies — public spending was cut and taxes raised.

Less than 40 years later the whole episode was repeated. When Brazil was no longer able to service her external debt (which in 1930 amounted to £253 million) as a consequence of the crisis which had hit the world market, and especially since the burden of debt service in real terms had increased unreasonably as a result of the general fall in raw-material prices and the consequent dramatic decline in her income from exports, Brazil once again took the same measures as she had tried before (in 1898 and 1914). A moratorium on interest and loan-capital (re)payments was announced and the terms of her external debt had to be modified. In 1931 Brazil obtained new loans to the value of £74.5 million. This sum enabled her to pay accrued interest amounting to around £75.5 million. Thus the new loan (today we would call it fresh money) was used basically, as it would be today, to service old debts with the inescapable consequence that the future burden of debt service increased still more. Accordingly, between 1931 and 1933, 55.4% of Brazil's income from exports had to be earmarked for debt service, that is handed over to her overseas lenders.

This game, like the one which the country would play 50 years later, could not continue indefinitely. When, in 1937, the US economy was plunged into a new recession and Brazil's export earnings fell radically as a result — after all, 45% of her total exports were supplied to the USA — interest and loan-capital (re)payments had to be suspended again. This time, however, Brazil declined to enter into negotiations for an agreement to have the terms of her debt modified, since this would of course only mean that her difficulties in servicing her debt would be deferred until sometime in the future. 'And nothing happened. Unbelievable as it may seem, apart from making verbal protests, the creditors waited until 1940, when negotiations were resumed and Brazil began to pay again . . .' (Singer) — and then only such sums as the country's financial position permitted.

How could this be? One obvious explanation is that suggested by Abreu when he refers to the structure of Brazil's external debt during those years. Around two-thirds of the debt were owed to Britain, the old-established financial centre of the world, and only 30% to US lenders. Looking at the balance of trade, however, we see that the USA had become by far and away Brazil's major trading partner, ahead of Britain, during the crisis-ridden 1930s. Thus the British 'had no economic levers to hand [with which to resist the moratorium] since they bought only 5% of our exports' (Singer). The USA, which could have exerted pressure, held back in order not to drive Brazil, under the pro-fascist President Getulio Vargas, into the arms of Hitler's Germany, with whom Brazil maintained intensive bilateral trading links in the form of barter transactions 'during those years in which Brazil was hungry for foreign exchange' (Abreu).

The debt crisis of the 1930s acted as a catalyst for the development of a new international economic order — the transition from the Pax Britannica to the Pax Americana. At any rate, when the dollar was named world currency at the beginning of the 1940s the financial burdens of the old British ruling order lost their value and were not to be borne by the dollar. This permitted the establishment immediately after World War II of a new regime of assistance and loans (such as Marshall Plan funds, development aid, World Bank loans) which forged the monetary irons which would successfully hold together the Pax Americana until the 1970s.

In Brazil the debt crisis of the 1930s was accompanied by a push for industrialization backed up by import substitution. A few examples: between 1925 and 1939 the percentage of imported textiles fell from 15.4% to only 1.8%; the percentage of cast iron from 22.9–0.8%; steel ingots from 32.1–8.1%; and cement from 89.6–10.5%. Brazil was actually able to compensate for this reduction in imports through her own production: between 1930 and 1939 real output rose by an average of 5.8% per annum, industrial output by a remarkable 8.7%. Towards the end of the decade the crude-oil industry was nationalized and the steel industry became one of Brazil's basic industries. The percentage of industrial output which was in the form of consumer goods fell (from 80.2% in 1919 to 69.7% in 1939), whilst during the same period the proportion of industrial output for which the capital and investment-goods industries were responsible rose from 18.0–27.8%.

During the 1930s, then, the debt crisis internationally acted as midwife for a new ruling order, that of the USA. In the debtor country itself it acted as a lever with which to cultivate national resources, with the result that at the end of the crisis and at the beginning of the long upturn in the world market Brazil's economy had been strengthened. Was there any prospect of the same happening during the debt crisis of the 1980s?

Industrialization: vain attempts at catching up

Brazil's economic successes are, admittedly, fragile; this is immediately obvious if one compares the various industries participating in the world market, which expanded rapidly after World War II. Brazil's industrial structure was strong enough to allow her to replace major imported goods with her own goods in collapsed markets but not to increase exports in competition with the already developed industrialized nations. In order to implement the Fordist industrialization model in Brazil, the country had to accept two developments which would be crucial to its economic future:

- The country had to be opened up to direct investment from transnational firms. This happened mainly from the mid-1950s on and remained a characteristic feature of the subsequent decades until the outbreak of the debt crisis. As a result, the modern sectors of the Brazilian economy are today still largely in the hands of foreign capitalists. This is true, for example, of the motor industry, where foreign concerns account for 57.2% of the nominal capital, for the pharmaceutical industry (66.2%) and for the rubber industry (96.4%).
- The exclusive nature of the accumulation model (this was more significant, since it was in part responsible for the long period of political stability which Brazil experienced after 1964 under the military regime). The model excluded large sections of the population from its bounties; it was concentrated in the states of the central south and was extended to Brazil's peripheral regions in the northeast and the north only very much later, if at all; it favoured large-scale investment projects and the shopping baskets of the middle classes, not those of the lower classes. As a result, the World Bank today estimates that nowhere in the world is inequality in the distribution of income and in the quality of life greater than in Brazil. The social equivalent of this economic exclusion was exclusion from social benefits and political participation, a phenomenon which O'Donnell analyses in the context of the theory of the 'bureaucratic–authoritarian state'.

Yet unlike the other military dictatorships in Latin America during the 1960s and 1970s for which the 1964 *putsch* had served as a model, the Brazilian military attempted to develop the country through a combination of large-scale investment programmes and even issued National Development Plans (PNDs).

The second PND of 1974 is of particular significance, since it was devoted to the establishment of large-scale projects in: the power-producing industry; the steel industry; in nuclear science (nuclear power being regarded as the substitute for crude oil); and in the transport infrastructure, amongst other sectors of the economy. These large-scale projects, which were to cost around US$232 billion, could be financed successfully only if the government could fall back on overseas savings, in this case loans from international banks. The logic was thus inescapable: Brazil would have to incur new debts abroad in order to realize its national plans.

In the mid-1970s this did not appear to be a problem: international interest rates were very low and comparatively high raw-materials prices promised high foreign-currency earnings for the projects once completed, in particular for extractive projects. One accurate criticism levelled by Conceicao Tavares *et al.* is that all of the large-scale projects were actually planned on the assumption that the international commitments accruing from the loans raised by Brazil during the 1970s could be discharged by 'mobilizing her wealth'. With surplus foreign currency it should be possible to kill two birds with one stone: to set aside financial resources for the country's development and, as the then minister of planning, Delfim Netto, put it most clearly, to enable Brazil, as a nation-state to finance the servicing of loans raised abroad. The major purpose of the large-scale projects was to procure foreign currency in order to reduce the economy's vulnerability, which had been clearly revealed after the first crude oil shock.

It is immediately obvious that this ensemble of large-scale projects was aimed at the perfection of a Fordist industrial model: a nation becomes a *grande potencia* through the establishment of a heavy industrial base and its accompanying infrastructure (which permits import substitution), and through export-oriented projects which are intended to procure the foreign currency which may well be needed for any process of industrialization. Though it may not have been admitted openly, the whole process was modelled on that which the industrialized nations had already undergone and on the form of industrialization which had enabled the Soviet Union to catch up with the capitalist world since the end of the 1920s. However, Soviet industrialization had been achieved in dissociation with the world market, largely within a war economy and without the pressure to meet the criteria for microeconomic capital utilization, whereas the Brazilian project of 1974 had to be carried out under conditions of increasing dependence on the development of the world markets, including those for goods, but in particular those for productive capital and private credit. Furthermore, the hopes of the masses for an increase in their level of consumption and for political freedom could not be ignored until the projects had been completed; the military regime had already lasted too long. The strike movements which aroused new interest in the industrial centres, especially in São Paulo, at the end of the 1970s demonstrated clearly the social limits of the industrialization model selected, though initially it was possible to keep within these by means of political and military repression. When the New Republic replaced the military regime in 1984 the large-scale projects were seen as more of a burden than a legacy which would enrich the nation. In addition, although the projects were being worked on to a significant extent by state-owned concerns, they were oriented towards profit and were necessarily therefore subject to the conditions set by the world market on how capital was to be employed. The difference between this and the push for industrialization in the USSR is therefore striking; yet at the same time the boldness of undertaking an industrialization project of the traditional type at the end of the long Fordist cycle is clear: in a period of world economic development in which trade in the First World is already being restructured in favour of new industries, Third World countries such as Brazil are attempting to catch up with the old model.

Bearing in mind the magnitude of the projects, Barros de Castro's and Pires de Souza's assertion that the 1974 option was 'without doubt extremely bold' — Conceicao Tavares *et al.* even talk in terms of the plan being 'desperate' — is completely understandable. After all, the sums invested approximately equalled Brazil's entire GNP for 1983, which at 1980 prices amounted to US$240.2 billion and at current prices amounted to US$208.42 billion. But there are other reasons which support the theory of 'boldness': first, Brazil's high growth rates — between 1970 and 1982 manufacturing industry's net product rose from US$19.235 billion to US$43.300 billion, or by 125% — had until then been based primarily on the development of the consumer-durables industries. Between 1976 and 1980 the volume of industrial production as a whole grew by an average 6.1% per annum, that of the consumer-goods industries by 11.5%. However, investment was now being targeted on the infrastructure and basic industries. This shift had undoubtedly been necessary, since unless the investment-goods and capital-goods industries were developed it would hardly be possible for Brazil to sustain the high growth rates in the consumer-durables industries, especially if during the debt crisis access to finance for imported investment and capital goods should become more difficult.

Second, one has to remember that the large-scale projects and the push for growth in industrial production which they triggered were intended to take Brazil forward at the very time, the second half of the 1970s, when the entire world market was in the midst of a recession; the prospects for an export-oriented strategy were thus not as good as they might have been. Arguing the need for an anti-cyclical investment policy, those who advocated the large-scale projects in eastern Amazonas interpreted this as an opportunity. After a period of investment aimed at establishing the ore-extracting industries during the 1970s it was fully expected, according to the classical model of the industrial cycle, that there would be a new boom at the beginning of the 1980s, in the course of which the raw-materials markets would cease to be depressed and the prices required if the projects were to be profitable would be reached. Evidently the calculations were made on the basis of a world-market development model such as the one which had been dominant during the boom and until the beginning of the 1970s, without the possibility of a long-term period of stagnation (Phase B of the long cycle) ever being seriously considered.

Third, emphasizing metallurgy and petrochemistry during the energy crisis meant that Brazil was concentrating on sectors which used a great deal of energy. This necessarily required an expansion in the domestic supply of energy. Barros de Castro *et al.* maintain that the planning of the large-scale projects was not without a 'high dose of economic rationality': growth at any price was the order of the day in order that the underdevelopment in Brazil's industrial structure, quite unlike those of the industrialized world, could be eradicated in a kind of *tour de force* through the creation of a heavy industrial base.

Barros de Castro *et al.* even interpret Brazil's undeniable success in achieving large balance of trade surpluses in 1984 and 1985 as a sign of the success of the import substitution and export orientation introduced under the 1974 option. Doubts have, however, been voiced about this theory, for until 1985 successful foreign and domestic trade was possible with capacity utilization of just 77%. But when maximum capacity is reached then it can only increase through new investment, and that inevitably conflicts with a country's requirement to service its debts.

Simply for reasons of competitive capacity, funds have to be put aside for investment purposes, for initially import substitution is oriented towards a certain pattern of demand, just as export orientation is geared to a certain range of products. Thus this kind of modernization is initially an adjustment to world-market conditions and is designed to allow a country to catch up. Such conditions are highly dynamic in view of the technological and social reshaping of the development model. However, in order to speed up the process of import substitution and export orientation, permanent investment must be undertaken which will allow modernization of the productive system, including the infrastructure and political and social institutions. To this extent Conceicao Tavares *et al.* are correct when they claim that the New Republic which replaced the military dictatorship had to bear the burden which it inherited from that dictatorship.

Because of the financial trap built into the scheme for externally-financed export orientation and import substitution, there was competition for funds: should they be used to service the debt or for necessary investment? Fishlow warns against the illusion that it is possible to project the export successes of Mexico (which were ruined in 1986 by the collapse of oil prices) and of Brazil into the future; at the end of 1986 and the beginning of 1987 the warning proved to be justified when Brazil's export surplus decreased so much that she could not continue to finance even the interest on her external debt.

The state-owned concerns lead the economy into debt

The process which began with the planning and establishment of Brazil's large-scale projects implied a partial nationalization of the economy by a government which, like other military juntas in the politically repressed Latin America of the 1970s, otherwise adhered to the free-market economy philosophy, for the realization of projects which would become profitable at best in the long term required either state subsidies or the involvement of state-owned concerns. Thus it happened that the state-owned industries in Brazil's energy-producing sector, in the crude-oil industry and in the telecommunications sector, amongst others, were given a key part in bringing the projects to fruition, despite the fact that a de-nationalization campaign was being run in Brazil in 1975/76. At any rate, during the second half of the 1970s the percentage of both nominal capital and turnover for which state-owned industries (as opposed to private national and foreign firms) were responsible increased.

As such, it was decided that their function should be to lead the economy's demand for loans; indeed, Brazil's state-sector industries became the international banks' most powerful borrowers. The government supported this process of indebtedness with a series of decrees; because of the difference between the interest payable on internally and externally raised loans, it became extremely attractive for Brazilian firms to fall back on overseas savings (that is on external loans from the internationally operating banks). The high domestic interest rates thus served not to mobilize domestic savings to finance investment or to fight inflation, but as a means of bringing pressure to bear on concerns to raise their loans on the Euromarket. This permitted

the formation of a gigantic mechanism for dealing with financial transactions which dollarized the domestic credit system and made domestic monetary policy dependent on the destiny of the dollar on the international financial markets. (Conceicao Tavares *et al.*)

As long as interest rates on the international credit markets were low, then resorting to overseas savings seemed to be excellent business (Conceicao Tavares *et al.*) for the country: it appeared that Brazil's long-term dream of becoming a great power could be financed with short-term loans. This was, of course, a risky venture, for its success depended on the development of parameters which it was not in the power of national policy-makers to control: on future trends in interest rates, raw-materials prices and the dollar rate.

Whereas at the beginning of the 1970s around three-quarters of the loans raised abroad were still being obtained by private national and multinational businesses, by the end of the decade this figure had fallen to about a quarter. For the public sector, in particular the energy-producing sector, the trend was in precisely the opposite direction. This confirms that in Brazil, as in many other debtor nations, debts, and therefore also debt service, were being nationalized. Interest rates became a major cost for the state sector, especially after some rose above 20%. This cost was passed on to some extent in the price of the product (although at first charges were held steady). This in turn pushed the rate of inflation up to a new, higher level: immediately after the *putsch* in 1964 the military had been able to reduce the rate of inflation, which stood at about 100%, to a new level of around 20%, but after 1975, following the first oil-price shock, the rate of inflation showed a constantly upward trend and finally reached the 400% mark as the Cruzado Plan was announced in February 1986. Paradoxically, one of the conditions imposed by the IMF these days is that deficits run up by the state sector, which after all were originally the other side of external borrowing, should be reduced.

Thus from the very beginning there were problems inherent in the planning and execution of the large-scale projects covered by the 1974 option. The intention was to reduce the overseas dependence of the Brazilian economy by establishing capital- and investment-goods industries and a material and social infrastructure at home; yet this objective could only be achieved by integrating the economy extensively into the monetary world market and thereby dollarizing it. As IBASE points out, Brazil would, in fact, have had to put almost half of her gross investment into the projects for a period of ten years after the planning first began if it had been necessary to finance the projects provided for by the second development plan out of domestic savings. If other investment in the economy was not to come to a standstill, then either domestic (government and private) consumption quotas had to be restricted, or Brazil had no option but to fall back on overseas savings.

It was a risky game, and when at the beginning of the 1980s international interest rates took off

> the procurement of foreign currency . . . became a matter of economic life or death for the Brazilian Government to which all other economic and development policy objectives had to be subordinated. (Sangmeister)

It became clear that Brazil's export surplus would have to be used almost exclusively to finance interest payments; there was nothing left over for the country's economic development. The projected development model of national dimensions therefore ran aground; the economic projects did not yield the 'political surplus value' expected by the military. Having seen its results, Bresser Pereira, appointed as the new finance minister in April 1987 after the resignation of Dilson Funaro, has described the 1974 model as a paradoxical 'model of highly industrialized underdevelopment'.

February 1986–February 1987: from the Cruzado Plan to the suspension of interest payments

Shortly after the Mexican shock of August 1982, Brazil found that she too was unable to meet her debt-servicing commitments since her foreign currency reserves had fallen to just under US$2 billion. The availability of fresh money from the banks and the IMF was dependent on the country concluding an agreement with the IMF, which the Brazilian Government sought to avoid, for on 15 November 1982 more or less free elections were once again to be held in the country for the first time since 1964. Following the elections, on the 17 December 1982, however, a Letter of Intent (which was even published and thus the subject of fierce public debate in Brazil!) was handed to the IMF.

Brazil promised economic policies aimed at reducing inflation, cutting the budget deficit, increasing the profitability of state-owned concerns or reducing their deficits, controlling wages and boosting exports. In 1983 she obtained US$5 billion from the IMF and had old loans refinanced and new loans worth US$4.4 billion granted by the private banks. Brazil had to pay dearly to have her old debts refinanced, for not only did she have to pay a 2.5% spread over and above the LIBOR rate (2.25% higher than the Prime Rate) but also 1.5% brokerage; these terms were less favourable than those which Mexico had been able to negotiate.

Nothing had been gained but a new deadline, for just a few months after the joint signing of the Letter of Intent the IMF discovered that the economic policy objectives upon which Brazil had set her sights for 1983 could not be met. The subsequent years brought no improvement. Brazil's economic policies were limited basically to attempts at raising new loans from the international banks in order to meet interest and loan-capital (re)payments, which, despite a positive balance of payments, grew from year to year. The 'tail is wagging the dog', wrote Brazil's best-known financial journalist, Joelmir Beting: the Brazilian economy, whatever impressive successes it may have been able to boast since 1984, was programmed simply to transfer debt service.

Despite the fact that between 1980 and 1985 Brazil paid US$96.58 billion in interest and loan-capital (re)payments, her net indebtedness rose during this period from US$53.85 billion to US$93.13 billion (US$108.8 billion at the beginning of 1987). In 1980, Brazil's external debt amounted to just 26% of her GDP, but by 1985 this had risen to 47%. This rise was, admittedly, the result not only of an increase in the external debt but also of a fall in GDP (in its US dollars equivalent) from US$283.14 billion in 1982 to US$220.20 billion in 1985. Accordingly, between 1977 and 1981 2.7% of Brazil's GDP had to be set aside for debt service. For 1982–5 this figure rose to 5.5%. This is outrageous when one considers that in the 1970s, the 'decade of development policy', the industrialized nations had committed themselves to transfer 0.7% of their GDP as development aid, a target which few of the countries has ever reached. As a consequence of this transfer of resources, which was roughly equivalent to the USA's net rate of saving (!), the rate of investment fell from 22.5% in 1980 to 16.3% in 1985. The target is actually having a counterproductive effect, since it prevents the growth which the IMF hopes to stimulate in order to solve the problem of debt service.

Under these circumstances it was not surprising that poverty increased in Brazil despite the boom the country experienced between 1983 and 1986 which saw GDP grow at 4.5% in 1984 and by a remarkable 8.3% in 1985. Of course, it has to be said, in order to prevent hasty conclusions being drawn, that these rates of growth were achieved when the economy was operating at 23% below capacity. The number of poor people in Brazil doubled, from around 10 million in 1979 to 20.3 million in 1985 (the definition of a poor person was earnings of less than 95% of the minimum wage — and that was already low enough — on the basis of official exchange rates less than DM100 per month). Of the 52.4 million wage workers in Brazil 29.3% earned up to the minimum wage, and

Figure 13.1
Brazil: balance of payments
(US$bn)

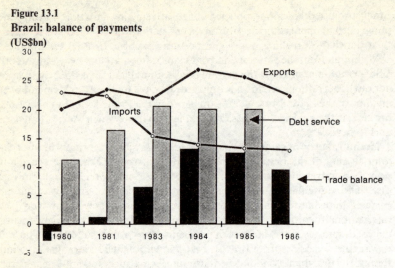

Source: Banco Central do Brasil

another 22.5% up to twice the minimum wage. If one adds to that the 12.9% who received no formal pay at all then it is clear that 64.7% of the workers had a standard of living which fluctuated 'between destitution (up to the minimum wage) and intense poverty (up to twice the minimum wage)' (Jaguaribe).

The price of the external loans which were intended to bring the country greatness and affluence was thus high and paid in the form of impoverishment and pauperization. Since it was not possible to service the debt, as planned, from the foreign-exchange proceeds of the projects which the external loans financed, consumption and investment funds had to be tapped for that purpose. This created a vicious circle: a reduction in investment damaged the country's medium-term competitiveness and therefore also her export opportunities (judged to be so hopeful during the previous few years). Together, a lack of imports, the financial sector's hypertrophic structures and institutional arrangements designed to index government loans meant that rapid growth was accompanied by both impoverishment and galloping inflation (in January 1986 the monthly inflation rate was more than 15%). It was vital for Brazil to break out of the vicious circle once and for all. The Cruzado Plan of February 1986 was an attempt to do just that.

On 27 February 1986, Law Number 2284 unleashed the 'heterodox shock' (Lopes). This was intended to call a halt to inflation, which was approaching the 500% per annum mark. The plan provided for the replacement of Brazil's unit of currency, the cruzeiro, with the cruzado through the deletion of three zeros; an end to the practice of indexing government loans and wages; a ban on the inclusion of index clauses in sales contracts; the freezing of wages and prices (though with the significant exception of interest rates, which were not tabulated); and the fixing of a rate of exchange between the cruzado and the dollar (US$1 = CZ13.77), although this last point did not mean that it was possible to eradicate the black market for foreign currency, i.e. the sphere in which currency speculation took place.

Although this programme was accepted euphorically at first by the inflation-weary population, it did not, however, function properly. Attempts at checking inflation resulted in a deterioration in quality, shortages and increases in the price of goods whose prices were not fixed. More important still was the fact that inflation was not merely a monetary phenomenon, but also a sign of the structural imbalances in the economy. As the Argentinian economist Juan Carlos Lerda, who also worked on both the Austral Plan and the Plano Tropical recalled, these imbalances become apparent when inflation is brought to a standstill. The plan might therefore have a boomerang effect in the medium and long term. Why? Galloping inflation encourages, indeed induces, speculation, if for no other reason than for the purpose of defending income and wealth against brutal depreciations of the currency. The aim of the plan was first and foremost to spoil these opportunities both for many members of the middle classes and for the financial system as a whole, so that liquidity squeezes would be sure to occur in the banking sector. The losses which would probably be sustained in the financial sector had until then deterred the government, which already tabulated prices and wages, from tabulating interest rates (the price of credit). Although interest rates had fallen immediately after the reform, they could not be allowed to drop too far, for in such circumstances traders can find it profitable to hoard goods and keep supply short. Moreover, it can act as an incentive for capital to leave the country. Thus cutting interest rates, something which is actually necessary if the rate of inflation is to be reduced, is a tricky business. As can be read in any text book, however, high real interest rates are a sign that inflation, although checked, will at some time explode again in the form of price rises.

No one needed an extraordinary talent for prognosis to foresee the early failure of the Cruzado Plan. But it was the hope of finding a much-needed way out of the spiral of inflation and squeezes on foreign trade which caused many critical economists, formerly members of the opposition and some of whom held high-ranking posts in the government after 1984, to regard the plan's quiet and fragile glass-bead game as the bell which would ring in a new era after the humiliation of Brazil's various restructuring agreements.

This was not possible. The old-established belief that there were still numerous ways in which firms could evade government regulations proved correct. The motor industry, for example, cut deliveries because of a shortage of spare parts and thus reduced the supply of new cars, and suppliers of primary products would not deliver at the fixed prices. Meat disappeared from the shops, because the price had been set too low. Either the quality of products worsened or the quantity available for the price was reduced, all quite normal reactions from resourceful businesses to fixed prices. Of course, the government's control bureaucracy could not even begin to deal adequately with these many forms of evasion, even though it could impose penalties and fines, some of them draconian. The original idea of control by the people — of ensuring that fixed prices were observed through an unparalleled mobilization of the population — could have worked but only if the political parties had been willing to agree to the people participating in pertinent economic decisions. This would have upset completely the precarious balance of power between the military and the political parties and within the party system itself in the New Republic created in 1985.

The Cruzado Plan failed essentially, however, as a result of two structural deficits in the Brazilian economy:

- The agrarian reform which governments had been promising for decades had never taken place. Only this could provide the peasants with the land for which they hungered and prevent their migration to the towns and economic growth centres, whose infrastructures could not cope; only agrarian reform could relieve the agricultural sector of the burden of having to export so much and increase the supply of agricultural produce on the domestic market, that is relieve inflationary pressure.
- More than 5% of the goods produced domestically had had, for a long time, to be exported simply to service the country's debts. An economy with external debts cannot fight inflation successfully if debt service exceeds output (and therefore has to be financed out of increases in the current national product); failure is inevitable.

The enthusiasm with which the Cruzado Plan was received was followed by deep, even depressive, frustration.

The Brazilian moratorium of February 1987 (the *calote*) was unavoidable; first, the Cruzado Plan could not solve the internal problem of raising funds for debt service, and second, Brazil could not continue to realize huge balance of trade surpluses like those of 1984/5 and thereby solve her production of funds for debt-service problems with foreign earnings. Foreign earnings were not sufficient even to pay the interest due to the international banks, let alone the loan capital. Raising new loans in order to be able to pay the interest would merely have deferred the structural problem until a later date and worsened the terms of debt service still further. The giant's debts have flung him to the ground. The next act will be about how the banks aim to deal with debts receivable from Brazil or whether and how Brazil will resume servicing the debts which she has incurred during the 1980s, as she did 50 years ago in 1940 after the moratorium of 1937. Unlike 50 years ago, of course, Brazil's 1987 moratorium is just the tip of the iceberg as far as the debt crisis is concerned, a sign that the relations between creditors and debtors in general cannot continue as they are. This was emphasized when the ministers of the co-ordinating committee of the non-aligned nations met for a summit in Georgetown one month after the moratorium. Brazil, then, is no isolated case . . .

Recommended Reading

Abreu, Marcelo de Paiva (1984) 'Argentina and Brazil During the 1930s: The Impact of British and American Economic Policies', in Thorp, Rosemary (ed.) *Latin America in the 1930s*, Oxford, 1984.

Barros de Castro, A. and Pires de Souza, F. E. (1985) *A Economia Brazileira em Marcha Forcada*, Rio de Janeiro.

Bresser-Pereira, Luiz (1985) *A divida e a inflação*, São Paulo.

Branford, S. and Kucinski B. (1988) *The Debt Squads: The US, the Banks and Latin America*, Zed Books.

Conceicao Tavares, Maria da and Assis, J. Carlos de (1985) *O grande salto para a caos*, Rio de Janeiro.

Fishlow, Albert (1985) 'A crise da divida: una respectiva mais a longo prazo', *Revista de Economia Politica* 5(3), July/Sept., pp. 26–49.

IBASE (1983) *Carajàs. O Brazil hipòteca seu futuro*, Rio de Janeiro.

Jaguaribe, Helio *et al.* (1986) *Brasil, 2000*, Rio de Janeiro.

Hurtienne, Thomas (1985) 'Wirtschaftskrise, internationale Verschuldung und Entwicklungspotentiale in Lateinamerika', *PROKLA* 59, 15(2), pp. 34–64.

Lopes, Francisco L. P. (1986) *O Choque heterodoxo —Combate á inflacao e Reforma Monétaria*, Rio de Janeiro.

O'Donnell, Guiellermo (1980) 'Desenvolvimento Politico ou Mudanca Politica?', in *Pinheiro, Paulo Sergio (co-ord.), O Estado Autoritario e Movimentos Populares*, Rio de Janeiro, p. 23ff.

———, Schmitter, Philippe and Whitehead, Laurence (1986) *Transitions from Authoritarian Rule*, 4 vols, Baltimore/London.

Sangmeister, Hartmut (1984) 'Brasilien: Modell einer Krise — Krise eines Modells', *Vierteljahresbericht (der Friedrich-Ebert-Stiftung)* 97, Sept., p. 241ff.

Schatan, Jacobo (1986) *World Debt: Who is to Pay?* Zed Books.

Singer, Paulo (1985) 'A Economia Mundial e o Brasil em crise', in *Programa Nacional de Pesquisa Economica*, mimeo, Rio de Janeiro.

World Bank (1985) *World Development Report*, Washington DC.

Werneck, Rogério C. Furquim (1983): 'A Armadilha financeira do setor público e as empresas estatais', *Forum Gazeta Mercantil, FMIX Brasil. A Armadilha da recessao*, São Paulo, pp. 139–46.

Wood, Robert (1986) *From Marshall Plan to Debt Crisis*, Berkeley.

14. Central America (Guatemala, El Salvador, Honduras, Nicaragua, Costa Rica, Panama): The Role of External Debt in a Geopolitically Disputed Region

Eugenio Rivera Urrutia

The scale of indebtedness

If one takes a bird's-eye view of it, indebtedness in Central America (Guatemala, El Salvador, Honduras, Nicaragua, Costa Rica and Panama) looks a great deal like that in the rest of Latin America. During the 1960s the level of indebtedness was relatively low and debts consisted mainly of obligations towards multinational financial bodies which were lending their resources to these countries on favourable terms (as far as both the period over which loans were to be repaid and interest rates were concerned). In 1970 the total indebtedness of the six Central American nations amounted to US$1,349 million or US$88 per inhabitant. The total amount owed was not even 25% of these countries aggregate GNP, although it did exceed the value of a year's exports.

In 1974 the situation began to change: as a consequence of the simultaneous rise in the prices of crude oil and imported manufactured goods, and because of the fall in prices of the region's exports, which was itself the result of the decline in demand which had been caused by the general recession in the world economy. Between 1973 and 1978, Central America's total debt increased by 205%. During the same period indebtedness per head rose to US$219. Between 1979 and 1986 there was a further thrust, and the external debts of the Central American nations increased from US$6.4 billion to US$23 billion.

A second increase in the price of crude oil, rising international inflation, a rapid increase in interest rates and the world-wide recession between 1981 and 1982 formed the external framework for the process which plunged the Central American economies into the most serious crisis in their recent history. At the same time, the intensification of political conflict, the wars, the problems which the Central American nations faced with regard to their industrial structures, and economic-policy errors were the major internal causes of a liquidity crisis in the region. There is, then, no automatic link between an intensification of political conflicts and the escalation of the debt problem. The causes are more complex and many faceted.

It was partly chance, then, that Costa Rica was the first country in the region which found itself unable to pay its debts. As Table 14.1 illustrates, in absolute terms this country's indebtedness was some two or three times higher than that

Table 14.1
Central America's total debt (billions US$)

	1979	1980	1981	1982	1983	1984	1985	1986
Guatemala	0.934	1.053	1.305	1.560	2.130	2.463	2.644	2.530
El Salvador	0.939	1.176	1.471	1.710	1.891	1.949	2.003	2.120
Honduras	1.180	1.510	1.708	1.986	2.162	2.392	2.615	2.390
Nicaragua	1.136	1.588	2.566	3.139	3.788	3.901	4.616	5.260
Costa Rica	2.233	3.183	3.360	3.497	3.848	3.955	4.084	4.000
Panama	—	4.756	5.047	5.960	5.924	6.537	6.500	6.450
Central America	6.422	13.266	15.547	17.852	19.743	21.197	22.462	23.240

Source: Gallordo y Lopez (1986); CEPAL.

of the other countries within the *Mercado Comon Centroamericano* (MCCA) —Central American Common Market. After 1978, Costa Rica's debt increased rapidly. This trend had begun when the government of the country was taken over by a coalition in which monetarist Neo-Liberal ideas held a great deal of sway and the notion of opening the country up to the world market was raised to the rank of a political programme. However, in order to acquire very cheap imports the new government stuck to a completely overvalued rate of exchange. Its domestic budgetary and monetary policies were restrictive. Every increase in government spending or individual demand was geared to the acquisition of imported goods. As a result of liberalization in the economy it had become possible for Costa Rica to raise funds on the international monetary and credit markets in order to finance these imports. After 1979 the burden of interest on loans raised in this way increased rapidly: as a consequence, the country's external debt grew by 24.7% in 1978, by 19.4% in 1979 and by 42.5% in 1980. The abnormally high rate at which interest charges increased on the international monetary and credit markets — in 1979 the Prime Rate and the LIBOR rate stood at an average of 12.5%, in 1980 at 14.8% and in 1981 at 17.2% — intensified the negative effects of Costa Rica's debt policies. This combination of Neo-Liberal policies on the domestic front and the risky and inadequately-backed lending policies of the international banks ultimately led to Costa Rica becoming totally incapable of paying her external debt, and in September 1981 she imposed a unilateral moratorium on the (re)payment of interest and loan capital.

Until 1979 the other Central American nations had relatively small external debts, partly because of their extremely restrictive budgetary policies, partly because of the minor role which the state played in the economy and finally because they were under only slight social pressure to step up government expenditure on social welfare. All this was reflected in government spending which accounted for only a small proportion of the GDP.

Within the group of countries Panama was a special case. Although in 1986 her external debt was very large in absolute terms (more than US$6 billion) this was attributable mainly to the country's role as an international financial centre. Thanks to generous tax laws, a number of off-shore banks had set up in Panama and capital which was on the move internationally tended to collect in their accounts.

Nicaragua proved also to be a special case. Although in 1979 her debts totalled only a little more than US$1 billion, as early as 1980 the new government was forced to enter into restructuring negotiations. The post-revolutionary reorganization of the country and the Sandinistas' intensifying conflict with the US-backed Contras resulted in a rapid increase in Nicaragua's indebtedness, so that in 1985 she was Central America's most heavily indebted nation with the exception of Panama. There are a number of factors responsible for this expansion, and Nicaragua's need for external financing on credit is more than evident if one looks at changes in her income from exports and balance of trade deficit. Between 1981 and 1986 the cumulative balance of trade deficit rose to US$2.4 billion. During the same period the value of Nicaragua's external debt increased from US$2.5 billion to more than US$5 billion. Whilst growth in the GDP virtually came to a standstill between 1981 and 1986, external indebtedness rose by an average of 20% per annum. What this rapid increase in indebtedness concealed was a whole string of structural and political problems: whereas previous import levels were maintained, the value of exports fell sharply as a result of the country's armed conflicts, the USA's refusal to buy Nicaraguan goods and Nicaragua's inconsistent exchange-rate policies. The trade balance was permanently in deficit.

The burden of debt service: a region incapable of paying its debts

The expansion in Central American indebtedness during the 1980s can be divided into two stages. Until approximately 1983 the indebtedness of the countries in this region, with the exception of Costa Rica and Panama, increased rapidly. Annual rates of increase of 30% were not rare. After 1984 the rate at which new debts were incurred slowed down, and in Guatemala, Costa Rica and Panama the total debt even diminished in some years.

The burden of debt service was nevertheless onerous. Between 1981 and 1985 the Central American nations (excluding El Salvador) (re)paid US$4.3 billion in interest and US$4.7 billion in loan capital. The actual scale of the burden of debt service becomes particularly obvious if this is compared with the value of the region's earnings from exports.

For example, in 1985 Guatemala and Costa Rica each had to spend more than half of their export proceeds on debt service. As far back as 1981 the Central American nations were using an average of 30% of their income from foreign trade to cover loan-capital and interest (re)payments. This massive transfer of resources was largely responsible for the unfavourable trend in the region's GDP during the 1980s. Whereas between 1970 and 1980 real GDP increased by an average of 2.7% per annum in Guatemala, El Salvador,

Honduras and Nicaragua, between 1980 and 1986 the average rate of increase per annum in this group of countries was negative. Whilst the economies in Guatemala and El Salvador had negative annual growth rates of 1% and 2% respectively, the rates of growth in Honduras, Nicaragua and Costa Rica were a little under 1%. In the case of Nicaragua even these figures are deceptive: if 1979 had been included in the calculation then the figures for this country would also have shown a decline in output in subsequent years. If poverty in the majority of these countries was already oppressive in 1980, then it is only too easy to imagine the current situation, in which declining or stagnating output is accompanied by continuous population growth.

Despite having made great efforts to pay debt service, during the 1980s the whole of Central America has been unable to pay its debts. A country's inability to pay its debts has three indicators. It is clear from the trend in exports that there is no sign of the problem easing. In 1986 exports stood at the same or in some cases a lower level than that of 1981. Most serious of all is the situation in Nicaragua, where exports have fallen to half their 1981 value. Guatemalan exports stand at around 14% below their 1981 values, and the level of El Salvadorian exports is the same as in that year. Even Costa Rica, a country which has taken a multitude of orthodox measures of adjustment in order to boost exports, only recorded a small increase in exports of 7%, or 1% per annum. Only in Honduras and Panama was the trend better.

Figure 14.1
Debt service of the Central American nations
(US$m)

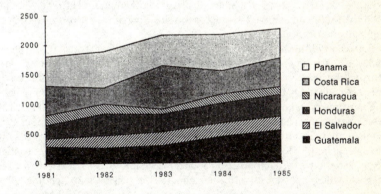

Source: ECLAC

The second indicator of a country's inability to pay its debts is the ratio between its total accumulated external debt and its exports. Although in some cases there were signs of an improvement in this ratio in 1986 (see Figure 14.1), it nevertheless remained at around the same level as in the period between 1982 and 1982, when the inability to pay debts first became a problem.

It is without doubt the third indicator, the ratio between debt service and exports, which has the most force of expression. During the 1980s this ratio has worsened seriously. Whereas in 1981 the countries of Central America had to use on average 30% of their earnings from exports for debt service, by 1985 almost half of their export proceeds were being devoured by loan-capital and interest (re)payments.

Naturally, the fact that a country is unable to pay its debts primarily affects that country's creditors. Nonetheless, the accompanying enormous decline in output, wages and employment also represent a serious problem for the other countries of the region, for each of these factors intensifies the social problems with which this region is confronted and so reduces the prospects for the democratization of Central America and of a political solution to the Central American conflict being found.

The process of restructuring: IMF conditions and the role of the USA

When, after 1981, the current accounts of every country in the region began to go seriously into deficit, the IMF attempted to prevail upon their governments to implement measures designed to limit demand, to devalue their currencies and to pursue policies geared towards structural adjustment. In the period between 1981 and 1983 every country in the region, with the exception of Nicaragua, implemented restrictive stabilization policies, mostly on the basis of agreements with the IMF. Costa Rica was the only country which concluded a further agreement with the Fund after 1984 (in April 1985). The pattern of events was very different in this region to that in Mexico and several other South American countries, which one after the other entered into agreements with the IMF, and is linked to the continuous flow of funds from the USA to Central America.

Between 1983 and 1985 the region began to adopt more expansive policies (in 1983 in Costa Rica, from 1984 on in El Salvador). Financial backing from North America was of crucial significance for Central America's success in checking a further decline in GDP and later in actually managing to make a slight recovery. The flow of funds from the USA to the Central American region (other than Nicaragua) increased in value from US$236 million in 1981 to more than US$1 billion in 1985. But as early as 1985 the situation was to change again: the flow of funds from the USA eased off. This trend intensified after 1986 and was accompanied by an increase in the burden of debt service, an increase which contrasted with the stagnation in private bank lending. As a result, El Salvador and Guatemala were each finally forced to initiate a process of currency devaluation, which reached its peak in 1986. The devaluations were accompanied by strong inflationary pressure. Subsequently every country in the region took new measures to limit demand. Despite the financial backing which the USA provided, primarily as a result of her geopolitical interests in the region, the Central American nations saw no sign of recovery in their economies until 1987.

Returning to Costa Rica; it is possible to distinguish two phases in her relations with the international financial organizations. During the first, which fell within the term of office of Rodrigo Carazo, the country broke two agreements with the IMF. The financial backing which she was receiving from the USA was not adequate to enable Costa Rica to offset the social costs associated with the process of adjustment.

The second phase, on the other hand, was notable for the fact that Costa Rica was able to meet the objectives laid down in the two IMF agreements, mostly thanks to the huge influx of financial backing from North America.

The Honduran case stood out primarily for the fact that the Suazo Government managed to avoid implementing the austerity measures and adjustment programmes which the IMF and US IDA actually regarded as inevitable. Unlike in Costa Rica, where the IMF was the government's major negotiating partner, Honduras negotiated mainly with the US IDA. The subordination of the country at international level, in particular her acceptance of the US military presence, helped to give Honduras a great deal of room for manoeuvre in her exchange-rate policies.

The distinguishing feature of the situation in Guatemala was that the military government and the employers' association joined forces on the issue of tax reform. But here too financial backing from the USA played an important part. That the country's transition from military rule to civilian government went so smoothly was thanks to the fact that the Guatemalans used the election to win sympathies in the USA and to become beneficiaries of US policies. We are nevertheless still waiting for proof of this government's ability to succeed.

For obvious reasons, Nicaragua's development looks rather different from that in the other Central American countries. Despite the narrow scope of the *economia mixta* (mixed economy), state intervention has increased. Attempts at gaining a broader base of support within society for the revolution have been increasingly hampered by the undeclared war being conducted by the USA through the Contras. This has led to a certain contradiction between revolutionary rhetoric and the measures of adjustment which have been taken over the last few years and which do not differ substantially from those whose implementation the IMF has insisted upon in the other countries. Largely responsible for this, of course, is the country's high dependence on external funds.

The economic and social consequences of the adjustment policies

First it should be emphasized that the measures of adjustment implemented in the region are by no means clearly and unambiguously monetarist in nature. They differ from monetarist measures of adjustment in the severity of their implementation and in the fact that they are less doctrinaire in their attitudes to the role of the state and of the market. Instead, the military and political conflicts in the region have forced them to take more account of questions of legitimacy and social consensus. Nevertheless, they have struggled for the structural changes recommended by the IMF just as hard as the monetarist remedies typically applied in the *cono sur*, the southern cone of Latin America.

It is important to avoid making two contradictory assumptions, the first that the process of structural adjustment has advanced rapidly. Detailed analysis shows clearly that there has been little progress made towards adjusting economies to suit the new circumstances. The pressure for adjustment has in fact been weakened by the financial backing of the USA. War and the need for governments to maintain, or if possible extend, their support within society have meant that political considerations have also had a hand in this. Accordingly, the region has both preserved the openly protectionist structure of its economies and continued to support a great range of measures designed to subsidize production for the domestic market, in particular in the foodstuffs sector. It has proved impossible for this institutional system to be modified into the new export-oriented economic model as quickly as the IMF had hoped.

Yet it would be wrong to assume that no progress had been made in the process of adjustment. In fact, the measures adopted have tended to reduce the state's influencing control. Bit by bit the market has replaced state regimentation, moves have been made to open up to the outside world and the sale of non-traditional exports to third markets has increased, although at the expense of sales to the Central American Common Market and of traditional export goods. The pressure exerted by the US IDA and the international financial organizations has led to greater liberalization within the financial system and to economies being opened up more and more to overseas investment. The proposal contained in the Baker Plan that debt service should be effected through the selling off of interests in domestic concerns (debt-to-equity-transactions) is an expression of this trend.

The economic and social costs of adjustment have been increased by the effects which adjustment policies have had on the stability of the region's currencies. The freeing up of prices was intended to create a price structure throughout society which would permit rational decisions to be taken on the question of investment. The criticism is often levelled at measures of this kind that where market structures are oligopolistic and where there is protectionism the freeing up of prices merely results in an uncontrollable rise in prices. Where the freeing up of prices goes hand in hand with a liberalization of the financial system, the inflationary effects of both measures are increased still further. This also explains to a large extent the appearance of an inflationary trend in Central America, a region which had until then known only relative monetary stability. Another destabilizing effect of transformation policies is their negative effects on state income and expenditure. Under such policies, exports are supposed to be promoted primarily by means of subsidies and tax relief. However, trade concessions often include the abolition of import duties. A combination of this and the problems existing in the region has meant that every change in fiscal and spending policy has resulted in grave budget problems. The events which took place in Costa Rica in 1979, in Guatemala in 1983, in Honduras in 1984 and in El Salvador in 1987 are eloquent proof of all this.

It would seem that it is fast becoming impossible for the countries of Central America to stabilize their economies by the monetarist method: for one thing, the political demands of the IMF and World Bank for reductions in public spending are constantly being undermined by US aid in the form of political funds (or in the case of Nicaragua by the USA's financing of the Contras). For another, the Central American nations will not be able to take the option of both eradicating their burden of debt and abandoning their protectionist isolationism by increasing their export quotas until someone comes up with a comprehensive programme for the promotion of economic development in this region: the expansion in their exports has already come to a standstill because of the strain necessarily imposed on the budget by all export-promotion policies. As long as there is no support for endogenous, structural-development options in these countries it is safe to assume that the only competitive advantage which exports from the region will enjoy will be based on the fact that its wages are lower than elsewhere. On the other hand, the alternative — for the region to concentrate all of its efforts on supplying the North American market — would result in Central America becoming more dependent on the market and political decisions of the USA.

Recommended Reading

CEPAL, (various years) *Estudio Economico de America Latina.*
Gallardo, Maria Eugenia and López, Jos Roberto (1986) Centroamerica. La crisis en cifras, FLACSO — IICA, SAN JOSE.
González Rubí, Jorge (1985) Centroamerica. Crónica de una deuda anunciada Síntesis del documento de la CEPAL: Centroamerica: el financiamiento externo en la evolución económica, 1950–1983, Mexico marzo de 1985 en Comercio Exterior, Vol. 35, Mexico, junio.
Stahler, Richard y Arana, Mario (1987) Deuda externa y políticas de estabilización y ajuste estructural en Nicaragua Avance de Investigación, presentado en Seminario Regional sobre Deuda externa y politicas de estabilización y ajuste en Centroamerica y Panamá, San Jos 19–20 febrero.

15. LLDCs (Least Developed Countries): The Fourth World in the Debt Trap

Rainer Tetzlaff

It would not be unreasonable to assume that the countries of the Fourth World are too poor to be able to run up large debts internationally; after all, this lack of resources makes them even less attractive to overseas lenders than other countries, since it means that there is not much to be got out of them in the way of profits. This seemingly plausible assumption is, however, not always supported by the facts. There are indeed countries which are poor in resources among the heavily indebted (either in relative or absolute terms) nations. For example, in 1986 Sudan, a country whose exports are limited to cotton and hazelnuts, was the twentieth most heavily indebted Third World nation with an external debt of US$10 billion. Four other African countries are also members of the major debtors' club: Algeria (US$18.4 billion), Egypt (US$16.0 billion), Nigeria (US$14.8 billion) and Morocco (US$11.0 billion).

The five countries named above are, in fact, endowed with raw materials (crude oil or phosphate) for which there is demand on the world market. But even those agricultural states in Africa which are poor in resources have managed to raise loans of all kinds abroad, and these have now plunged them into a serious solvency crisis. Structural adjustments are the magic words with which the World Bank and the IMF are attempting to drag these countries out of their debt-related quagmire. The thinking behind the strategy is that if national production is brought into line with the pattern of demand on the world market then the increase in these countries' exports will enable them to earn enough foreign currency to settle their debts. As such it resumes the historical process, which began with colonialism, of compulsorily exploiting the value of the non-European economies.

What are LLDCs?

Since 1971 some of the less developed countries (LDCs) have been referred to by the UN as least developed countries (LLDCs) and are frequently also known, as a group, as the Fourth World. Before inclusion in this group (whose members are given preferential treatment by some aid organizations) countries have to meet three criteria:

- GDP per head has to be less than US$250 (this guiding figure was originally set at US$100);
- industrial output has to account for less than 10% of GDP; and
- the literacy rate for those over the age of 15 has to be less than 20%.

The 36 countries concerned have a population of approximately 300 million, just under 9% of the population of the whole Third World, but according to estimates account for only 20% of the world's 'absolutely poor'. This term is used by the World Bank to describe people in the developing nations who are forced to live at a level below the statistically calculated subsistence level. Because of their wretched nutritional circumstances, living conditions and state of health, such people are condemned to absolute poverty and an early death. It is estimated that there may be as many as 750–1,000 million of them throughout the world. They live predominantly on the land, from where they are migrating in ever-increasing numbers to the slums in the proliferating large cities. The majority are concentrated in four Asian countries: India, Pakistan, Bangladesh and Indonesia. Yet only Bangladesh is included in the LLDC category. Although more of the absolutely poor live in India than in the rest of the Fourth World together, it is not an LLDC. As such, to equate the Fourth World with the poor world is not accurate.

Table 15.1
Least Developed Countries (LLDCs)

Africa:	
Benin	Tanzania
Botswana	Togo
Burundi	Uganda
Cape Verde	Upper Volta (Burkina Faso)
Central African Republic	
Chad	*Asia:*
Comoro Islands	Afghanistan
Djibouti	Bangladesh
Equatorial Guinea	Bhutan
Ethiopia	Laos
Gambia	Maldives
Guinea	Nepal
Guinea-Bissau	Samoa
Lesotho	Yemen (Arab Republic)
Malawi	Yemen (People's
Mali	Democratic Republic)
Niger	
Rwanda	*Latin America*
São Tomé and Principe	Haiti
Sierra Leone	
Somalia	
Sudan	

It is worth noting that even though these countries have to an increasing extent been both incorporated into the international division of labour and structurally integrated, their capitalization is far from complete. Foreign-currency loans and development aid are helping considerably to ensure that the Fourth World maintains its position, albeit an inferior position, in the world economic order.

Sudan in the debt trap: geopolitical considerations in the struggle for power

Let us now look in more detail at the case of Sudan, the most heavily indebted nation of the Fourth World. We should ask what has made Sudan, which neither mines mineral resources nor operates lucrative industrial plants, so attractive to overseas lenders of capital? Do these lenders really believe that they will ever get back from this economically unstable country, which exports only hazelnuts and cotton in any great quantity, the capital which they have lent? That overseas banks, export firms and development agencies have been prepared to provide loans to oil states such as Algeria and Nigeria, and to Morocco, one of the world's major producers of phosphate, seems far more understandable since these countries, being rich in resources, can after all offer their lenders certain material guarantees of being repaid. In the case of countries with no exportable minerals, such as the Nile states, Egypt and Sudan, things look a little different: here it is geopolitical considerations and power politics which have led the Western industrialized nations to make loans available to countries which — economically speaking — lack the preconditions which would enable them to utilize capital productively.

Sudan is important to the NATO countries, since it acts as a barrier to the presumed expansionism of Soviet policies on Africa and the Near East. In the west the country, Africa's largest in terms of area, borders on Libya, which has been governed since 1969 by Colonel Gaddafi who is widely known to be no friend of the USA or Egypt. In the east it has a common border with socialist Ethiopia, which since 1974/5 has maintained close political and military links with the USSR. As a coastal state on the Red Sea, on which the USSR maintains a military presence in several ports (in particular in Aden in the Yemen), it is also closely allied with the anti-socialist regime in Saudi Arabia, which keenly observes political (and religious) developments on the opposite side of the Arabian Inland (or Red) Sea. In this political hotspot with all its powerful East–West tensions the development strategists of the West considered it opportune to back and stabilize the anti-communist regime of Colonel Numeiri (1969–85) with loans and military aid. These loans from Western European and Arab states were used primarily to finance large-scale development projects.

The list of these projects, which were expensive and completely overstretched the country's financial and administrative capacities, is long. Examples of projects which smacked more of development gigantomania than development-policy good sense include:

- the Kenana Sugar Project (estimated cost: US$750 million);
- the Jonglei Canal in Southern Sudan, which is still under construction and which is to help drain the Sudd swamp along the Nile and open up new opportunities for irrigation in Egypt and northern Sudan (more than US$1 billion);
- the planned crude-oil pipeline from Kosti to Port Sudan, which is to carry oil pumped by the US firm Chevron on to the world market (US$900 million);
- the planned oil refinery in Kosti (US$1 billion);
- the planned Meroe Fill Dam, which will supply hydro-electric power (US$600 million); and
- the Rahad Irrigation Project, co-financed by the World Bank, for hazelnuts and cotton (US$346 million).

Tripartite co-operation on development policy between Sudan, which was to become the breadbasket of the Arab world, the Arab oil states and the West continued long after it had been proven that the corrupt military regime in Sudan preferred to keep its own people away from development-policy work than to mobilize them. When the unsuccessful dictator Numeiri (who provoked another civil war in 1983) was finally toppled in 1985 by the indignant masses (led by trades unionists, teachers, doctors, students and military officers), his regime simply disappeared, but the people were saddled with the debts which it had run up, debts to the value of US$10 billion. For generations to come the Sudanese will have to suffer under this huge financial burden.

Tanzania: the social effects of IMF conditionality

Just what austerity policies can mean in concrete terms for people in a Fourth World country can be seen from the Tanzanian experience. This East African country has the highest debt per head of the population in the Fourth World and is one of the states whose governments refused for years to implement the austerity measures recommended by the IMF.

In the 1970s, Tanzania was regarded as a promising example of socialist reorganization by a post-colonial society. This reorganization was to be achieved through reform of the agricultural sector. Under the *ujamaa* (a form of socialism based on familyhood) ideology of the Unity Party Tanu, poor farmers were to be given the opportunity to meet their basic needs through their own efforts, not by utilizing external loans. 'Money is the weapon of the rich', declared the shrewd party leader and ruler of the country, Nyerere, when he prescribed self-reliance for the Tanzanians. This principle of 'putting one's trust in one's own efforts' met with so much acclamation in the West that Tanzania received more foreign aid per head than any other country.

It was clear from the beginning that, like the Nile's sandbox, Sudan, Tanzania had little that was of economic value to the OECD countries, but political and military support for national independence movements in southern Africa, calls for a New World Economic Order and initiatives in the field of world-wide disarmament meant that the unaligned Tanzania was much-courted politically. However, politically motivated help from abroad was unable to check the economic decline of what had been traditionally an agricultural exporting country. On the contrary, in the beginning it actually accentuated the still-unsound nature of state bureaucratic intervention in rural life.

Four factors in particular brought Tanzania to the brink of financial ruin:

- Periodic bad harvests, droughts and famines, which in 1974 (the first year of disaster) alone reduced foreign-currency reserves by around DM250 million.
- The military campaign against Uganda, which was forced upon Tanzania by the dictator Idi Amin and which devoured approximately DM2 billion, more than 50% of which showed up in the books as foreign currency payments for weapons and ammunition.
- A systematically unsuccessful agricultural policy which offered farmers (other than the co-operatives which exported coffee) hardly any incentives to increase production, combined with a policy designed to drastically restrict imports and which forced down industrial output until firms were operating at less than 40% of previous capacity. The regenerational effects of the shortage of consumer goods which this caused strengthened agricultural producers in their resolve to restrict production for the market.
- What is more, the years of unsuccessful negotiation between IMF experts who stuck firmly to their principles and no less ideologically devout Tanzanian state officials prevented the rehabilitation of the ailing economy. Imports were dramatically restricted, new investment was no longer forthcoming. Finally, in 1982, a serious economic crisis forced the Tanzanian Government to make a move towards accepting the IMF's recommendations. The Fund demanded a 300% devaluation of the Tanzanian shilling, a reduction of almost 200% in subsidies on agricultural produce (especially maize), the dismissal of 10% of the civil service (27,000 people) and an end to free medical provision and free education.

When, after the resignation of state president Julius Nyerere in October 1985, the inevitable happened and the IMF was able to get its programme implemented, the effects of IMF conditionality quickly made themselves felt. Women and children were its major victims. Unlike the 25% devaluation of the US dollar in June 1986, the prescribed devaluation of the Tanzanian shilling increased the number of unemployed in the towns, the number of farmers ruined by price rises and above all the costs of all those producers who were dependent on imported raw materials, fuel, spare parts and machinery. According to a church organization in Dar es Salaam the consequences of the devaluation would be that:

Farmers will undoubtedly experience a net loss of earnings, since they now have to pay more for agricultural inputs; for education, which until now has been free; and more in development tax; as well as higher prices for some goods. Their extra outgoings will amount to far more than they earn by exporting their crops.

Furthermore, planned development projects could 'not be undertaken as a direct result of the devaluation of the national currency'.

As a complete episode, the Tanzanian drama teaches us something about the developmental dilemma facing the have-nots, who were integrated into the international division of labour during the colonial age without their permission and cannot free themselves from the snare of dependence and external debt. Even long years of refusal by a (weak) state with an internationally respected president to abandon a socialist (and non-self-financing) alternative in favour of the dominant market-economy system, which requires the opening up of the country and adjustment to world-market conditions, does not guard against the danger of external intervention. The financial world is one built on blood and tears!

Looking at two heavily indebted LLDCs, Sudan and Tanzania, the IMF and the World Bank would surely conclude that development-policy good sense (or the law governing the productive use of overseas capital) has been offended against. In theory, external loans should, of course, function in such a way that a borrowing country is able to meet its own development objectives more quickly and economically with their help than it would without external aid and must be such that they can be repaid. The ability to (re)pay interest and loan capital in the future depends on whether external loans are invested in such a way that the projects which they fund will be profitable enough and the growth in a country's GDP which they stimulate will be strong enough to enable that country to raise the funds which it needs for debt service. Loans should thus not be used thoughtlessly to fill gaps in current import statistics, nor should they be used in such a way that they stimulate the domestic market alone. Overseas funds should be invested in a manner which ensures that adequate foreign currency is raised for interest and loan-capital (re)payments. This is often an ideal which it is not within the power of the governments of debtor nations to realize.

Dependence and vulnerability through raw materials exports

The above problem points up one of the dilemmas facing the countries of the Fourth World, and it is a dilemma to which there is no easy solution: how can they earn foreign currency if the international demand for the goods which they have been producing since the days of European colonial rule, namely monocultural products, is stagnant or even in decline? 'Monocultural products' describe plant-based raw materials and luxury foodstuffs (such as cotton, sisal, coffee, cocoa and tobacco) which were and are cultivated on large areas of land (often they are the only useful plants grown) and are destined for export in order to satisfy demand in the industrialized nations of the North. What would have become of textile production in Europe, for example, if there had been no cotton imports from Egypt, Sudan or Chad? For decades Bangladesh and Tanzania (previously German East Africa, then British Tanganyika) supplied sisal and jute for the production of ships' ropes and hard-wearing containers. Islands such as Mauritius, Jamaica and Cuba were forcibly transformed by the former colonial powers into suppliers of cane sugar (and rum). The bulk of these industries' profits, which were only possible because labour was acquired at artifically reduced prices (colonial forced labour), flowed into the colonial metropole; profits were thus lost as a source of investment which might have allowed diversification of production in erstwhile colonies. Yet this was the only way to reduce the vulnerability caused by one-crop agriculture systems, a vulnerability which abandoned the countries affected to unpredictable fluctuations in the demand for and price of monocultural products on the world market. The story was repeated in the tropical and sub-tropical countries which export mineral substances such as copper, iron and tin.

After such countries had gained political independence, domestic politicians attempted, on the advice of the World Bank and other development-aid institutions in the West, to maintain and further extend this form of social reproduction (that is the exportation of raw materials for the world market). In doing so they ended up in a developmental blind alley which had serious consequences for the political, national sovereignty which they had just won; for this development path ultimately led them into the debt trap.

Here we should mention the World Bank's unfortunate role in instigating industrial projects with dubious prospects in terms of profitability. Essentially since the (in)famous Nairobi speech delivered by the president of the World Bank, Robert McNamara, in 1973 (in which he announced that the Bank would be tackling 'poverty-oriented' development projects and that total lending to Africa would be doubled every five years), the Bank's management has prevented its experts from watching out for possible aid projects which could meet the objectives which it has set itself. Moreover, development schemes have been set up (with the help of manipulated feasibility studies) which were to prove to be faulty business investments.

The stock advice given by World Bank experts to several governments in Africa — that they should install the same types of sugar refineries as part of a programme of industrialization through import substitution — has become notorious. When sugar prices crashed on the world market as a result of overproduction but the operating costs rose steeply and unexpectedly (when machinery, spare parts and petrol became more expensive), it dawned on the planners that they would be unable to save foreign currency in this (capital- and technology-intensive) fashion or earn foreign currency by exporting surpluses. Costly development projects involving both the cultivation of hazelnuts, coconut palms, pineapples, flowers and citrus fruits and the production of textiles and clothing and financed from abroad were encouraged in much the same way.

The risk of faulty planning by others — it is, of course, rather difficult to forecast volume and price trends for products from the Tropics — is naturally borne by the borrowing-country alone.

The debt crisis in some LLDCs thus merely reflects productive relations which are unsound and anachronistic from the point of view of the balance of payments: cotton is being replaced increasingly by synthetic fibres; sisal production (in Tanzania) is being reduced more and more all the time because plastic materials produced from crude oil serve the same purpose and are often cheaper. Even where cane sugar is concerned, patterns of consumption in the Western metropole are beginning to split the industrialized nations from their former colonies: as a sweetener, glucose extracted from maize serves the same purpose as sugar and is being increasingly substituted for sugar imports from the Third World. In Sudan, which built the most modern sugar refinery in the Third World in the 1970s at a cost of around US$700 million, the costs of production today exceed sugar prices on the world market, with the result that sugar production has become one of the industries which the government subsidizes. This country's attempts to substitute domestically produced goods for industrially-manufactured imported goods, as other countries have done, has contributed greatly to her overindebtedness.

There are signs that the developing nations' beef trade is also suffering in a similarly ruinous manner: traditional exporters such as Argentina (an NIC) and Botswana (an LLDC) are now barely able to sell their beef at a profit.

The terms of trade and human dignity

At the same time as the demand for many raw materials from the Fourth World is falling, however, prices are rising for the kinds of products which the tropical and sub-tropical countries import: foodstuffs, fuel, manufactured goods and chemical products, including fertilizers and pesticides (both products which are essential to the Green Revolution, the strategy for modernizing the agricultural sector which the World Bank has been propagating). As a result, the price gap between the LLDC's imports and exports is widening dramatically. These unfavourable terms of trade mean that the LLDCs are losing billions in possible earnings from exports at fair raw materials prices (that is such prices as would keep pace with the trend in prices for manufactured goods). Moreover, their balances of payments are moving into the red, and there is nothing left over for the new investment which they need so badly. Were this trend to continue, then the future could only be described as grim for the Fourth World: processes of self-industrialization would be abandoned (the spectre of de-industrialization); development policy would degenerate into a mechanism for exerting pressure on countries to earn foreign currency for the purpose of servicing their debts; and the fairy-tale objective of countries being able to meet their own basic needs through their own efforts would vanish into thin air. On the intravenous drip of international development aid, the weakest developing nations would then come to be regarded by the creditor nations of the West as hardship cases and would be politically disenfranchised.

Any policy designed to alleviate need in the Fourth World must begin by looking at the question of causes. Observation of this kind has shown that it is external, world-market-dependent factors which have the greatest bearing on the overindebtedness of the Fourth World. The governments of dependent developing nations which are poor in resources have little influence over these factors (raw-materials prices, world market demand, interest rates, amongst others) and, accordingly, it is only right and proper that Western (and, if affected, also Eastern) industrial nations should also be called to account when it comes to finding a solution to the debt crisis. That only the weak should have to adjust, even to catastrophes for which they are not themselves to blame (external shocks), contradicts the law according to which the international development partnership is supposed to operate. The sensational declaration issued by the Papal Commission Justitia et Pax in January 1987 on 'an ethical approach to overcoming the international debt crisis' emphasized the responsibilities which the creditors have towards the debtors:

> Those sections of the population most badly hit by the consequences of indebtedness need clear signs that the measures taken as a solution are just and effective . . . However, from a moral point of view no government can ask its people to suffer privations which are irreconcilable with the dignity of man.

Much of what is part of daily experience in the Third World is irreconcilable with the 'dignity of man'. A great deal would have been achieved if the people in the poor countries of the world were at least granted the right to survive — to have their basic material needs met. This would include respect for the natural environment of the rural poor, which is often destroyed these days by the influx of modern technology for the benefit of a minority within society and at the expense of the less modernization-friendly majority. The introduction of tractors into semi-arid regions of Africa and Asia, for example, has enabled some investors to earn huge profits rapidly, but has quickly caused the soil to turn to slag and left it exhausted (this is why we talk of 'agricultural mining'). Enormous fill dams which force whole villages to disperse, and industrial forestry plantations which deny the poor free access to the resources (such as firewood, structural timber, berries) in what was previously natural forest are further examples of impoverishment aid.

What we must therefore demand is that the environmental and social acceptability of projects financed by external loans is proven beforehand. It would be better for unacceptable development projects (those with destructive consequences) to be dropped, even if the export interests of the industrial nations are limited by this in the short term.

Above all, it is not reconcilable with the dignity of peoples that having won the political independence for which they have struggled they are then faced once again with the threat of political recolonization. The fact that social reforms in poor countries cost money and that countries which are striving towards reform therefore often grope their way into the debt trap more easily than they might otherwise have done (as did Tanzania, Jamaica and Chile) is exploited by the creditor states, which apply 'gentle force' to ensure good economic-policy and political conduct in the global East–West conflict.

Recommended Reading

Biermann, W. (1987) 'Das Ende der sozialistischen Tranformation. Die Verschuldungskrise Tanzanias', *Informationsdienst Südliches Afrika*, April.

German Bundestag, (1986) Committee for Economic Co-operation, hearing of 5 November in Bonn: *Einfluß de von der Weltbank und dem IWF geführten Anpassungsprogramme auf die entwicklungspolitische Zusammenarbeit*, BT-Drucksache 10/470.

Körner, P., Maaß, G., Siebold, Th. and Tetzlaff, R. (1986) *The IMF and the Debt Crisis: A Guide to the Third World's Dilemma*, Zed Books.

Nuscheler, F. (1985) *Lern- und Arbeitsbuch Entwicklungspolitik*, Bonn.

Onimode, Bade (ed.) (1989) *The IMF, The World Bank and the African Debt: Vol.1: The Economic Impact; Vol. 2: The Social and Political Impact*, Zed Books.

Pressedienst der Deutschen Bischofskonferenz (Press Service of the German Bishops' Conference) (1987) *Dokumentation*, Bonn, 26 January.

16. Mexico: Five Years of Debt Crisis

Raúl Rojas

The outbreak of the crisis

When Mexican Minister for Economic Affairs, Jesús Silva Herzog, declared a 90 day moratorium on the country's debt service payments in August 1982 he could not have imagined that by doing so he was opening a new chapter of Mexican history — the decade of debt crisis. Although in the two previous years other Latin American countries had actually gone bankrupt, the international banks refused to recognize the global crisis until, that is, the apparently unthinkable happened. This time it was not a small country which had run into financial difficulties; this time the country which had become unable to pay its debts was the world's second biggest debtor and, moreover, the strongest link in the chain of indebtedness: the crude-oil-rich Mexico. August 1982 became a milestone in banking history and marked the birth of the 'Mexico syndrome', for from that moment on a global banking crisis could not be ruled out.

In Mexico itself the historic nature of the events was barely recognized. The government regarded the whole thing as a temporary problem of liquidity which would be mastered within a few months. This liquidity squeeze would, however, prove to be Mexico's most serious crisis since the restive years of the Mexican Revolution. Fifty years of uninterrupted growth had forged the legend of the 'Mexican economic miracle', and in the course of the ecstasy unleashed by the discovery of crude oil during the 1970s the ruling Institutional Revolutionary Party (PRI) had allowed itself to be seduced by a number of fanciful visions: it talked both of managing the 'opulence' and of transforming Mexico into an industrialized nation by the year 2000. Instead, the 1980s will go down in the country's history as a lost decade, a period in which the expansion of the country's real wealth came to a standstill while the population continued to grow. In 1990, Mexico's GNP differed only slightly from her 1981 levels of output, whereas during the intervening period almost 15 million more Mexicans were born.

Five years after the 1982 collapse it is possible to take stock for the first time. The picture looks disastrous. In the past five years output has not increased. Nor has Mexico's external debt diminished. Inflation and indebtedness have spiralled. Not a single month has passed over the last few years in which negotiations have not taken place with the banks and the international financial institutions on the subject of old loans. The process of permanently restructuring Mexico's debts has merely disguised the country's actual inability to pay those debts.

Figure 16.1
Annual rates of growth in Mexico's GNP, population and external debt

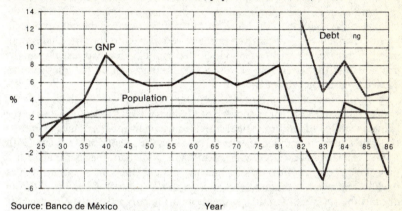

Source: Banco de México   Year

Figure 16.1 reveals at a glance the drama of the present crisis. The cyclical nature of the growth in Mexico's GNP is clearly recognizable. In three of the periods given (1940–45, 1960–65, 1975–81) the growth rates recorded were above average; but what is most important is that over five decades the mean average rate of growth was around 6.7% per annum. This figure, which is regarded in Mexico as a historic rate of growth has shaped the nation's policies and economy for many years. In the past, periods in which annual rates of growth have been less than 5% have been viewed as something approaching a recession. In 1982, however, the rate of growth in Mexico's GNP was negative for the first time since the 1920s. Since 1982 the country's GNP has not grown at all; regardless of this stagnation, however, the country's external debt continues to increase. The causes of the Mexican economic crisis can be broken down into three closely related problem areas:

The import-substitution crisis. Mexican industry had expanded too quickly and in chaotic fashion and by the end of the 1970s it had become virtually impossible to solve the problems in the infrastructure which had arisen as a result. For decades Mexico's import substitution policies had concentrated on creating a highly developed mass consumer-goods industry. The state had taken over unprofitable or capital-intensive branches of industry and made cheap raw materials, electricity and infrastructure available to Mexican firms. The deficits which had accrued had been financed from year to year by new domestic loans and from the 1970s onwards by loans from overseas. From a book-keeping point of view, however, the accumulated deficit meant that by

1970 the large state-owned industries were on the brink of bankruptcy. Despite, or perhaps because of, the hothouse conditions under which national industry operated, import substitution did not become a self-financing process. The establishment of the consumer-goods industry was financed by foreign currency earned either in the agricultural sector or from the production of raw materials, but not from exports of manufactured goods. The volume of capital goods imported remained high: there has been no substantial improvement in the ratio of imports of capital goods to total imports since 1958. In fact, the chronic overvaluation of the Mexican currency encouraged the import of such goods. Though the fact that the borders were closed to imported consumer goods but (at least partly) open to imported capital goods was justified on the grounds that the latter were necessary for rapid growth. In the long run this caused even greater problems.

Mexico's industrialization was financed by means of a three-pronged transfer of resources: from agriculture to industry; from the state-owned to the private sector; and, during its final stage, from overseas to the domestic front in the form of private and public external loans. As the splendour of the late 1970s approached, the Mexican Government's far-sighted strategists argued for a new policy: export substitution. Industry should, they maintained, finance itself by exporting manufactured goods on a massive scale. Cheap credit from abroad and the huge quantities of crude oil being pumped after 1976 eased the situation and deferred the crisis until a later date. Overseas indebtedness and crude oil enabled the old and largely failed accumulation model to survive for a few more years. Consequently, when the crisis broke at the beginning of the 1980s, it was many times more uncontrollable than it would have been if the necessary corrections had been made much earlier.

The agricultural crisis. As a result of extensive growth, agricultural output had been rising steadily since 1930. By the end of the 1970s almost half of Mexico's territory had been divided out between the *campesinos*, and this led to an increase in the area of land under cultivation. Nevertheless, productivity in the agricultural sector increased only very slightly each year, and the rates of increase lagged way behind those in industry. Controlled agricultural prices ensured that the agricultural sector delivered cheap foodstuffs and raw materials to the towns. As a consequence, the rates at which goods were exchanged between the agricultural sector and industry worsened steadily, and the agricultural sector was systematically exploited. It became a source of accumulation for industry, since price controls set in motion a transfer of resources; until well into the 1960s it provided the foreign currency required by the accumulation model; and it supplied the towns with the workers for which they hungered, with the bulk of their reserve armies of labour. During the 1960s, however, this scheme for plundering the agricultural sector clearly began to reach its limits. Since then (with the exception of a few years) agricultural output has expanded more slowly than the population. Moreover, since 1970 the agricultural sector has not been able to perform its function as a procurer of foreign currency, and Mexico's agricultural trade balance has alternated between being negative and positive. Even traditional foodstuffs have had to be imported in large quantities from the USA. Initially, Mexico's growing external debt and her crude-oil revenues were able to make up for her lack of resources.

Dependence on the foreign-trade sector. The success of the Mexican economy has always been measured in terms of how much the actual growth rate differed from the historical rate of growth. What was important was not that expansion should be regular and harmonious, but that the process should be one of permanent growth. The plundering of the agricultural sector and the import-substitution crisis permitted the emergence of an economic system one of whose structural characteristics was imbalance between the various branches of the economy. In addition to highly developed industrial branches, there were others which produced their goods under completely outmoded conditions; in addition to the state-owned industries which produced at a huge loss, there were others which were able to earn exceedingly high profits; in addition to branches of industry with many producers, there were others, such as the motor industry, in which only four or five large firms divided up the entire market between themselves. The susceptibility to crisis of this system was disguised until 1981 by Mexico's dependence on foreign trade. As part of the economic cycle, cheap imports became responsible for temporarily stabilizing existing imbalances. In this sense the foreign-trade sector did not merely complement the national economy, but was instead an irreplaceable component part of it. Since the peso was overvalued, imports were able to penetrate the entire economic mechanism and create an apparent balance. In 1981 the balance of trade deficit (without crude oil) climbed to almost US$15 billion. When it was no longer possible for Mexico to sustain the rate at which imports were increasing, a serious crisis became inevitable. This was the mortgage on the future which had been raised during the decades of *desarrollismo* (a policy of growth at any price).

The Mexican crisis of 1982 was not a phenomenon which can be explained in terms of external factors alone. Naturally, the Mexican Government emphasized the effects of external shocks, in particular high interest rates, the fall in crude oil prices and the lack of patriotism displayed by entrepreneurs who allowed capital worth several billion dollars to flee to the USA. Indeed, the effects of the two shocks cited cannot be ignored: for a while in 1981 the US Prime Rate (the preferential rate of interest for 'first-class names') stood at over 20% and was still 15% in 1982. Also in 1981 the price of crude oil fell by US$4 a barrel and this set in motion a downward trend which reached its lowest point to date in 1986.

The causes of the Mexican crisis are, however, primarily homemade; the external shocks merely acted as a catalyst for them. The high US Prime Rate only had such a catastrophic effect on Mexico's industry because in the previous 20 years that industry had been transformed into an insatiable import-devouring machine and because the imports which it devoured had been financed by external loans since the end of the 1960s. The fall in the price of crude oil was only a disaster for Mexico because the country's entire development until the year 2000 depended on crude-oil revenue once the agricultural sector had lost its role as the provider of foreign currency. Mexico's entire development model had long teetered on the brink of a huge crisis which was only postponed because of her crude-oil revenue and the cheap loans available in the 1970s. When, at the beginning of the 1980s, the USA drove interest rates up and the Reagan Administration began to divert the flow of credit away from the Third World and to the USA it became impossible to postpone that crisis any longer. The Mexican débâcle is therefore more than simply a debt crisis. It is a crisis whose roots are buried deeply in the whole pattern of the economic development of the past few years.

Let me explain the link between external, uncontrollable shocks and the homemade conditions capable of causing a crisis by means of a vivid example. When an earthquake transformed parts of Mexico City into a heap of ruins on 19 September 1985 no one could dispute the fact that the earthquake was unforeseeable. The effects of the earthquake could not, however, be laid at the door of nature alone. Fifty years of obsession with growth had turned Mexico City into a Moloch, an industrial monster, in which 25% of Mexico's total GNP was produced in the tiniest of areas. The agricultural crisis had been driving the *campesinos* from the countryside and into the town for years; even today 3,000 come in search of work each day. Not only did the earthquake destroy buildings, it also laid bare the infrastructural madness of Mexico's capital city. What happened in the debt crisis was very similar: the external shocks merely triggered the current desperate situation. Its deeper-seated causes, however, are to be found in the history of the last few decades, in attempts to speed up growth without tackling the structural causes of poverty and misery. The ruling party cannot shirk responsibility for this by blaming external factors.

A monument has been erected to the old policies. That monument is known as the Mexican debt figures.

Table 16.1
Mexico's total external debt
(US$ m)

Year	Private debts	Public debts	Total
1970	1,829	4,262	6,091
1972	2,691	5,065	7,696
1974	4,471	9,975	14,446
1976	6,208	19,604	25,808
1978	6,983	26,264	33,247
1980	14,832	33,813	48,651
1982	21,459	58,874	80,333
1984	14,500	74,500	89,000
1986	14,000	83,000	97,000
1987	14,000	90,000	104,000

Source: Banco de Mexico.

The first stage in the management of the crisis

After the moratorium of August 1982 the Mexican Government took the bull by the horns. On 1 September the entire banking system was nationalized and a complete system of foreign-currency import and export controls introduced. Carlos Tello, a representative of the left-wing of the PRI, was appointed as president of the Mexican central bank. Within the space of only three months Tello attempted to correct the faulty trends of the previous period. Interest rates for small investors were raised from 4–20%, interest was to be paid to savers on their bank-account deposits, and interest rates on some loans to industrialists were reduced in the hope that this would encourage increased investment. On the foreign-exchange front attempts were made to stabilize the rate of exchange of the Mexican currency, and this was set at 70 pesos to the dollar, though in the last few days of August the currency had sunk to more than 100 pesos to the dollar. At the same time, a controlled exchange rate was also established between the peso and the dollar. This controlled rate was to be used for foreign-currency transactions relating to strategic imports or the debt-service payments made by firms in Mexico to overseas banks.

At the heart of Tello's 90-day programme was a set of stabilization measures which within a few months were to lead to a new expansive economic cycle. The top priority was to control inflation and devalue the currency. However, the interest rates set were actually negative, that is lower than the rate of inflation. Between August and November interest rates fluctuated around the 70% level, whereas the annual rate of inflation stood at 100%. These unrealistic interest rates were justified at the time with the argument that inflation was falling, that is to say the nationalized banks did not set interest rates with reference to previous rates of inflation but with reference to those expected by the monetary authorities. In the long run this led to a still greater exodus of capital and to the dollarization of the economy.

The final *coup* pulled off by Tello and President Lopez Portulli at the end of his term of office was that they managed to anchor their nationalization of the banks in the country's constitution. At this time (November 1982) it was already known that the recently-elected new president intended to reverse partially the nationalization of the banks. So whilst the new government team was preparing to assume power, a bill was sent to Parliament and passed with all speed. At the same time, Mexico opened negotiations with the IMF. The Letter of Intent addressed to the director of the Fund was, however, totally ambiguous. The only thing that was clear was that Mexico needed new loans immediately to tide her over the next few months. The IMF promised US$3,600 million, and the USA also participated in Mexico's rescue with several commercial loans and by purchasing Mexican crude oil (for the purpose of increasing her strategic reserves). But by then it was already clear that any concrete agreements would have to be concluded with the next government.

On 1 December 1982 the new government assumed power. The first thing it did was to part-reprivatize the banks. The Constitution was remodified as swiftly in December as it had been in November. The system of *economia mixta*, that is a state-controlled market economy, ceased to be a political programme and passed into the law of the land. Tello's measures were overturned. The currency was devalued once again and interest rates raised. Plans were made to sell off the bulk of the state-owned firms to the private sector. Agreements were concluded with the IMF, and the government committed itself to achieve a graduated reduction in the rate of inflation and the budget deficit over the next three years. In short the new phase was to be a restrictive one.

At the same time as these domestic economy measures were being taken, negotiations were opened with the international banks at two levels: with the aim of concluding an agreement on short-term public loans (due by December 1984); and for the purpose of settling the matter of Mexico's private debts.

The international banks were particularly disturbed by this second point. Many Mexican businesses had neither paid interest nor repaid loan capital on their external debts since 1982. As Table 16.1 reveals, there was almost US$15 billion at stake. Of this, US$2.3 billion, an amount equal, for instance, to just under two-thirds of the total Bolivian external debt, was owed by just one Mexican firm, Grupo Alfa. The banks therefore demanded some form of government security for the private debts before they were prepared to open negotiations.

The government responded by creating FICORCA, a special fund which was to serve as an intermediary between Mexican firms and the banks. The Mexican firms could pay interest and loan capital into FICORCA in pesos, and FICORCA then handed over the appropriate sum to the creditor bank in dollars. Should the Mexican firms not have the money for these payments they could even obtain loans from FICORCA. In the long run this mechanism could be used to convert dollar loans into pesos. Industrialists were able to profit from this transaction in two ways: the peso/dollar exchange rate set for these transactions was extremely favourable (30% cheaper than the floating exchange rate); and the interest rates charged on the peso loans were lower than the market rates. In addition, they were calculated in such a way that at the beginning of the repayment period only small payments had to be made. Thanks to FICORCA, things moved on apace, and on 28 June 1983 the governments of 16 countries signed a rescheduling agreement covering the private debts of 1,200 Mexican firms. It was agreed that the due dates should be extended to six or seven years with grace periods of at least three years.

The first government loans were rescheduled in August 1983, after long negotiations. The due dates on short-term debts amounting to US$20 billion were extended by eight years (with a four-year grace period) and an agreed surcharge of $1\frac{7}{8}\%$ over and above the LIBOR rate or $1\frac{3}{4}\%$ over the US Prime Rate. The agreement was extolled as a breakthrough by both the banks and the Mexican Government. During the first few months of the year Mexico had realized a substantial balance of payments surplus (for the first time in 20 years), and it was thus expected that the government's restrictive economic policies would last only a short time. In May 1983 the Mexican Government had even published its National Development Plan, under which it was envisaged that from 1984 onwards Mexico would once again be able to tread her previous growth path. The two years 1982 and 1983, with their negative growth rates, were to go down in history as exceptions, as statistical discrepancies. It was hoped that by 1989 GNP would be increasing by 5% per annum. The first rescheduling agreement had created the required room for manoeuvre, and Mexico would now remain capable of paying her debts until at least the end of 1984. Negotiations were, however, set to continue, as Mexico's debt structure after 1985 continued to give cause for concern.

Figure 16.2 illustrates how the due dates on outstanding loans were pushed into the future (to the right of the figure) after the first Mexican rescheduling. The first curve shows the 1982 position, that is how many millions of dollars were supposed to be paid each year (loan capital only). After the first rescheduling (the second curve) the due dates on Mexico's loans were concentrated in the period 1984–94. Nonetheless, payments totalling US$10 billion were due in 1985 and, since it was impossible to effect these, a new round of negotiations had to be opened. Even before the ink was dry on the first rescheduling agreement, then, negotiations were already being conducted for a second rescheduling (the third curve of Figure 16.2), one which would cover not merely short-term loans. In the meantime, however, the media were already thinking aloud in terms of an end to the state of emergency. Just one year after the Mexican August the world appeared to be getting back to normal again.

Figure 16.2
Mexico: Debt structure after three rounds of restructuring

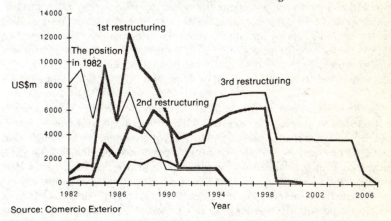

Source: Comercio Exterior

The second stage: more rescheduling and the new oil crisis

After the first stage in the crisis long-term projects began once more to be placed on the agenda. It had become clear from the National Development Plan and from many of the speeches delivered by President de la Madrid just what the new strategy for the country's development would look like. The objective was to tie Mexico into the world market and transform her into an exporter of manufactured goods. On the domestic front the market economy was to be strengthened. This meant that state intervention in all spheres was to beat a retreat. Fewer subsidies, fewer public-sector firms and less government were to go hand in hand with the liberalization of the domestic market, with the aim of transforming Mexico into a kind of Latin American Taiwan. It was time for Mexico to make use of her locational advantages. In particular, the government hoped to tie the country into the US market in the medium term by encouraging overseas investment and through the establishment of *maquiladoras*, or 'world market factories' on the border of Mexico which would produce directly for the US market. In order to create better circumstances for her assault on the world market, Mexico was also to become a member of GATT.

But first the second rescheduling agreement, which involved US$48 billion which would otherwise have fallen due in or after 1985, had to be concluded. In the middle of 1984 it looked like agreement could be reached, but suddenly interest rates in the USA were raised from their 1983 low of 11% to 13%. If interest rates were to rise again to 20% Mexico would once more become unable to pay her debts, and the second rescheduling agreement would be placed in jeopardy. Acting swiftly, Mexico, Brazil and Argentina called a meeting of the indebted Latin American countries in Cartagena, Columbia. The meeting was not convened primarily with the aim of taking concrete measures against the international banks, but first and foremost for the purposes of developing a common strategy for negotiating with them. The international banks recognized the risk associated with a consultative meeting of this kind. Just a couple of months later they agreed a second rescheduling agreement with Mexico on more favourable terms than the first. However, almost twelve months were to elapse before the rescheduling agreement was finally signed, for more than 500 international banks were involved. The agreement had to be ratified by all of them, and this formality alone took a year.

At the beginning of 1985 it looked as though the Mexican Government's calculations would prove to be correct. Debt (re)payments were under control, and the GNP was rising again after two years of recession. It was thought that crude-oil revenues would safeguard future payments, and the new National Industrial Plan proclaimed with complete confidence that by the year 2000 Mexico would be a 'medium-sized industrialized nation'. The optimism was premature. In February 1985, OPEC decided no longer to maintain a reference price for crude oil; the market price fell immediately. As early as March the Mexican Government was forced to announce its first measures of adjustment: the national budget was cut by 4%, and 236 state-owned firms were released for reprivatization.

In July 1985 the price of crude oil fell again. Repeated cuts in the national budget were imperative: 22,000 civil servants were dismissed, and several subsections within ministries were abolished and not replaced. By this time it was already obvious that Mexico would not be able to meet any of her obligations to the IMF. It was proving impossible to push inflation down to less than 50%, and the national budget deficit could not be reduced even to 5% of

GNP. Nevertheless, Mexico eventually reached agreement with her hundreds of creditors, and in the August of 1985 the second rescheduling agreement was finally ratified. The due dates of the debts which it covered were extended over 14 years so that until 1998 Mexico's debt structure would be more constant (see the third curve in Figure 16.2). However, this debt structure, which had been negotiated a year before, could only be financed with crude-oil prices at their old level. The disruption of the crude-oil market in 1985 rendered the whole agreement more than doubtful.

In fact, by this time the IMF was no longer particularly delighted with the outcome of Mexico's economic policies. In its view, these were still too expansive, despite all of the austerity measures which had been introduced, and on 18 September 1985 the Fund decided to refuse Mexico the last tranche of her US$3.6 billion loan on the grounds that the country had not met its obligations. One day later Mexico City was devastated by an earthquake. With one stroke Mexico had lost US$4 billion, not to mention countless human lives. Less than three weeks after it had been announced that Mexico would remain solvent until the year 2000 the government imposed a new moratorium, the second since 1982, on the repayment of over US$1 billion-worth of loan capital which would fall due in the coming weeks. The second rescheduling agreement was suddenly no longer worth the paper on which it was written. Mexico demanded the unthinkable of the banks: this time US$12 billion in fresh money was needed if the country was to maintain the pretence that it was able to pay its debts. The answer came back promptly: the new magic formula for dragging the indebted nations out of the quagmire was a plan proposed at the IMF meeting in South Korea: the Baker Plan.

The third stage: economic aftershocks and the third rescheduling

After the débâcle of the September, the Mexican Government increased the pace of its planned economic revival. From day to day it became clearer that the country's debts could not be financed by crude oil. In 1982 crude-oil revenues still exceeded US$15 billion, whereas interest payments amounted to US$11 billion. In 1985 the gap between the two figures narrowed, and in 1986 annual crude-oil revenues fell below the level of annual interest payments for the first time since the outbreak of the crisis (see Figure 16.3). Mexico's crude-oil crisis reached its most serious point when OPEC decided no longer to maintain a fixed price, but to fight for market shares. The price of crude sank temporarily to less than US$10 a barrel, despite the fact that some countries (including Mexico) curbed their output. By this time it was already evident that Mexico was not going to receive the US$12 billion which she had demanded exclusively from the banks: the big banks announced that they would make available a maximum of US$4 billion. The rest would have to be financed by the IMF and the World Bank. In the course of 1986 both institutions declared themselves willing to make available several billion dollars. However, the banks still hesitated to throw new money after old. In the meantime Mexico's economy had been plunged deeper into crisis. Inflation was rising sharply, GNP fell again by a remarkable 5%, and crude-oil prices stood at a lower level than at any time since 1976.

In Mexico itself the trauma of the earthquake had made certain that despite the rescheduling agreements the external debt could not be (re)paid in this way. Left- and right-wing parties, churches, entrepreneurs and trades unions joined forces to demand a new moratorium. The public pressure on the government became intense during these first few months of 1986, but the official policy did not change. Confronted directly with the intransigence of the banks and more sensitive than the rest of the government team to public pressure, the minister for finance began to talk of the possibility of taking tougher measures. His stance became more radical from day to day, and his tone more and more bitter until, in June 1986, President de la Madrid dismissed him. There was no room in this government for strategies of non-acceptance. The old policies must be continued, whatever the cost. The banks understood the new signals coming from Mexico and arranged with the new minister for finance for the conclusion of a third rescheduling agreement on spectacular terms: the due dates of US$47 billion-worth of loans were extended for 20 years (final curve in Figure 16.2).

Figure 16.3
Mexico: Proceeds from exports of crude oil and interest payments

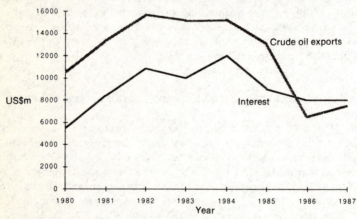

Source: Banco de México

The interest rate surcharge on this US$47 billion was reduced to 13/16% of 1% over and above the LIBOR rate, and most importantly of all a grace period of eight years was agreed, which meant that with the new debt structure no substantial loan capital repayments would be due until 1994. For the first time Mexico was forging ahead into the twenty-first century, and the present government (1988–1994) will not, providing that nothing else unexpected happens, have to bother with a new rescheduling agreement until 1993. The international banks were less satisfied with the arrangement. They were once again expected to lend US$6 billion in fresh money to Mexico, and the 13/16 of

1% interest-rate surcharge was described as an exception which would not be repeated. In fact, the banks had given in to the Mexican Government's blackmail. With its latest rescheduling agreement the government was able to buy another term of office for the ruling party. Until 1994 loan-capital repayments on the external debt had been reduced to a tolerable size. It is widely accepted that after that a fresh agreement will be required to regulate everything anew.

The banks' dissatisfaction manifested itself in the slowness with which many small banks ratified the agreement. It was March 1987 before all of the banks involved had signed and Mexico could receive her US$6 billion. Just a couple of weeks earlier only US$300 million had been needed to tie up the entire package, but a couple of the small banks had seemed determined to resist the Mexican attempt at blackmail. So Gustavo Petriccioli, Silva Herzog's successor, pulled a new rabbit out of the debt-management hat: Mexico could lend herself the US$300 million! Then the whole package would be sorted out, and the agreement concluded: future generations have the US president of the Fed., Paul Volcker, to thank for the fact that it did not come to this, for it was he who found other, more effective methods of bringing the small, wilful, American banks to their senses.

The final act: the industrial 'reconversion'

This report on Mexico's failed economic policies over the last five years naturally raises the question of whether it would not have been possible for Mexico to pursue different policies. Or to put it more clearly: why did Mexico never resort to confrontation with her creditors, as countries like Peru, Argentina and even Brazil did for a time? Why was there no serious attempt to transform the Cartagena Group from a forum for discussion into a debtors' cartel?

There are three reasons:

- The bulk of Mexico's external debt is owed to US banks. A Mexican moratorium would have hit these banks more than any others and provoked a response from the US Government. But of all the Latin American countries it is Mexico which has the most stable trading relations with the USA: two-thirds of Mexico's foreign trade is conducted with her northern neighbour. It would therefore have been possible for the USA to exert a great deal of economic pressure on Mexico.
- It would also have been possible for the USA to close its border to Mexican migrant workers and illegal immigrants.The safety vent in the North would then have disappeared and turned into direct political pressure on the Mexican Government. Only a government with political legitimacy could have coped with a conflict of this kind, yet political legitimacy is just what the PRI has most lacked since 1982.
- In addition, Mexico always attempted, with success, to have herself treated

as a special case in her negotiations with the banks. In 1987, Argentina and the Philippines were still trying to get the same concessions from the banks as Mexico had done, but they have not managed to obtain all of the benefits contained in the Mexican rescheduling package. Mexico was consciously treated by the banks as a 'strike-breaker' in order to prevent the indebted nations from ever forming a united front.

There is one more factor which is vitally important, namely the Mexican Government's new industrialization strategy, which has become known as *reconversion industrial* (industrial reconversion). Industrial reconversion is geared towards transforming Mexico into an exporter of manufactured goods. In actual fact what the Mexicans are attempting to do is to tie themselves in to the American market. Mexico is to become a paradise of cheap labour in order to attract new investment from the USA. The new world-market factories will extend the Southern USA into Northern Mexico. The new economic policies are no longer concerned with how the country can be developed domestically, but rather how it can be industrialized from outside. Development policies are no longer adopted in the Cabinet, but rather in the board rooms of General Motors, Ford, IBM and General Electric.

It was, then, not so much the fear of what might have been if Mexico had declared a moratorium, but much more the fear of what would no longer be which made a moratorium impossible in practical terms. It was not so much the fear of reprisals against current production, but of reprisals against the Mexican Government's dreams for the future which made Mexico into a permanent strike-breaker. Miguel de la Madrid will undoubtedly go down in Mexican history as a tragic figure. His government elaborated the boldest plans for the future and for Mexico's union with the world market. This government wanted to go beyond the traditional limits of Mexican politics, to eradicate protectionism and to overcome the Mexicans' fear of contact with the USA. At the core of its strategy was the creation of world-market factories and the financing of the industrial reconversion from crude-oil revenues. This, however, was the first nail in the coffin, for after 1986 crude oil could only partially finance interest payments. The second nail in the coffin was the ruling party's loss of legitimacy.

No one asked the Mexicans themselves whether they cared to pay for union with the USA with the lowest real wages since 1955. The social costs of the industrial reconversion are being borne by workers and *campesinos*, who now live in the most wretched conditions. So far this has provoked no political rebellion in Mexico, but the PRI is not finding it as easy to govern as it did during the years of prosperity. In 1985 and 1986 the PRI was only able to win the various elections for governorships by means of electoral fraud. Time was running out for the PRI. Yet time is just what a policy of industrial reconversion requires, and the PRI has gained this time through the most recent rescheduling agreement. It will not be Miguel de la Madrid, but his successor (personally selected and designated as such by him), who will have to put the new policies into effect by 1994. The social costs of the reconversion will be borne for better or for worse. On this point the PRI will not brook any argument.

Thus there will inevitably be a new, violent outbreak in Mexico. Different policies are only possible with a different government, yet no government has so far lost an election in Mexico since 1810 (the year in which Mexico gained independence). Elections change nothing. The Mexicans know that.

Recommended Reading

Huerta, A. (1985) *Economia Mexicana. Mas alla del Milagro*, Mexico.

Rojas, R. (1984) 'We pay mañana: Die Verschulding Mexikos und die heutige Krise', in *Peripherie* 15/16.

Tello, C. (1984) *La Nacionalizacion de la Banca en Mexico*, Mexico.

17. The Philippines: The IMF's Intractable Regular

Niña Boschmann

'Head of central bank deceives IMF over foreign-currency reserves: US$600 million less in the coffers than believed.' This is the sort of news which since 1983 has made the public, already sensitive to the diverse and spectacular inability of other states to pay their debts, aware of the Filipino debt crisis. Closer examination reveals, however, that the problem is by no means a recent one. The Philippines has had balance of payments deficits for decades; this Southeast Asian country received its first stand-by credit from the IMF as early as 1962. In 1969 the first debt restructuring took place in Manila, and so far the country has had to conclude no less than 19 stand-by agreements with the IMF in order to restore equilibrium to its balance of payments.

Despite these loans which, like others elsewhere, were subject to rigid conditions, and despite the unparalleled involvement of the World Bank (the Philippines has now become its eighth biggest customer), the country was unable either to stabilize its economy in the way that the Neo-Liberal IMF had suggested or to control Marcos' system of favouritism. After 20 years of dictatorship and a quarter century of IMF policies the Philippines is now Asia's most heavily indebted nation after South Korea and has debts totalling US$28 billion.

The Aquino Administration, which has been in office since February 1986, has failed to draw radical conclusions from this. It behaves well towards the country's creditors and hopes in exchange to be able to restructure its debts on easy terms and to secure enough new loans from the commercial banks and public development aid to enable it to consolidate its own power base.

So far it has had considerable success: in the autumn of 1986 the IMF abandoned demands for drastic economy measures for the first time ever. The terms which were negotiated with the commercial creditor banks in March 1987 are the most favourable granted to any country other than Argentina and Mexico since the beginning of the 1980s.

More American than the USA

IMF intervention in the Philippines began as early as 1949, when the country went through its first serious balance of payments crisis, three years after it was formally granted independence. In contrast to other Asiatic countries, the Philippines had no industry to speak of before World War II. Unlike Japanese imperialists, the American colonial power regarded the islands primarily as an outlet for the USA's finished goods and as a supplier of sisal, sugar and mineral substances. To all intents and purposes US goods could be imported into the country duty-free and in unlimited quantities. In 1946 the US resident commissioner to the Philippines claimed before the US Congress that the Philippines were 'more dependent on the USA than any actual federal state'. In order to maintain this state of affairs, the country was forced to commit itself the very same year under the Bell Trade Act not to impose duties on US imports after independence, not to introduce foreign-exchange controls and to grant American entrepreneurs the same rights as local ones at least until 1954.

The consequences of this regulation were that between 1946 and 1949 Manila had an average annual deficit in its trade with the USA of US$273 million. Even the IMF acknowledged that it was scarcely possible for the Philippines to establish any industry of her own under such circumstances. Since the majority of the funds available during the post-war period were used to finance the recovery in Europe, the IMF (contrary to its later credo) advised temporary import and foreign-exchange controls.

The 1950s: Filipino first — the heyday of import substitution

After 1950 the Filipino Government acted promptly to introduce the measures recommended (Filipino First Policy), but under pressure from the Americans these were restricted in one crucial area: foreign-exchange controls were not to be allowed to imperil the repatriation of American profits.

So although in the 1950s a large amount of light and lightish industry was established in the Philippines, the proportion of the country's GNP accounted for by processing industries rose from 8% in 1950 to almost 18% in 1960, and there was a reduction in the amount of consumer goods imported. Because imports of primary products were increasing at the same time and profits were being transferred back out of the country, neither the chronic trade balance nor the balance of payments deficit was reduced. Often the foreign-exchange controls hit Filipino industrialists harder than they did US investors. On the other hand, branches of American firms profited just as much as Filipino entrepreneurs from the import controls on competing manufactured goods. Most of the goods produced were of American design put together on an assembly line. Hardly any industries at previous or subsequent stages in the production chain were developed.

In 1958 the first open conflict took place between a Filipino Government and the IMF when the then governor of the central bank applied to Washington for new loans to cover the country's balance of payments deficit. The IMF, which nine years before had voted for the introduction of foreign-exchange and import controls, now demanded, in view of the strengthened position of American investors in the Philippines, that they be abolished again.

The 1960s: import liberalization causes record deficits

The governor of the central bank refused to implement the measures demanded by the IMF. He submitted a graduated plan of his own — and lost against his own government. In 1961, Diosdado Macapagal won the presidential election with a decidedly pro-American campaign and implemented the Decontrol Policy on the grounds that the US Government and the IMF had pledged US$300 million to support the measures. In 1962 the Philippines concluded its first stand-by agreement with the IMF for US$40 million in SDRs, devalued the peso by 100%, abolished major duties and curbed the availability of internal credit. The consequences were drastic: within the space of two years, 1,500 Filipino entrepreneurs had gone bankrupt. Overseas investors, on the other hand, were to be granted particularly favourable conditions.

After 1965 the newly-elected President Marcos kept to the same path. In 1967 the Investment Incentives Act was passed, and in 1969 the first export production zones were founded in the province of Bataan.

Yet the external stimulus was still lacking. Whereas before the implementation of the Decontrol Policy the Philippines' external debt had stood at US$275 million, by 1969 it had climbed to just under US$2 billion. After the extremely expensive and violent presidential election of 1969, which ushered in Marcos' second term of office, another acute balance of payments crisis broke out. At the same time the first US$250 million-worth of restructured debts became due. In order to obtain the new loans which she so urgently required, the Philippines was forced to free up the exchange rate of the Filipino peso, and in 1970 this led to another devaluation. In the same year the rate of inflation rose to 14%, its highest for twelve years.

At the same time as the economic situation was deteriorating, the political system, a two-party élite democracy, was also plunged into crisis. The old-established clans fought each other with ever more violent methods; the number of strikes increased; a radical and nationalist student movement gained in strength; and bombing raids shook the capital city.

The 1970s: cronyism under martial law

As a result of the favourable trend in world-market prices for the Philippines' major exports, her macroeconomic situation improved again in the early 1970s. In 1973 the country even realized a balance of trade surplus.

After the declaration of martial law in September 1972 the political situation also seemed to stabilize, at least as far as the creditors could tell. Politicans no longer slaughtered each other, but disappeared for the most part into prison or went into exile; a new constitution safeguarded the economic power of the USA and the increasingly strong student and trade-union movement was crushed. With his mixture of repressive law and order policies and limited programmes of reform (the Policy for a New Society) Marcos even temporarily managed to secure the support of the urban middle classes.

Fresh money flowed in torrents: whereas in the 1960s the Filipinos received an average of US$30 million in new loans each year, in 1971/2 they received US$90 million. In the period between 1977 and 1981 the value of new loans actually rose by an average of US$420 million per annum.

The World Bank in particular became much more involved. In the hope of being able to carry out a process of technocratic export-oriented modernization like those carried out in the four Southeast Asian NICs (South Korea, Hong Kong, Singapore and Taiwan) with Marcos, the Bank made available more than US$2.6 billion for 61 projects between 1973 and 1981. The Philippines climbed from 30th to 8th place in the league table of the Bank's 113 borrowers; in exchange, the government gradually incorporated into its development plans the World Bank's four basic principles: increases in the productivity of small farmers as a hedge against revolutionary movements; attractive terms for overseas investment in the processing industries; further liberalization of foreign trade; and targeted investment in energy and infrastructure projects.

Several costly large-scale projects, including fill dam systems, a nuclear power station and an elevated railway for Manila, were begun. The only independent initiatives taken during these years were the 11 Major Industrial Projects. These large-scale and ambitious schemes worth US$6 billion, including a steel plant, a petrochemical complex and a copper smelting plant, were intended both to help to portray Marcos as a nationalist on the home front and to create the basis for a new heavy industry.

Two months after the declaration of martial law Marcos issued a decree which created the investment incentives required for the export production zone (EPZ) established two years before. In addition to various tax privileges or forms of tax relief and preferential foreign-currency allocations, these incentives included a ban on strikes in certain industries which were classified as essential and a particularly low minimum wage. Another 12 EPZs were to be set up by the beginning of the 1980s.

Marcos backed up this reorientation of the economy in favour of labour-intensive export production by devaluing the peso and stifling domestic demand simultaneously, by oppressing the trades unions and by raising the price of both oil products and consumer credit. The proceeds from the export of textiles and semi-conductor products, and from other non-traditional exports, actually rose 26-fold from US$95 million in 1970 to US$2.4 billion in 1982 (or to over 50% of the country's total export proceeds).

Yet still the boom lasted only a short time. By the middle of the 1970s the Philippines were once again recording balance of trade and balance of payments deficits, and in 1975 the country was forced to apply for an IMF stand-by credit through the Extended Fund Facility (EFF). Not until years later did it become known that in the then top-secret Letter of Intent Marcos had committed himself to continue to pursue the current course, to increase taxation and to work towards increases in the volume of mineral substances and processed agricultural produce exported.

For all that, the deficits did not diminish. On the contrary, the demand for credit assumed ever greater dimensions. Almost annually the country had to negotiate with the IMF for new stand-by credits. However, increases in the price of oil, which represented a heavy burden on other states, barely made any difference to the level of the Philippines' indebtedness, since in the 1970s these could be offset almost completely against the increased income from tourism and remittances from the umpteen thousands of Filipinos who had migrated to the Gulf States. More significant, or so the World Bank maintained at the end of the 1970s, was the fact that a much higher proportion of the new industries' output had been imported than had been assumed (often only 15–20% was added to the value of goods during processing in the EPZs); and what had developed under Marcos was not an even halfway efficient dictatorship bent on development, but one of the most corrupt kleptocracies in the Third World.

The World Bank's 1979 *Poverty Report* recorded an increase in income concentration and a massive process of impoverishment among the broad mass of the population. In 1980 the real wages of urban workers were 36–47% lower than in 1970. On the other hand, during effectively the same period (1970–82) the value of imported luxury goods rose from US$22 million to over US$1 billion per annum.

Imelda Marcos' notorious addiction to luxury was just the tip of the iceberg. External loans, the raising of which was no longer subject to parliamentary control, were increasingly seen as just another source of finance for the government, the state-owned sector and privileged individuals. According to a confidential report by the World Bank, over US$3 billion of funds which had entered the country in the form of loans had been sent abroad illegally between 1970 and 1983. According to more recent estimates, this figure had actually risen to US$5–10 billion by the time the dictatorship was toppled in 1986. Those who benefited from this dictatorship bent on enrichment were a relatively small number of entrepreneurs, the Cronies, most of whom had not been particularly successful from a business point of view before martial law, but who took control of whole branches of industry during the 1970s under the privileges granted to them by Marcos.

As part of this process, the structure of the debt also changed. Whereas before martial law three-quarters of the loans from official sources (governments, the World Bank, the IMF) were granted to the government on soft terms for concrete investment schemes, in 1981 only a third of all current loans was tied to projects. The proportion of capital provided by private lenders increased, interest rates rose and the loans were spread over shorter periods. In 1980 the Philippines had external debts of US$12 billion, six times more than before martial law.

1981–86: the dictatorship during the crisis

Between 1981 and 1983 increasing protectionism in world trade, reductions in the price of the Philippines' agricultural exports, especially sugar, and an increase in the level of interest rates began eventually to make the house of cards more and more shaky. The interest rates charged on the country's loans soared to more than 20%, the GNP came to a standstill, capital flight increased. The assassination in August 1983 of opposition politician Benigno Aquino as he returned from exile finally buried what was left of the domestic and overseas investors' confidence in the government.

The Philippines' seventeenth IMF stand-by credit, which was granted in the spring of 1983 and was worth a record US$503 million, was tied to a rigid savings programme which required the abandonment of the 11 Major Industrial Projects, reductions in the number of people employed by and wage cuts in the state sector, an increase in the taxes on tobacco and petrol, further import liberalization and tariff reductions, the freeing up of the exchange rate and a drastic restriction of new debts and the budget deficit. The World Bank in particular pressed increasingly vehemently for the Cronies to be deprived of their monopolies and tax privileges.

In order to give the dictatorship time to put the measures into effect, the creditor banks granted the Philippines a provisional three-month-long moratorium on interest and loan capital (re)payments in the autumn of 1983. Yet Marcos did not prove particularly co-operative. In December 1983 it was revealed that the governor of the central bank had deceived the IMF as to the value of the Philippines' foreign-currency reserves.

Not until the summer of 1984, when the parliamentary elections were over and it became impossible for the Philippines to avoid coming to a basic understanding with the IMF since this was set as a precondition for the restructuring of the country's debt (which had by then risen to more than US$25 billion) did the dictatorship yield. The banks extended the moratorium.

Within a few months the exchange rate fell, new taxes and duties were introduced and the (11) Major Industrial Projects sacrificed. In the autumn of 1984, on the strength of all this, the IMF made available a further loan of US$650 million which was to be paid over in stages once the success of these measures had been verified.

But the downward advance could be halted no longer. In 1984 the GNP fell by 6%, inflation reached a record high at 60%, 1,500 firms declared themselves bankrupt and 90,000 workers were dismissed. In view of the constant influence of the Cronies and the growing strength of both the guerillas and the urban opposition, overseas investors left the country in droves. Twenty firms left the export production zone alone, and the number of people employed there fell from 26,000 to 16,000.

In consideration of this situation, the IMF decided for the first time ever no longer to content itself with short-term measures of stabilization. Both the Fund and the World Bank were of the opinion that the third tranche of the 1984 loan (US$106 million) and the second tranche of a loan of US$925 million negotiated with the banks should not be paid over until the sugar and coconut monopolies, the major sources of income of Marcos' two most powerful Cronies, had been abolished. In fact, in the autumn of 1985, under pressure from the technocrats in the Cabinet, Marcos finally declared his willingness to do this. Moreover, the dictator's image was to be cleaned up by means of a presidential election scheduled for February 1986. Before then, however, political events assumed an unstoppable dynamism of their own. On 25 February 1986, two weeks after the country had gone to the polls, which had been rigged by means of unprecedented bribery and other fraudulent practices, Marcos was toppled by a combination of popular insurrection and military revolt.

Figure 17.1
The Philippines: external debt and rates of growth in GNP 1980–86

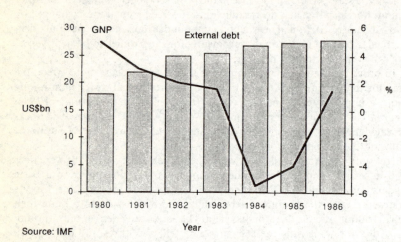

Source: IMF

Liberalization and restructuring — a way out of the crisis?

When the bourgeois–liberal coalition led by Corazon Aquino, the widow of the assassinated Benigno Aquino, took office it found yawningly empty coffers and consequently reacted with coolness to the creditors' demands. A week after his appointment Finance Minister Jaime Ongpin explained:

> At the moment our first priority is to feed the population. That concerns me considerably more than the question of how we pay our debts. We did not create them, and the creditors are at least as responsible for them as we are.

The idea of a 'selective debt repudiation' was put forward primarily by the minister for planning, Solita Monsod, and backed by some of the president's left-liberal advisors. These maintained that loans which had been granted as a result of corruption should not be repaid. The most obvious example related to the nuclear power station built by the US firm, Westinghouse, near the export production zone in Bataan. In order to pay for this outmoded model, which for good measure had been erected in a region threatened by earthquakes, the Filipinos had raised a loan of US$2.1 billion, even though there was no question of the station being put into service, for reasons of safety alone.

Westinghouse had only been commissioned for the project, which had been the subject of controversy even under Marcos, after paying a bribe of US$80 million.

Under pressure from the conservative faction in the government and in view of the increasing urgency of both restructuring a good deal of the country's overseas liabilities (now amounting to US$28 billion) and obtaining the capital requirements for projects of her own, Corazon Aquino decided eventually in favour of good conduct. In July 1986 she declared: 'All debts will be honoured.' At the same time the government voluntarily met a number of demands made previously by the IMF and the World Bank: the Cronies' monopolies were broken up and any property which they had acquired illegally was confiscated; a government commission attempted to get its hands on some of the dollars which Marcos and his associates had managed to get out of the country; more than 1,200 commodities were reincorporated into the import-liberalization programme begun in 1981 under the supervision of the IMF; and new incentives were created for overseas investors under the Omnibus Investment Code.

In the autumn of 1986 the government inaugurated a sweeping programme of privatization and a debt-equity-swap as possible market-economy-based methods for reducing the burden of debt and attracting overseas capital. Just as Aquino embarked upon her first visit to the USA, 77 state-owned businesses, including the National Oil Company, a steel plant, a hotel and the national airline, were offered for sale internationally.

In return for this kindness, however, the Aquino Administration expected to be treated equally obligingly during restructuring negotiations. The IMF's usual austerity policies would be totally incompatible with political and economic stabilization. In the first nine months of 1986 the country paid just US$3 billion (around 80% of its export revenues) in interest. In the coming years, however, the Philippines would be required to pay at least US$7 billion in order to finance the programmes which were being planned, in particular for the resumption and extension of Marcos' agrarian reform (with compensation, of course) and for a job-creation programme drawn up by the end of 1987 for the improvement of the agricultural infrastructure. The extra income which it was thought this would generate should then stimulate the economy from the demand side during the all-important election year (and contribute to the victory of the forces of moderation in parliament and in the town halls). In view of the Philippines' strategic importance in the Pacific and the policies being pursued there, interest rates would have to be set on the basis of the terms granted in the first instance to Mexico. The strategy proved effective. In October 1986 the IMF approved the country's nineteenth and latest stand-by credit of a full US$500 million (including the last tranche of the previous one, which had been frozen under Marcos), without insisting on its usual recessive and drastic cure, and at the end of March 1987, after a few diplomatic tugs-of-war, the 483 commercial creditor banks also yielded. The US$13.2 billion in commercial loans (almost half of the total debt) due to be repaid between 1987 and 1992 was rescheduled. Repayment will now be spread over 17 years with a

Figure 17.2
The effects of IMF strategy on the Philippines

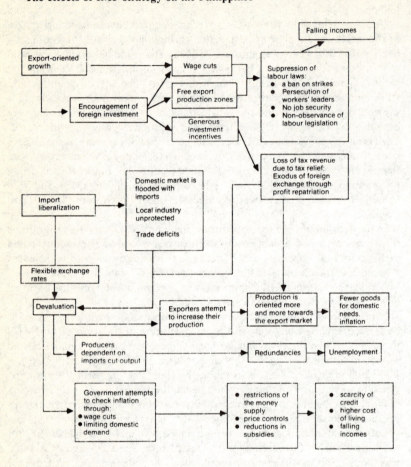

Source: M. T. Diokno: 'The IMF and How it Affects the Filipino People', *Third World Studies Papers* 36.

seven-year period of grace. The interest rate was fixed at 0.875% over and above the LIBOR rate, whereas until then the rates charged had been 1.6–1.7% above LIBOR. At the time 1 per cent less above LIBOR meant a saving of US$80 million per annum. The new rate is the lowest which has been granted to any debtor nation since Mexico and Argentina.

Even after this triumph the final days of the debt trap are still a long way off. The Philippines is still having to use 25–30% of her export proceeds to service her debts, debts which basically financed the luxurious lifestyle of a dictatorship bent on enrichment. From a political point of view, too, there is an element of selfishness on the part of the creditors and the USA in this method of settling debts. In the coming year a fresh round of negotiations will be conducted on the subject of the American military bases on the archipelago and there is no cheap alternative for the USA. If the money continues to flow the likelihood increases of the administration in Manila proceeding according to the motto: you don't bite the hand that feeds you.

Appendix: the effects of the IMF's policies

Taking the Philippines' seventeenth IMF stand-by loan as an example, the Filipino university lecturer Maria T. Diokno has gone into the effects (on her country) of the policies decreed by the IMF (see Figure 17.2). The Fund's standard requirements for reducing balance of payments deficits are: the liberalization of foreign trade (for which read abolition of import barriers of all kinds); an increase in exports; and the freeing up of exchange rates.

Attempts are made to increase exports by making the products concerned cheaper. In countries like the Philippines this is generally achieved by means of a concerted low-wage policy which incorporates a ban on strikes, repressive labour laws and the persecution of trades unions. The result is that the real wages of employees fall.

What is more, the country has to be attractive to overseas investors, for it is these who have access to the necessary technology and know-how. Overseas investors receive generous incentives and are given preference over local producers. Consequently, the government loses tax revenue (since taxes are not levied out of consideration) and foreign currency (since profits are repatriated).

As a rule, the freeing up of exchange rates leads to depreciation, which makes exports cheaper but also makes imports more expensive. The latter has recessive and inflationary effects. Industries which are dependent on imports have to reduce their output, and this then leads to redundancies. Where this is not the case, the higher costs burden prices. In order to get a grip on inflation, the government attempts to prevent further wage increases and to curb domestic demand. Price controls and subsidies are abolished, and the money supply dries up. This leads once again to price rises, reductions in real income and a short supply of credit. The recessive tendencies are strengthened by the flooding of the domestic market with imported consumer goods which compete with those produced locally.

Other possibilities, such as concerted bans on imports and foreign-exchange controls, are rejected by the IMF as being 'not in line with real market conditions'.

Recommended Reading

Diokno, Maria Theresa (1983) *The IMF and How it Affects the Filipino People*, Third World Studies Papers 36, University of the Philippines, September.

Snow, Robert (1983) *The Bourgeois Opposition to Export-oriented Industrialization in the Philippines*, Third World Studies Papers 39, University of the Philippines, October.

Magno, Alexander (ed.) (1984) *Nation in Crisis — A University Inquires into the Present*, Quezon City.

Far Eastern Economic Review (various editions).

18. Poland: Out of the Crisis with Violence and Reform

Friedhelm Wachs

The failure of Gierekian Keynesianism

Poland is one of a group of internationally indebted countries in which the debt crisis has had not only economic but also far-reaching political consequences. The imposition of martial law in December 1981 was closely linked with the failure of attempts to modernize the Polish economy. Party chief Gierek had initiated these attempts in 1971 as a response to the violent clashes which took place in December 1970. In 1979, in the course of this process of modernization which was intended to help Poland catch up with the industrialized world, the country experienced a serious economic crisis (and a drastic reduction in its national product) which was to drag on for several years and reached its lowest point in mid-1982: Poland's economy had fallen back to its 1974 level.

The Gierek Administration proved incapable of reacting economically and politically to this crisis. The strike movement which had emerged in 1979, originally as a protest against massive price rises, quickly formed itself into the trade union *Solidarnosc* and led a protracted struggle for power with the government and the Party, which was pushed into a corner in a previously unimaginable manner. Unlike in the previous crises (1956, 1968, 1970 and 1976), the political leadership was no longer able to appease the population with economic concessions and shake-ups within the existing power structure. Consequently, on 13 December 1981 the military under General Jaruzelski took over the political and economic leadership of Poland, replacing the government with a military council known as the *Wojskowa Rada Ocalenia Narodowego* (WRON). Up until this point in time the Polish post-war economy had been shaped by two different economic strategies, both of which had failed, and a string of unsuccessful reform programmes.

From the end of the war until the mid-1960s, Poland's dominant economic strategy was the Stalinist development strategy. Its objective was to develop the country from an agrarian into a modern industrialized nation in the shortest possible time. To this end the government encouraged heavy industry in particular. The entire economy was organized by means of strongly centralized and *dirigiste* planning methods.

The strategy failed for three basic reasons:

- It encouraged wasteful and extensive growth and over-investment. A great deal of capital expenditure was undertaken, but few of the projects were completed on time because of shortages of materials. Moreover, the new capacity created in this way was often underutilized.
- The government encountered resistance, sometimes active resistance, from the population, partly because consumer goods remained in short supply and of a poor quality and also because of the regularity with which it planned and put into effect drastic price rises for these goods.
- The unrealistic approach of the inflexible bureaucracies charged with planning and steering the strategy also served to obstruct it; they had no conception of the problems facing the industries and their only response to shortages was to procrastinate, often for months. After the bloody unrest which followed the price rises in December 1970 and the spring of 1971, Poland's planners developed a Five Year Plan for 1971–5 whose basic objectives were to improve the standard of living of the population and to make the Polish economy more competitive on the world market.

At first this Gierekian Keynesianism produced an investment boom in the consumer-goods industry. Gierek, who led the Polish United Workers' Party (PZPR) as its first secretary from 1971 until 1980, wanted to increase demand inside the country with the help of loans (from the West) and to stimulate productivity by increasing wages.

Figure 18.1
Poland's economic indicators
(1978=100)

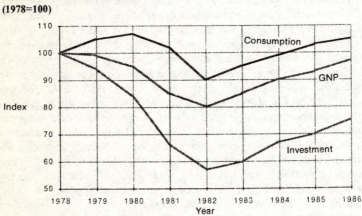

Source: HWWA

The government discovered that consumption and foreign trade were both factors which affected growth (see Figure 18.1). Western governments and commercial banks overwhelmed Poland with capital, for two reasons: they believed that centrally planned economies were better able to cope with any financial difficulties which might arise than systems geared towards the free market, and they banked on Poland being able to increase exports of her rich deposits of coal, copper and sulphur; on the basis of the 'umbrella theory' they assumed, although nothing had been said to this effect, that the Soviet Union would vouch for Poland's debts. At the beginning of the 1980s both assumptions proved to have been erroneous. Productivity in Poland's raw-materials and energy-producing industries and in her various processing industries could be increased only for the short term, and the Soviet Union was neither willing nor able to take responsibility for the country's debts.

As a result, Poland's debts increased 20-fold between 1971 and 1980, from US$1.2 billion to US$24.7 billion. Gierek's strategy for transforming the Polish economy from a closed into an open economy firmly integrated into the international division of labour through investment policies financed by external loans failed. Anticipated successes did not materialize: although capital expenditure, wages and prices rose, capacity utilization remained at a much lower level than had been expected. The original objectives of the strategy had not been met: it had proved impossible to recover the cost of imported machinery and technologies, of expensive licence fees and related loan repayments, from a corresponding increase in exports. This would have required a more efficient economic control mechanism than the one which existed. At the same time, over-investment in certain sectors was fast becoming the major characteristic of the Polish economy, and the government's investment strategy actually augmented the resulting imbalance in the domestic economy. In order to forestall social and political unrest, the government repeatedly granted wage increases and introduced subsidies on foodstuffs, financing these increasingly with Western loans. The upshot was inflation at a rate previously unknown in the socialist countries: 103% in 1981. Poland's trade balance with the West accumulated between 1971 and 1975 to reach US$6.79 billion and between 1976 and 1979 to reach US$9.05 billion. The country's external debt increased rapidly.

Militarization

When the military took control on 13 December 1981 it was less the political than the economic leadership of the country which it assumed. The first act of the military council WRON was to install military representatives responsible to the appropriate ministries in almost every concern. The ministries in turn were controlled by the military. At the same time WRON suspended the trade union *Solidarnosc* before banning it once and for all in October 1982, and forbade all strikes. All men between the ages of 18 and 45 were drafted into work. Through these measures WRON not only disarmed its most powerful adversary on the domestic political and economic-policy fronts, *Solidarnosc*, but also won the trust of Western banks and governments. Its economic rehabilitation programme could thus be introduced unhampered and overseas capital kept in Poland. Despite all this, the USA responded to the imposition of martial law by implementing a politically motivated trade boycott which crippled those branches of the economy which were dependent on imports. Other Western governments also tried to exert pressure on Poland, either directly or through the banks. The effects are difficult to assess. According to Polish figures, the total damage inflicted ran to US$15 billion.

In order to obtain new loans, however, Poland was expected to provide security which she could not produce and which the banks hoped would be forthcoming if Poland joined the IMF. During its term of office the Polish military did everything in its power to make it possible for the country to join: it increased prices for foodstuffs and services and cut investment; export-orientation of the economy formed the basis of its policies.

Poland and the IMF

Poland had been a founding member of the IMF in 1944 at Bretton Woods, but had withdrawn at the beginning of the 1950s partly because she regarded the USA as having too much influence on IMF policy and partly because she did not agree with the general policies of the Fund. In November 1981, Poland reapplied for membership. The Polish leadership hoped that this would improve the country's credit worthiness, especially with the Western banks. When martial law was imposed, the application process was suspended.

Not until 30 May 1986 was Poland permitted to rejoin the IMF. The quota approved for the country was roughly the same as it had been when the Fund was founded. Poland paid the Fund US$770 million, of which 22% was in convertible currency, and received in exchange US$680 million in SDRs. Henceforth Poland would be able to obtain from the IMF loans totalling a maximum of 450% of her own SDRs (or up to US$4 billion).

Poland could not, however, obtain loans from the IMF and the World Bank, which she also joined, until 1988. World Bank loans are intended to be used for material- and energy-saving programmes, for the processing of agricultural produce and for projects which boost exports. Given Poland's export structure at the time, this meant increased dependence on the West. Poland was to be required to yield her autonomy, particularly in the foodstuffs sector, in favour of an export-oriented economy.

The scale of indebtedness

Whereas in 1971, Poland had debts of US$1.2 billion, by 1976 this figure had increased ten-fold to US$12.1 billion. By 1980 Poland's mountain of debt had doubled again to a total of US$24.7 billion. During this period the loans were restructured several times.

The loans had been raised in convertible and non-convertible currencies. At the end of 1986, Poland was indebted to the USSR to the tune of 6.5 billion roubles and also owed US$33.5 billion in convertible currencies. Of this, 90% was owed to Western banks and the Paris Club. Taken together, the amount owed to the two COMECON banks, the International Investment Bank, the Bank for Economic Co-operation and the Soviet Union amounted to US$2.5 billion, and that owed to the Arab states to US$700 million. In addition, Poland had short-term business loans repayable over less than two years. There is no overview available of the exact creditor structure of these debts.

More than 500 commercial banks have participated in granting loans to Poland. Only around 40% of the loans are payable in US dollars, another 20% each in deutschmarks and Swiss francs, the rest in some 14 other currencies. Fluctuations in the dollar rate make an exact overview of Poland's liabilities impossible. For example, in 1986 the debt rose by US$4.2 billion, of which only US$900 million consisted of unserviced loans and US$194 million of new medium- and long-term loans. The remaining US$3.1 billion-worth of new debt had accrued as a result of the decline in the dollar rate. The devaluation of the US dollar against the Western currencies increases the value of loans payable in these currencies.

Since in 1986, Poland received hardly any new loans from the countries in the West, 95% of her imports had to be paid for immediately in convertible currency. Only 5% could be financed with Western loans. Poland's rouble debt therefore continued to increase, even though an agreement between the USSR and Poland was intended to limit the debt to 6.5 billion roubles until 1990. For 1987 alone the two countries agreed an increase to 7.2 billion roubles. According to Polish figures, in 1986 Poland paid almost US$2 billion to her creditors; between 1982 and 1985 the figure was US$5.6 billion plus 900 million roubles.

Since restructuring agreements lead to an accumulation of payments obligations, it is expected in Poland that the debt will not peak until 1993 and will then amount to at least US$50 billion.

Attempts at attracting capital into the country through joint ventures appear to have been unsuccessful because: Polish firms and Poland's economic bureaucracy have little interest in joint ventures, since these mean that their work is then regulated and that they have to give up their powers; and those Western firms which invest in socialist countries are offered more favourable terms in the Soviet Union and Hungary.

Debt rescheduling negotiations

At the beginning of the 1980s it became obvious that Poland was on the verge of being unable to pay her debts. As a result, in 1981 Poland initiated rescheduling negotiations with Western banks and governments for the first time ever. Whereas in December 1981 the governments which belonged to the Paris Club broke off negotiations after the first agreement, negotiations with the banks continued even during martial law. Between 1981 and 1984 the banks conducted four rounds of negotiations, and these resulted in a package designed to reschedule US$7.7 billion in debts. It was agreed that Poland could postpone the repayment of 92% of her accumulated debts until 1987 if she would settle her outstanding interest of around US$800 million and declare her willingness to continue with the interest payments in the future. In 1986, in a further round of negotiations, US$800 million worth of the bank loans due in 1986 and US$1.2 billion of those due in 1987 were rescheduled. At the same time it was arranged that 80% of the debts would be repaid in 1991 and 1992 and 15% would be serviced immediately with the help of newly raised loans.

Negotiating over government loans and loans guaranteed by governments turned out to be considerably more difficult. As early as the end of December 1980, Poland began negotiating with the Paris Club for the rescheduling of debts amounting to US$10 billion. In March 1981 the Polish Government called a halt to the repayment of all debts owed to the Paris Club. On the strength of this, agreement was reached on 27 April 1981 over the rescheduling of loan capital and interest amounting to US$1.8 billion. Repayment was to begin in January 1986 and would be spread over six years.

After the imposition of martial law, the negotiations were not resumed until 1984, but after 18 months of negotiation a second agreement was signed on 15 July 1985. Under this agreement, Poland was granted a five-year grace period for the loan capital and interest amounting to US$14.7 billion which she had not paid between 1982 and 1984. Once this grace period came to an end, all debts covered by the agreement were to be repaid between 1990 and 1996. Before the agreement came into force Poland had to remit US$650 million in interest.

A third agreement was signed on 19 Nobember 1985 and covered the rescheduling of US$1.6 billion in loans and interest due in 1985. These loans were to be repaid over five years from 1991. Although a fourth agreement, which dealt with a further US$900 million worth of debts, was concluded on 7 March 1986, it was not signed by Poland.

These four agreements alone will thus deal with a total of US$16 billion in loan capital and interest (re)payments by 1996, with US$1.8 billion to be repaid between 1986 and 1989, and US$14.2 billion between 1990 and 1996. To this will be added interest of US$1.4 billion for the first period and around US$2 billion for the second, as well as further commitments accruing from other liabilities.

While the Polish Government has given absolute priority to the servicing of private bank loans, at the beginning of the second quarter of 1987 it did not meet those payment obligations to the creditor nations which arose out of the rescheduling agreements concluded between 1981 and 1985. At the same time, Polish government representatives cast a glance at the payment moratorium declared by Brazil and took the view that any easy terms which are granted to one debtor nation should also be applied to the other debtor nations, including Poland. Repayments of US$3 billion per annum after 1990 were out of the question. Further negotiations would therefore have to be conducted on the subject of more favourable interest rates and the rescheduling of long-term loans.

The effects of indebtedness

The repayment of external loans demands the acquisition of foreign exchange, and it was felt in Poland that the agricultural sector should be making a contribution to this. By exporting the produce of large industrial pork and veal farms Poland hoped to create a source of convertible currency on the world market. Western loans were used to finance increased production. However, Poland did not produce the quantities of fodder which this kind of export trade required and soon became dependent on imports of grain and fodder. This placed a burden on the trade balance and increased the country's indebtedness.

In order to restore equilibrium to the trade balance the military ordered a reduction in grain imports. This meant, however, that supplies destined for the population could no longer be guaranteed, since the farmers, who generally worked on very small-scale farms of only five hectares each and in this way worked 77% of Poland's total usable land, sold only one-fifth of their own grain production to the state, even though the purchase prices had more than doubled. They used what they kept back for private animal husbandry. The effects of the US embargo were also felt by the farmers. As poultry farming was reliant on US maize, output fell by 70% between 1981 and 1983, and since imports of animals for slaughter had been reduced by one-third, the meat rationing which had been introduced in 1981 could not be abolished in 1986.

The situation in industry was also dramatic. Some 13% of all industry was unable to work in the first half of 1982 because of shortages of materials, including raw materials. Although in 1986 industrial output once again reached the 1979 level, most of the increases were achieved in the investment-goods sector. Like the consumer-goods industry, the foodstuffs industry lagged way behind demand. In 1986 there was a shortage of fridges, deep freezers, televisions and radios, cotton clothing, shoes, and many other items. Even toothbrushes and shaving foam were often not available. The consumer-goods industry was still regarded by the government as being of tertiary importance.

The crisis in the construction industry was also catastrophic, despite there being a considerable need for living space. Whereas in 1979, 198,000 new homes were completed, by 1986 this figure had fallen to 126,000, the same level as in 1965.

Since exports of raw materials could not be increased to any great extent, the Jaruzelski Government was only able to realize a balance of trade surplus by curbing imports severely at the expense of supplies for the population and for industry. Since vital raw materials and semi-finished products could no longer be imported whole branches of industry, especially in the manufacturing sector, were temporarily shut down independently of the US trade boycott.

The policies of the military government

Repression and reforms are the traditional responses of the Polish political system to social dissatisfaction, and the Jaruzelski Government resorted to these also when the going got tough. Whereas at first it disciplined the Church and *Solidarnosc*, and later obstructed independent movements associated to some extent with the Church, in 1982 the military government embarked upon a programme of economic reform, the Three Ss: self-dependence, self-financing and self-administration. This reform was designed to awaken in the population a sense of responsibility for Poland's desperate economic situation and was to be put into practice in two stages. Self-dependence (*samodzielność*) was to be effected through fewer indexes, fewer handicaps and fewer binding sections being incorporated into the Plan, and thus through fewer binding development guidelines, de-bureaucratization and the dismantling of the middle-management level (the consortia). Self-financing (*samofinanzowanie*) meant that firms were to manage their own expenditure and essentially bear the risk of bankruptcy, finance a proportion of their investment from their own resources and be allowed to own foreign exchange.

These two Ss represented the first stage. Today even experts cannot say whether and to what extent they were actually put into effect because virtually every provision was modified, replaced by others or counteracted: fearing that the firms' freedom in the field of pricing and employment policy could fuel inflation, the government introduced regulations which effectively enabled the state to set prices after all. Self-financing was strictly regulated and burdened with taxes, which were constantly being replaced and which were levied on the basis of purely fiscal, non-economic considerations. Sometimes it was better to make a loss than to realize a profit, and this thwarted all attempts at attracting investment. The holding of foreign exchange was limited or forbidden many times, and the right to decide how profits should be employed, so vital to investment and financial independence, was also regulated by the state.

By the beginning of 1987 it was already doubtful whether the second stage would ever be put into effect and thus whether self-administration (*samorzad*) would ever become a reality. In 1982 a Council of All Employees and a General Congress of Workers had been established by law and workers given a say in production plans, investment, the way in which profits were used, mergers and so on. The employers were supposed to identify more strongly with state-ownership and therefore improve their productivity. Self-administration was intended to serve primarily as a psychological and ethical lever. Whether it will have any great measure of success has yet to be seen.

Price reforms

Time and time again massive price reforms of sometimes several hundred per cent were instituted by Poland's planners. Since the population reacted violently, often with strikes, to these kinds of increases, they were generally only put into practice in a directly or indirectly reduced form. Where this was not the case, the government tended to fall. So far both Gomulka and Gierek have failed because of their attempts at price reform.

Prices were raised in order to reduce the value of state subsidies and in an attempt to draw the income of the entire population into the economic process. Although by the end of 1986 the government had succeeded in reducing the proportion of the national budget which was spent on subsidies to 30% (from 50.5% in 1982), it did not succeed in absorbing purchasing-power through higher prices. The reason for this is simple: the total value of goods available accounted for only 86% of the funds which the population actually had at its disposal. In addition, supplies of some major consumer goods were short, with the result that the Poles spent only 76% of their disposable incomes. The rest of the money will not flow into the economic process unless there is an improvement in the supply of consumer goods.

On the other hand, the negative effects of price rises had to be counteracted through the paying of subsidies to the younger sections of the population and to large families which had extremely small disposable incomes. Whilst reductions in subsidies were being achieved primarily through cuts in the grants given to firms, in 1986 price subsidies for essential consumer goods increased by 46% over the previous year. In addition, deficiency payments of between 1,200 and 2,100 zloty per month were made to groups earning less than 13,000 zloty in order to compensate them for the price increases. In April 1987 a further price rise came into force which was intended to increase the price of foodstuffs by an average of 14% and coal by 100%. After huge protests, in which even the new state-organized trade union, the OPZZ, took part by threatening strikes, prices rose by (only) 50% for coal, 23% for electricity, 25% for petrol and gas and 9.6% for foodstuffs. At the same time additional deficiency payments and wage increases were announced. Even this price reform does not appear to have had the desired effect, since consumer goods continue to be in short supply.

Although the Jaruzelski Government repeatedly blamed external influences for its financial difficulties, the key to the Polish economy's recovery appears to lie in Poland itself. If the mechanisms for controlling the economy and individual firms are not made more effective then Poland will not be able to export even enough to enable her to repay her debts. Continuous reform has so far not noticeably taken Poland a single step forward. The restoration of equilibrium to the trade balance or the realization of a balance of trade surplus at the expense of productivity can no longer be regarded as a sign that the Polish economy is recovering. It should also not be assumed that Poland will be able to obtain any significant follow-up financing for expiring loans, or even for new projects, over and above her entitlement under IMF quotas, since an accumulation of her liabilities at the beginning of the 1990s would considerably intensify the financial crisis. Poland will basically have to continue selling semi-finished goods and so become more and more engulfed in the economic crisis. There is as yet no end in sight to the Polish dilemma.

Recommended Reading

von der Lippe, Peter (1985) 'Die Wirtschaftspolitik der Regierung Jaruzelski 1982–1984', in Dieter Bingen (ed.), *Polen 1980–1984. Dauerkrise oder Stabilisierung?*, Baden-Baden.

19. Portugal: Indebtedness on the European Periphery

Claudia Preußer

From colonial power to the poorhouse of Europe

Portugal was and is an underdeveloped capitalist country on the European periphery, in part because of her internal economic structure and also by dint of her very individual form of world-market integration, for although Portugal was herself a colonial power for 500 years and a leading international power in the sixteenth century, she took up typical colonial trading relations with England, that is she exchanged colonial raw materials and agricultural produce for England's industrially finished goods. Not until the middle of the nineteenth century did she initiate a hesitant programme of industrial development on the basis of investment from abroad, above all with capital imported from England. Railways, transport routes and channels of communication were established along the coast, as were small businesses in the textile and preserved food industries; tobacco processing, cement factories and chemical plants sprang up around the ports. Nevertheless, in terms of capital intensity, the concentration of capital, the extent to which the production process was mechanized and the number of workers employed, the level of industrialization was extremely low. By the end of the nineteenth century over 60% of the active population were still small farmers. No more than 20% were waged agricultural or industrial workers.

The agricultural sector had come to a standstill, since the big landowners, who had become intermingled with the commercial and financial bourgeoisie, had no interest in developing agricultural production. This lack of interest resulted in agricultural labourers emigrating, imports of foodstuffs, rising prices and hunger. Portugal's colonial trade permitted the formation of a small, affluent financial and commercial bourgeoisie, but not of a domestic industrial bourgeoisie or of a significant proletariat. The constitutional monarchy had suffered a huge loss of prestige, certainly by 1890, because of its inability to enforce its rights in southern Africa, but even in the country's first republic, which was established not long after (1910–26), Portugal's economic and social structures remained largely intact.

Salazar's *Estado Novo*

The parties which dominated the first republic were unable to create a stable political climate. The military *coup* of 1926 reflected the heartfelt convictions of the various bourgeois factions and brought the republic to a radical end. Yet even the military did not succeed in getting a hold on the country's disastrous economic situation. Accordingly, after 1928 the military began to reintroduce civilian ministers into the government, among them António Oliveira de Salazar as minister for finance. Although his measures for restoring financial soundness to the state finances were successful, they were implemented completely at the expense of the workers and the agricultural labourers. During this transitionary phase following the first republic no bourgeois group was capable of assuming power. Only Salazar's corporative *Estado Novo* (New State) was able to mediate between them by preventing competition, protecting small and medium scale industry, allying itself with the agrarian oligarchy and not permitting investment from abroad. All of this led to further stagnation in the agricultural sector and seriously checked industrialization. Political parties and trades unions were disbanded and banned, and their place was taken by the corporative state with its controlled bodies. Censorship, political surveillance and brutal repression moulded the lives of the population.

The effects of the world economic crisis of 1929/30 were not felt in Portugal until some time later, as is classically the way in underdeveloped countries. Government projects for the improvement of the infrastructure in the 1940s were intended to concentrate industrialization on the motor industry in order to reduce Portugal's dependence on the world market. In the 1950s an attempt was made to implement a policy of industrialization geared towards import substitution, yet as early as the beginning of the 1960s Portugal was forced to open up to the world market because of both the lack of success which this programme achieved and the amount of money being spent on the colonial wars in Mozambique and Angola. In particular, Portugal had to allow investment from abroad.

Expansion in the industrial sector was founded upon state-guaranteed minimum wages which were held down artificially by means of fixed agricultural prices. During this period the textile industry did indeed expand, since the use of cheaper and less qualified workers of both sexes, a lower level of mechanization and cheaper raw materials from the colonies guaranteed easy profits. Until 1945 the capital accumulated through colonial exploitation and trade was concentrated in bank consortia which were involved privately in Portugal's few large-scale industries.

In a move, albeit a hesitant one, towards concentration in the 1950s, many small and medium-sized firms disappeared. Nevertheless, in 1960 49% of the active population still worked on the land, with only 28% working in industry and 23% in the service sector. At the outbreak of the colonial wars at the beginning of the 1960s, and with almost 50% of the national budget being spent on these, the economy entered its first phase of expansion, just as the textbooks on Right–Keynesian 'war-far-spending' had promised. At this time, however, the material resources and foreign currency needed for industrialization were being creamed off for the war, with the result that productivity in the Portuguese economy fell behind. So, in 1965 the country was opened up to capital from abroad. West German capital in particular, but also American, English and French direct investment, streamed first and foremost into the sectors responsible for electronic semi-finished goods, clothing, chemicals and tourism, and joined forces with the strongest Portuguese businesses.

This change and the resulting rapid industrial growth enabled Portugal to rise in rank during the 1960s from an agrarian developing nation to an NIC. Remittances from migrant workers and colonial profits meant that the country's chronic current account deficits could be more than offset, and gold and foreign currency reserves to the value of US$2.8 billion (1973) built up; the external debt was low at US$1.3 billion (1973), and the escudo was a stable currency. Behind these favourable overall economic indicators, however, lay serious structural defects: Portuguese industry was dependent on large volumes of imported capital goods and technologies; the fact that the agricultural sector was totally neglected made the import of large quantities of foodstuffs vital; productivity in the industrial sector was very low in comparison with that in the rest of the world; industry was only able to remain competitive because wages were much lower and imported raw materials from the colonies cheaper; the education system was mediaeval; the large number of emigrations left whole tracts of land to go to ruin; and the country's industrial locations were all concentrated in the Lisbon/Setúbal region and the Oporto/Braga area on the coast.

Salazar's death in 1968 coincided with the general dissatisfaction of broad sections of the population. The expanding industrial sector called for the removal of restrictions on competition, the financial sector demanded that investment be concentrated and credit restrictions lifted, and both called for the country to be opened up to the world market. When Marcello Caetano assumed office, it was these sectors which profited, for it was these sectors which needed a certain amount of liberalization as a prerequisite for an accelerated capitalist expansion. However, Caetano's attempts at 'renewal with continuity' and the accompanying relaxation of the state's control over legal bans and censorship brought strikes and campaigning movements, above all at the level of the firm.

The Revolution of the Flowers (1974)

When, in April 1974, the *Movimento das Forcas Armadas* (MFA) toppled the authoritarian regime after 48 years of dictatorship in the Revolution of the Flowers (the Captains' Revolution), it succeeded to a difficult estate. General Spinola's book *Portugal and Her Future* had repeated the views of a section of high finance and of the senior military that the way out of the existing serious economic crisis, which had been intensified by the colonial wars and the restrictive regime, was to introduce free capitalist market mechanisms and put an end to the colonial wars in neo-colonialist fashion. At the same time, top people and officers in the Portuguese army were developing deep-seated opposition to the system. This arose out of the futility of the colonial wars, but was a result also of their bad pay. The changed social composition of the armed forces (students, people from the lower middle classes) had also played a part. It was their reading, as part of their duties, of the programmes issued by the liberation movements which had led in 1973 to the founding of the MFA. When the MFA occupied strategic positions inside the country on 25 April 1974, the corporative regime put up barely any resistance, but after 48 years of political oppression the population greeted its liberation enthusiastically. The dismantling of the old regime brought independence for the colonies, civil rights and liberties for Portugal, and the disbanding of the notorious secret police force, PIDE. Of course, this transformation did not take place without disruption. The many conflicts which ensued as the various factions struggled for political power provoked two reactionary *coup* attempts, and six provisional governments were dissolved within the space of only a few months. By August 1975 the stance most often adopted by the military executive was a socialist one.

Economic change, 1974–75

The independence of Portugal's former colonies plunged the country into an even bigger economic crisis (as gold, foreign currency, cheap raw materials and jobs disappeared), and the unstable political situation caused capital to be transferred abroad, skilled workers to migrate and factories to be closed. Despite this, the Portuguese economy developed in almost exactly the same way as those of the rest of the OECD countries, which were also suffering from the effects of a recession.

Early in 1975 the new regime began to modify the structure of ownership in Portugal, partly through nationalizations, state administration of the country's concerns, the occupation of land and expropriation of large estates, and the workers taking over responsibility for the self-administration of businesses. In response to demands made by the trades unions, the Council of the Revolution voted in April 1975 to nationalize: the banks and insurance companies; the haulage trade; the transport sector; the energy-producing sector; and the primary-products industries. By the end of 1975, 226 firms employing a total of around 157,000 workers had been nationalized. A further 380 firms were indirectly nationalized as the result of the nationalization of the banks and insurance companies. Despite these measures, the nationalized sector of the Portuguese economy was no larger than that in other Western European countries; it was roughly equivalent in size to its French counterpart.

However, the regime's social reforms — the introduction of guaranteed minimum wages; the expansion of the health service, welfare state and education system; financial support for colonials returning to their native countries — and the subsequent costs of the nationalizations placed a great strain on the national budget. The reforms, which were financed through deficits, resulted in rising rates of inflation and the rapid disappearance of the gold and foreign-currency reserves which had existed in 1973. Increases of some US$300–400 million per annum before 1973 were followed by decreases of US$600 million and US$750 million in 1974/5; and though the trend later slackened its pace, it could not be reversed until 1985.

The crisis intensified primarily as a result of external economic factors — increases in the price of oil and world-wide recession — and the politically motivated boycott imposed by American and European financial and economic circles, but also because of falling output, the exodus of capital from Portugal and polarization within society. The government, in which the various political standpoints held by members of the military were represented, was tripped up by this finally at the end of 1975. Here we must not ignore the active part played by the USA, which perceived her geopolitical interests (air-force bases in the Azores, Portugal as the western flank of NATO in Europe) to be under threat. West Germany too, particularly the SPD, the Friedrich-Ebert Foundation, and the DGB (West German TUC), dipped deeply into their money-boxes in order to support the social democratic PS against the Communist Party (PCP).

Whereas in 1974/5 the economic leanings of the officers of the MFA had tended more towards corporative industrialization policies than a socialist planned economy (in as much as they foresaw assistance for small businesses, a socially assisted home building programme and investment incentives for big business), by 1975 the PS was advocating Neo-Liberal economic policies. Even before negotiations with the IMF began in 1977 on the subject of a stand-by credit, the PS implemented tough economy measures, almost as an advance concession: despite inflation of 30% it decreed wage guideliness of 15%, and cuts in the national budget hit social expenditure more than any other area. In addition, the withdrawal or restriction of the workers' only recently won rights (protection against summary dismissal, a guaranteed wage, the right to strike, autonomy in negotiating wage rates) served as a sign to governments abroad of the party's political will to pursue a stabilizing austerity policy.

Portugal under PS and IMF rule

By 1977 it became obvious that the PS had no interest in a sweeping reorganization of the economy when the medium-term economic programme backed by the PS minister for planning, M. Silva, failed as a result of opposition from within her own party. She supported a development policy for Portugal which would expand the country's semi-industrialized social structure and above all would endeavour to meet the basic needs of the entire population (a World Bank and ILO concept). The only alternative to IMF programmes and joining the EC, other than that suggested by M. Silva and the inevitable demands of the PCP for more extensive nationalization and a planned economy, was that put forward by the Left-Catholic presidential candidate, M.

L. Pintassilgo. She favoured close economic co-operation between Portugal, as a Third World country, and the African nations, first and foremost with the former Portuguese colonies and the crude-oil states.

There was, of course, no serious attempt at putting this strategy into practice, and in terms of its economic and social policies, the first PS Government (1976–8) under Prime Minister Soares moved instead considerably closer to achieving its stated aim of bringing external capital into the country and clearing the way for Portugal's membership of the EC. In 1976 the EC lent the PS Government US$1.2 billion, and the USA promised US$1.5 billion and made US$300 million of that available immediately. These loans had their social and political price. Despite the aforementioned advance concession made by the PS Government in 1976/7, governments and lenders abroad demanded a formal stand-by agreement with the IMF and a Letter of Intent covering the economic policies which the government intended to pursue. Thus the IMF made its first appearance as a mediator for loans amounting to more than US$750 million from Western governments. In 1978 the first PS Government, since toppled because of its austerity policies, in coalition with the CDS, which by then had become extremely right-wing, began to negotiate the IMF's conditions: a reduction of one-third in the budget deficit, a substantial devaluation of the escudo, wage guidelines of 20% and various increases in taxation (10–15% for income tax and 10% for turnover tax). After a great deal of negotiation, during which the PS Government played up the threat of Communism for fear that the IMF might not be willing to ease its conditions, the agreement came into force with slight modifications. In 1979 a new round of negotiations with the IMF was begun but never concluded, since this time the private banks gave Portugal access to the international credit market even without the IMF's blessing. In this way Portugal joined the group of countries which run up debts primarily with the private banks because their conditionality appears to be less strict than that of the IMF and other international organizations.

During the period 1980–83 the subsequent Portuguese Goverment, a right-wing coalition of the PSD, the CDS and the monarchists which was known as the *Allianca Democratica* (AD), sped up the process of restoring the capitalist system. Under its leaderhip, the agrarian reform fell through once and for all, real wages were forced back down, workers' rights withdrawn and the law on dismissal liberalized. The insurance companies and the cement and fertilizer industries were reprivatized and the banking sector opened up to private banks. Big landowners and factory owners whose property had been expropriated previously received generous compensation. Domestic and foreign capital recorded hefty increases in profits; but the national budget and balance of payments slid further into deficit, and the external debt doubled between 1978 and 1983 from US$5.9 billion to US$14.5 billion. In 1987 it stood at US$18.2 billion.

In 1983 a PS-led coalition government had once again to conclude a new stand-by agreement with the IMF. Under this agreement, Portugal committed herself in particular to reduce her current-account deficit from US$3.2 billion

(1982) to US$2 billion in 1983 and to US$1.25 billion in 1984 and not to allow her external debt of US$13.5 billion (1982) to rise above US$15 billion by 1984. The austerity measures which accompanied this brought a measure of short-term cosmetic success: the current-account deficit disappeared, but in 1983 domestic demand fell by 7%, investment by 7.5%, and unemployment rose from an (official) rate of 7.6% to 10.8%.

Portugal is a perfect example of the special role which a social-democratic government can play in such circumstances — by using the IMF as a scapegoat on the domestic front, when faced with opposition from potential voters from among the blue- and white-collar workers, in order to divert attention from the active part which the government itself was playing in implementing austerity policies. Though it was toppled as a government every time it met the IMF's conditions, it was the only government capable of carrying out a programme of this kind in post-revolutionary Portugal. Although the opposition shown by the workers, the unemployed and the peasants from the South during the many thousands of demonstrations, strikes and mass rallies which they held led to regular changes of government, it did not bring about a change in economic policy.

Portugal in the EC

Although the minority-party cabinet led by the PSD which has been in power since 1985 has been able to translate favourable conditions for foreign trade (a falling dollar and falling oil prices) into a positive current-account balance and to help the middle classes to catch up in terms of consumption, it has not been able to make use of this opportune moment to bring in urgently needed structural reforms. Just how vital these are is illustrated by Portugal's social and economic panorama after she became a member of the EC:

- According to official statistics, in 1985 unemployment stood at 10.8%, although for women it was 15.6% and for young people 25.4%. The trades unions and academics believe, however, that the figures were actually double those cited, since the statistics above cover half the population at most. At best 20% of those registered as unemployed received unemployment benefits. In 1985, 67% of new employees were given only fixed-term contracts, and a total of 12% of all contracts of employment were fixed-term contracts lasting two years or less. In addition, child labour (using children between the ages of 6 and 16) was widespread; according to the estimates of the trades-union umbrella organization, the CGTP, the number involved was over 200,000.
- Cuts in real wages were so serious that in the 1980s these fell back to their 1973 level. With the exception of the first years of the Revolution in 1974 and 1975, and of 1981, the growth in real wages has been negative every year.
- Social achievements have been few and far between, meaning that either the members of rural families have somehow had to keep their unemployed or

underemployed relatives from starving and/or the church has had to increase radically the number of people which its soup kitchens can cater for each day. For many, survival would not be possible without the blooming shadow economy; according to the Department of Labour, it produces one-fifth of the country's entire national product.

Although the balance of payments has been in the black since 1985 because of the falling dollar rate and the fall in the price of oil, the trade balance is still negative, since Portugal has to import far more than she exports. Moreover, Portugal's membership of the EC has caused more EC goods to invade the country, with the result that at the end of 1986 Portugal had a negative trade balance with the EC alone of around US$5 billion, more than 30% of her entire foreign-trade deficit. Although Portugal is still an agricultural country, she has to import more than 50% of her foodstuffs. Some 90% of her agricultural exports are wine, tomatoes and tinned fish. Portugal's major and second-most important industrial exports are vehicles and machinery, and clothes and shoes, and this illustrates Portugal's position in the international division of labour. Vehicle spare-parts are imported as semi-finished products and merely assembled in Portugal. As in the clothing and leather-goods industries, it is mainly the country's cheap labour which is being used, and Portugal's export advantage lies in that alone. In fact, Portugal has the lowest wage levels in Western Europe; an average labour-hour costs only US$3. At the beginning of the democratic process Portugal was still able to contain her current-account deficits with her own gold and currency reserves, but increasingly the country has had to raise loans from abroad. Since 1978, Portugal's debt has been increasing steadily, with the result that it is one of the highest in the world measured against the country's national product (80% of GDP). Measured against income from exports the figure is a remarkable 300%! At the moment Portugal is having to use as many resources for debt service as for the health service, the education system and home-building taken together. The AD Government made a considerable contribution towards increasing the external debt with its policy of abolishing subsidies to nationalized-services enterprises after 1980 and forcing these to run up large debts on the private capital market. At the end of 1983 more than 60% of the external debt was owed by state-owned concerns.

Although favourable foreign trading conditions since 1985 have given Portugal a positive balance of payments and the PSD Government has won unexpected popularity with the voters (over 40% according to opinion polls), this has not made a difference to the country's structural deficits, particularly in the agricultural and industrial sectors and in terms of qualification levels and dependence on technologies imported from abroad. Portugal's political class, which from government to government since 1976 has excelled in incompetence, corruption and nepotism, has no concept of an economic policy which might rescue Portugal from her position as a semi-industrialized peripheral country. Lisbon government and business circles expect that, by joining the EC,

Portugal will undergo a wondrous transformation and reach a standard similar to that in central, but so far it is only direct investment from abroad which has increased; this has doubled in value since 1987 and in 1988 was running at US$0.9 billion. The major investing country is Britain, followed by the USA. Whether Portugal's economic structure can be altered permanently with resources from EC regional funds and from the European Investment Bank is questionable. The way in which the debt is expanding, the obligation to service the debt and the establishment of Portugal as a cheap wage and tourist oasis do not augur well for structural change, but instead predestine the country for further conditional IMF programmes during the next crisis.

Recommended Reading

OECD Economic Surveys, *Portugal*, 1976–87/8, Paris.
Preußer, Claudia (1980) 'Portugals Gewerkschaftsbewegung . . .', in *Europäische Gewerkschaften*, Hellmann/Oesterheld/Olle, Berlin.
Silva, Manuela (1982) 'Stabilization Policies and Development', *Annalen der Gemeinwirtschaft* 2, pp. 187–98, Lüttich/Geneva.
Stallings, Barbara (1981) 'Portugal and the IMF: The Political Economy of Stabilization', in J. B. de Macedo *et al.* (ed.) *Portugal Since the Revolution: Economic and Political Perspectives*, Boulder.
World Debt Tables, World Bank, Washington 1988/9.

20. South Africa: Apartheid and International Indebtedness

Gerd Junne

Half of the gold produced in the world comes from South Africa. Moreover, half of the world's known gold reserves are concentrated in South Africa. This has meant that South Africa has always played a special part in the sphere of monetary policy and has long benefited from preferential treatment by the IMF. In 1982 South Africa received another record loan of more than US$1 billion. Since then, however, circumstances have changed dramatically. In 1985, South Africa got into such difficulty as a result of the withdrawal of private share capital and bank loans that the country had to declare itself incapable of paying its debts. Unlike in its negotiations for restructuring the debts of almost every other developing nation, the IMF has not played any significant part in solving the problems which have arisen in South Africa as a result.

The IMF's allocation of credit to South Africa before 1982

South Africa received her first IMF loan in 1957/8 on far easier terms than those offered, for instance, to Latin America during the same period. The many loans received between 1968 and 1970 were also granted on easy terms.

In 1975 South Africa got into considerable difficulty with her balance of payments, not only because of rises in the price of oil, but more particularly because American strivings for the demonetization of gold as part of the dismantling of the Bretton Woods system forced down the price of gold and thus substantially reduced South Africa's export proceeds. At that time, the sale of gold accounted for at least one-third of the country's total exports. The balance of payments problems did not arise, however, exclusively as a result of the changes in oil and gold prices. South Africa's expenditure on arms, which was linked partly to the country's geopolitical role and partly to the repressive measures necessary to secure the system of apartheid, played a major part. Between 1972 and 1975 the country's spending on armaments had virtually doubled. South Africa had imported a great many arms and a great deal of police equipment.

As far back as the mid-1970s the allocation of credit to South Africa was the subject of controversy in the Executive Committee of the IMF. It was argued that the country with the world's largest gold reserves must be able to solve its problems even without help from abroad. Indirectly, the executive directors delegated from the 17 African nations also criticized the apartheid regime. They pointed out that the rigidity of the labour market and denying the black population education to a higher level would mean that in future the country would be bound to face serious economic problems. During a debate on South Africa's application for credit in November 1976 (five months after the uprisings in Soweto) some of the executive directors expressed their suspicions that South Africa's cards had been marked. A study carried out by the IMF's secretariat estimated South Africa's loss of exports at exactly the amount which South Africa had requested from the IMF. However, none of the criticism made any difference to the USA's and Britain's continued support for South Africa's application. In view of the recent internal unrest and the presence of Cuban troops near the Namibian border, both of these countries had an interest in stabilizing the South African regime. This interest is explained not only by the strategic location of the country and her large reserves of strategically important raw materials, but also by the fact that direct investment (especially by Britain and the USA) in South Africa was then still among the most profitable in the world. The balance of payments credits which the IMF granted South Africa in 1976/7 were worth more than the assistance given by the Fund to all of the other African nations put together. During these two years only two countries received more money from the IMF: Britain and Mexico.

Figure 20.1
South Africa's external debt and the dollar rand exchange rate

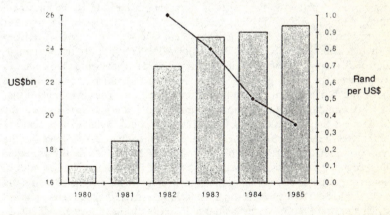

Source: South African Reserve Bank

At the beginning of the 1980s, South Africa again got into financial difficulties. The USA's international high-interest-rate policy had the effect of lowering the price of gold. Investments in gold do not bear interest. Whilst interest rates for investments in dollar bonds were high, investors were tempted to sell gold and switch to bonds. The South African balance of payments worsened dramatically as a result. Between 1980 and 1985, South Africa's external debt rose from just under US$17 billion to over US$25 billion. For this reason, in mid-1982, South Africa applied to the IMF for a stand-by credit of US$1.1 billion. By then, however, opposition within the IMF to the granting of the loan to South Africa had grown.

Many of the directors took exception to the soft terms on which the loan was to be extended. On the IMF's Board of Directors, where voting was generally unanimous, seven directors voted against the loan and nine were in favour of deferring the decision. With a tiny majority of 51.9% of the votes, the USA nevertheless succeeded in forcing through the loan.

Reaction to the mammoth credit of 1982

In the world at large the decision was met with harsh criticism, especially in the UN. The criticism was not without effect. In June 1983 the IMF's secretariat submitted a study which criticized apartheid from an economic-science point of view. Apartheid prevented the optimum use of available resources, in particular of the available labour force. Thus although apartheid had no short-term effects on the country's balance of payments position, it certainly had medium- and long-term effects. The report made it clear that in future South Africa would no longer have access to loans on the same terms as in the past.

The crucial change in the relationship between South Africa and the IMF was, however, primarily the result of increasing opposition to the apartheid regime from the USA. Whereas the Reagan Administration was altogether well-disposed to South Africa, congressmen, who were under pressure from both black and liberal voters, could not afford to support the system of apartheid. Opponents of the regime made use of the debate which took place in Congress on the raising of the USA's IMF quota and managed to get a clause about South Africa included in the law on ratification. The clause meant that the USA would be forced to oppose the granting of loans to South Africa in the IMF unless the US Secretary of the Treasury could convince the banking committees of the House of Representatives and the Senate beforehand that the terms on which the loan was to be granted would help to reduce the prejudice and repression caused by the system of apartheid. If one of the two committees should request it, the Secretary of the Treasury should be able to prove that the loans would help to dismantle (or substantially restrict) the pass laws in South Africa and that South Africa was not able to obtain the money elsewhere.

Although the extension of further loans to South Africa by the IMF did not become impossible in principle as a result of this move, in practice it was effectively halted. South Africa had to look around for other sources of credit. South African banks were encouraged by the central bank to raise loans abroad and in doing so to restore equilibrium to the balance of payments at the same time, and for a while this worked well. South African banks either borrowed money from overseas banks and lent it out again at home, or acted as intermediaries when overseas banks granted loans, predominantly short-term loans, directly to South African concerns. Short-term loans had the great advantage that the banks granting them did not need to show them separately on their balance sheets; they remained, therefore, largely invisible.

As volumes increased, however, these loans did not go unnoticed. The same opposition as had resulted in the legal clause concerning the granting of loans to South Africa by the IMF was now directed against the private US banks. Public and semi-public organizations (churches, municipalities) threatened to withdraw their deposits if their banks continued to extend credit to South Africa. As the losses which they incurred at home threatened to exceed the profits which they made in South Africa, the US banks began to revise their policies towards the country.

The unilateral moratorium on South Africa's debts

Another, more important, reason behind the withdrawal of capital from South Africa was that profits in South Africa had fallen dramatically. In order to restore equilibrium to the balance of payments, the South African Government had introduced drastic austerity measures. This had not only led to a serious recession but had also contributed to unrest in the black townships. The number of blacks without work rose to over three million in 1985. Although the austerity measures brought an improvement in the balance of payments, they worsened the situation in industry, where capacity utilization was decreasing. Between 1982 and 1985 industrial output fell by 13%. When profits followed, investment became less attractive. More and more firms withdrew totally from South Africa. Since 1984 substantially more than 100 overseas businesses have given up their direct investments. The most spectacular withdrawal occurred in August 1987, when the London Standard Chartered Bank sold interests worth DM460 million in a big South African bank.

Ironically, the IMF's policies had contributed to this withdrawal of overseas capital. The Fund had always argued for a liberalization of the capital market of the kind which had been introduced gradually since the stand-by credit of 1982. The abandonment of South Africa's two-tier exchange rate encouraged speculation against the South African currency, and the rand depreciated continually (see Figure 20.1). This in turn led to severe price rises in an economy in which imports accounted for around one-third of the national product, and these price rises necessitated economies in public spending and led to a reduction in consumption of 10%. This resulted in industry having difficulty selling its goods and in social unrest.

Due to the unrest in the black townships, the banks estimated that the political risks involved in investing in South Africa were higher than ever before. Logically, they demanded that loans to South Africa should be repayable over a shorter period and that interest rates should be higher. As a result of these higher interest charges, South African firms became more unprofitable still, and this precipitated the withdrawal of capital.

On 20 July 1985, with the unrest of the previous ten months having cost 450 lives, the Botha Government declared a state of emergency in order both to restrict press freedom and to enable it to suppress opposition from the blacks more effectively. These measures caused capital to flow out of the country in panic. Within the space of a week the value of shares traded on the Johannesburg stock exchange fell by 11 million rand. By the end of the month the rand rate had dropped to US$0.43. On 31 July the Chase Manhattan Bank decided to grant South Africa no new loans and not to extend the repayment periods of outstanding loans when they became due. Other US banks followed. Of South Africa's total US$14 billion in short-term debts, US$4.2 billion was owed to US banks. A considerable part of the loans were due to be repaid in August of that year.

Figure 20.2
The proportion of South Africa's external debt owed to the creditor banks of five countries, 1985

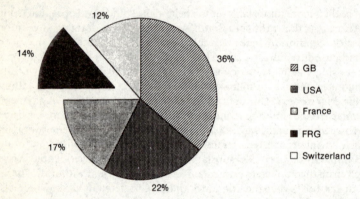

Source: South African Reserve Bank

Unlike the American banks, the European banks, which financed by far the greater part of South Africa's external debt, did not withdraw from the country. Some of them, including the Deutsche Bank and the Dresdner Bank, were even willing to fill the breach and extend total lending to South Africa. The Dresdner Bank granted South Africa approximately DM1.2 billion in loans, and between 1980 and 1985 had a share in 33 loans granted to South African debtors. However, President Botha's speech on 15 August 1985, which contrary to all expectations announced no sweeping political reforms, caused South Africa's credit-worthiness to hit rock-bottom. The flow of capital overseas became a streaming torrent, and at the end of the month the stock-exchange and foreign-exchange dealings were suspended. At the beginning of September, South Africa declared a unilateral moratorium on debt payments.

Indirect negotiations for the settlement of the debts

In the case of any country other than South Africa, the IMF would have played a disciplinary role in a situation of this kind. In the case of South Africa, however, its hands were tied. Supporting action was out of the question, and even to act as a mediator appeared unacceptable, since this might be classed as support for the apartheid regime. Nor was the IMF the only body unwilling to talk to the South African central bank. The private banks were reluctant. Due to the bad publicity which this would generate, the banks shied away from direct contact with representatives of the apartheid regime. Instead, the former president of the Swiss issuing bank and the BIS in Basle, Fritz Leutwiler, was recruited as an intermediary and given responsibility for negotiating the settlement of the debts. The negotiations dragged on for more than six months and did not lead to an official agreement. Since agreeing to a compromise might have been interpreted as support for the apartheid regime, the banks probably preferred that the outcome of the negotiations take the form of unilateral measures by South Africa, so that it appeared as if the banks' options were limited. Once again it is clear that double standards were at work here. In the event of a unilateral postponement of this kind by any other country the measures taken would have been far more drastic, for example seizure of property overseas. In the case of South Africa this was apparently not even considered seriously.

South Africa clearly has a special status among the debtor nations. At one time she was given preferential treatment by the IMF. At present the Fund wants as little as possible to do with her. The developments which have led to the country's inability to pay its debts are primarily political. The oppression of the black population and opposition to this have vastly reduced the credit-worthiness of the country's economy. Oppression requires high levels of spending on arms. It also militates against the training of sufficient numbers of qualified personnel, with the result that many products have to be imported and South African industry is not competitive on the world market. The fact that the South African economy's profits are falling is causing capital to be withdrawn, and this in turn is resulting in austerity measures which then fuel the political unrest.

The withdrawal of capital by the US banks was, however, not prompted by falling profits alone, for the European banks have clearly acted differently. The US banks are under great public pressure to restrict the loans granted to South Africa. What is more, this is the same domestic US public pressure which prevented the IMF from playing a similar part in the restructuring of South Africa's debts as it has played in restructuring the debts of other countries.

Recommended Reading

Harris, Laurence (1986) 'South Africa's External Debt Crisis', *Third World Quarterly* 8 (3).

Padayachee, Vishnu (1986) *The Politics of International Economic Relations: South Africa and the International Monetary Fund: 1975 and Beyond.*

21. Yugoslavia: The 'Socialist Market Economy' and the Debt Crisis

Hansgeorg Conert

In 1981, Yugoslavia's external debt passed the US$20 billion mark. Since then it has continued, with slight fluctuations, at this level, even though the Socialist Federal Republic of Yugoslavia (SFRY) has paid approximately US$30 billion in debt service over the last six years. Yugoslavia now finds herself in the midst of an economic crisis which was unleashed directly by policies designed to cope with her debts, as well as by world economic factors, but which have evolved from an economically defective development which began much earlier.

External indebtedness and debt management

Between 1971 and 1980, Yugoslavia's external debt, which had stood at only US$0.8 billion in 1960 and US$2.3 billion in 1970, grew by an average of more than 23% per annum. What were the causes of this? Here it is necessary to distinguish between the direct causes, illustrated by Yugoslavia's foreign-trade indicators, and the more general causes, which lie in the evolution of her economic structure and in her economic system.

External indebtedness on the part of countries or national economies generally evolves from a negative current account, from the fact that those countries' (or economies') foreign-trading relations require them to pay more in foreign currencies than they earn in foreign exchange. This is true of Yugoslavia.

Yugoslavia's balance of payments deficit is a result of the component parts of the balance moving in opposite directions. The trade balance, for example, has been negative since 1947. During the 1950s exports covered the cost of an average of 62% of imports; from the mid-1960s until the outbreak of the crisis in 1980 the balance of trade deficit increased regularly: from US$3.203 billion in 1966–70 to US$11.454 billion in 1971–5 and US$24.492 billion in 1976–80. It is worth noting, and significant in view of recent trends, that the volume of Yugoslavia's foreign trade and her foreign-trade deficit are distributed differently over three groups of countries whose level of development, economic systems and foreign-trading conditions are fundamentally dissimilar.

Yugoslavia's foreign-trade deficit is largely attributable to a deficitary trade in goods with the OECD countries. Whereas Yugoslavia's industrial finished

Table 21.1
Distribution of Yugoslavia's foreign trade and foreign trade deficit over three groups of countries, 1966–85 (%)

	1966–70	*1971–5*	*1976–80*	*1981–5*
OECD countries:				
% of Yugoslavia's foreign trade	59.5	56.9	51.1	42.0
% of Yugoslavia's foreign-trade deficit	87.8	80.9	77.5	108.5
*Socialist countries:**				
% of Yugoslavia's foreign trade	28.7	30.0	32.9	40.0
% of Yugoslavia's foreign-trade deficit	6.5	3.6	9.7	–25.1
Developing nations:				
% of Yugoslavia's foreign trade	11.6	13.0	16.0	18.0
% of Yugoslavia's foreign-trade deficit	5.7	15.5	12.8	16.6

* COMECON countries + Albania and the People's Republic of China.

products can easily be placed in the COMECON countries, her level of technological development, marketing and follow-up service, and the quality of her products are evidently not good enough to enable her to hold her own on the OECD markets.

This is also illustrated by the discrepancies which exist between the proportion of Yugoslavia's imports sold by and exports purchased by the groups of countries in Table 21.1: whilst between 1976 and 1980 trade with the OECD countries accounted for 51% of Yugoslavia's total foreign trade, this broke down into around 57% of Yugoslavia's imports and 41% of her exports. Trade with the socialist countries, on the other hand, accounted for 33% of Yugoslavia's total foreign trade — just under 28% of her imports, but 42% of her exports. The proportion of Yugoslavia's imports of machinery, plant and means of transport which came from the OECD countries was disproportionately high at regularly around 80%. As a result of increases in crude-oil prices during the 1970s and Yugoslavia's crisis during the 1980s, these accounted for only 15% of Yugoslavia's total imports in 1984, but in 1973 they had accounted for around a quarter. On the other hand, over the same period the proportion of Yugoslavia's imports which were reproductive goods (fuel, raw materials and semi-finished products) increased from 63–79%. Yugoslavia imports what is clearly a disproportionately high volume of these sorts of goods from the socialist countries, in particular from the USSR.

Yugoslavia would not be in a position to cope with this foreign-trade deficit without the positive balance on her invisible foreign-exchange operations since the beginning of the 1970s. The three main sources of her foreign-exchange revenue are transport services (more than 30% on average for 1966–70, falling to around 20% for 1976–80); tourism (rising from around 25% to 30% for the same periods); and transfers of foreign currency from Yugoslavian migrant workers (increasing from around 45% in 1966 to 50% in 1980).

With this foreign-exchange revenue Yugoslavia was able to provide cover for approximately 78% of her foreign-trade deficits for 1966–70 and almost 86% of those from 1971–5. In the period 1976–80, however, the cover ratio stood at only 65% (although it rose to 127% during the following five years as a result of severe import restrictions in the wake of the debt crisis). A major cause of the rapid increase in Yugoslavia's external debt at the end of the 1970s was thus the limited degree to which invisible foreign-exchange operations compensated for her balance of trade deficits.

Political and economic structural causes

In the Yugoslavia of the 1950s and 1960s, as in other socialist systems, the state had a monopoly on foreign trade. This monopoly was, in principle, intended to help avoid marked imbalances in foreign trade. However, in the 1970s the monopoly was increasingly relaxed. For example, commercial banks and large firms were given the right to raise external loans if they so decided. This development was the result of political and social trends dating back as far as the beginning of the 1960s, when Yugoslavia began to evolve both a mode of production peculiar to that country and productive relations which did not correspond either to the capitalist or the Soviet socialist structural model. Central and directed planning of the economy was abandoned; firms which by law were to be run by the workers themselves, were to take their own decisions and dispose of their profits as they saw fit. In terms of both the volume and selection of goods produced and their organizational and technical requirements, Yugoslavia's businesses actually became independent. Under this plan, their power to set prices was limited, although in reality it increased as time passed, and regional and local governmental authorities were able to influence investment decisions.

At the same time, the government began to open up the country to foreign trade, in stages, under the slogan 'integration into the international division of labour'. Decision-makers expected that for Yugoslavian industry this would result in technical development incentives and financial assistance, and that competitive pressure would promote higher productivity. This orientation towards growth and stimulating earnings and consumption strained the country's productive capacity to breaking-point. Individual demand for modern consumer goods, preferably manufactured in the West, increased as rapidly as public demand for both the construction of imposing administration buildings, sporting venues, cultural establishments and investment.

The economic and political autonomy of the individual republics, which had been strengthened by further moves towards decentralization between 1965 and 1969, intensified the rivalry between them as each endeavoured to persuade modern plants in the processing sector to relocate in their territory. This resulted in the development of at least three faulty structural trends:

- New industrial plants were constructed in an economically uncoordinated fashion and often without bearing in mind the economic and infrastructural conditions in the location concerned. Later it was widely bemoaned that this duplication of capacity was inefficient.
- Anxious for the country's investment to be repaid quickly and produce high returns and obsessed with the prestige of Yugoslavian products, the government encouraged processing firms but neglected the establishment of extractive industries and firms producing materials for production. By the 1970s at the latest it was clear that this had resulted in the country becoming dependent on imports of fuel, raw materials and primary products.
- The fact that the development needs of society as a whole and of the economy were ignored in favour of regional and sectoral requirements and market-economy considerations resulted in a reversal of previous policies designed to reduce traditional socio-economic developmental disparities. These began to grow rapidly again as a result of the debt crisis: whereas in 1947 per capita income in the Autonomous Province of Kosovo was 52% of the national average, by 1984 it had fallen to 33%.

The soft monetary and credit policies pursued in the 1960s and 1970s and the effects which these had on purchasing power strengthened demand pull in the Yugoslavian economy: 'Our habit of consuming more as a society than the National Product which we realize and of spending more as individuals than we earn was deeply entrenched' (Jovanov). With wages and investment competing for funds, works managements were often inclined to meet the workers' wage claims and to raise the funds needed for investment through loans. The proportion of their own funds which Yugoslavian firms invested was therefore always comparatively small; individual consumer demand was relatively high. The tendency to excessive demand and the structurally caused balance of trade deficit together caused the second endemic functional weakness in the Yugoslavian economy: the dinar's loss of purchasing power. Producers' prices and retail prices had been rising steadily since the 1960s, at an annual average rate of more than 18% between 1973 and 1979.

Despite these structural obstructions to expansion, Yugoslavia's success in promoting growth during the 1970s was considerable, especially compared with that of the OECD countries. Between 1971 and 1975 industrial output grew by an average of 7.8% per annum, between 1976 and 1980 by at least 6.7%. By the end of the decade, however, the rate of increase in real income was falling steadily. Accordingly, domestic growth began to come under increasing pressure.

The management of the crisis

When, in 1979, Yugoslavia's foreign-trade deficit increased by 167% over the previous year to US$7.2 billion and the balance of payments deficit rose by 291% to US$3.7 billion, the Federal Executive Council (central government) took measures which were aimed above all at increasing foreign earnings by reducing the trade deficit. These centred on the introduction of import restrictions and export drives directed primarily at the OECD countries. In the knowledge that the imbalances in Yugoslavia's foreign trade were ultimately caused by faulty structural developments in the country's own economy and that unless these were corrected there could be no long-term solution to the crisis, the Socio-Political Chamber, a permanent committee of the Federal Assembly, set up a commission at the beginning of 1982 whose job would be to examine the causes of this desperate situation and to elaborate a programme to overcome it. By the summer of 1983 the commission had compiled 17 reports, with conclusions, which were approved in summarized form by the Central Committee of the League of Communists of Yugoslavia (LCY) in July. This Long-Term Programme for Economic Stabilization was to be put into practice from early 1984.

For a long time more than a few Yugoslavian economists and politicians have regarded this programme, whose objectives were formulated more concretely than its recommended solutions, as having failed. This may be too wholesale an assessment; some of the Federal Executive Council's measures are taking hold, at least temporarily and/or to some extent, whereas others are having no effect at all. As part of a process which began in around 1968 and which was backed up by constitutional changes, Yugoslavia's component republics acquired a great deal of autonomy and have since not acted upon decisions taken by the organs of state where these have conflicted with their own interests — or have done so only with great leniency towards transgressions committed by their own local authorities or industrial organizations. This is a major problem.

The measures recommended by the programme may be summarized as follows:

- to regain control over the country's foreign earnings in order to be able to meet its international payments obligations, to provide a currency reserve and to restrict and prioritize imports;
- dinar devaluations, on the grounds that the introduction of a realistic exchange rate would prove beneficial to exports, especially those destined for countries with convertible currencies (although at the same time imports would become more expensive);
- the national bank should pursue restrictive monetary and credit policies, to which the commercial banks would have to adhere more strictly, in an attempt to stifle demand;
- surplus demand should be reduced by means of cuts in public spending (which could not be implemented) and by limiting the income of the masses

(which was not successful *per se*, but did succeed in real terms as a result of galloping inflation);
- in order to increase its accumulation capacity trade and industry should be relieved of the burden of paying taxation and rates;
- by making several changes in the law on joint ventures, terms of investment were to be improved for foreign, primarily Western, investors.

The Yugoslavian Government has negotiated with the IMF for new loans and for the restructuring of its existing debt every year since the beginning of the debt crisis in 1980. In February 1981, after a long period of negotiation, Yugoslavia obtained the largest loan (US$2.2 billion) which the IMF had ever granted. It was to be paid over in three tranches; before each payment there were to be fresh negotiations. Early in 1983, Yugoslavia conducted debt restructuring negotiations, in which the IMF took part, with representatives of 15 Western governments and a bank consortium, and also obtained a loan to the value of US$4.5 billion (Zurich Accord of 17 January 1983). On 20 March 1984 the country was granted a loan of US$2 billion, again with the co-operation of the IMF.

Figure 21.1
Yugoslavia: crisis in the socialist market economy

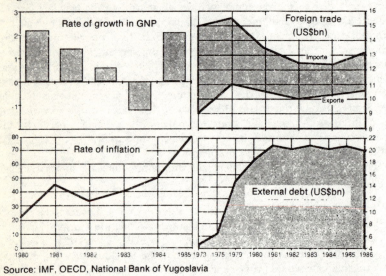

Source: IMF, OECD, National Bank of Yugoslavia

In March 1985 the IMF authorized a one-year stand-by credit for Yugoslavia of US$300 million as a prerequisite for the restructuring of payment obligations totalling US$5.7 billion which would become due between 1985 and 1988. In the course of these negotiations, Yugoslavia's creditors demanded that the country continue to work with the IMF 'on the basis of increased supervision of its economic performance'. Writing in the *Yugoslav Economic*

Review of November 1986, the Yugoslavian observer described this increased supervision as a 'process which would enable the IMF to examine the long-term efforts of the member countries to reduce their external debts' and which was expected to lead to more flexible management than that possible under the terms of stand-by credits, which Yugoslavia no longer wished to take up in the future. Yugoslavia was to account to the IMF quarterly, and the IMF was to carry out 'consultations' twice yearly.

Although the conditions imposed by the IMF were not publicized in detail, they were nevertheless specified and debated in the daily and academic press. Despite this, without inside information it is difficult to assess to what extent the IMF actually influenced Yugoslavian economic policy. Although there was unmistakable and substantial harmony between the economic philosophy of the IMF and Yugoslavia's austerity and stabilization policies, this is not necessarily proof that these were forced upon the Yugoslavian Government. As early as the 1970s leading Yugoslavian economists had argued repeatedly for monetary, credit and incomes-policy measures of this kind. It should also be remembered that even during the great economic debate conducted in Yugoslavia after 1959 it was the free-market orthodoxy which dominated. Criticisms of the market ceased to be voiced in the period which followed, even by economists in leading positions within the LCY. Moreover, the IMF was no less supportive after the declaration of the socialist market economy in Yugoslavia in 1952 than it was when the country took the more momentous decisions on liberalization in 1961 and 1965. During the 1950s the IMF's major concern was to ensure Yugoslavia's break with the USSR and to set the country on a path of its own. More recently the organization has been concerned to prevent Yugoslavia from turning increasingly to COMECON as a possible consequence of that region's markedly increased foreign trade with Yugoslavia. This situation has strengthened the hand of the Yugoslavian Government with regard to the IMF. Though a gradual divergence between the state and party leadership in Yugoslavia and the IMF (for example, over the scale and the deadline for price decontrol, the speed at which real interest rates, that is those above the rate of inflation, should be introduced and the extent of dinar devaluations) are becoming public, there is not much to indicate that any fundamental differences of opinion exist in relation to economic philosophy over and above differences of this kind, or that the Yugoslavian Government is therefore having to submit to the power of the IMF.

The consequences of crisis management

The economic effects of attempts by the Yugoslavian Government to find a solution to the crisis, in particular the debt crisis, since 1981 have been less positive. Although between 1981 and 1985 Yugoslavia's foreign trade deficit fell by an average of almost 24% per annum, from US$4.8 billion to US$1.5 billion, behind these figures there lurked a serious discrepancy in the regional structure of Yugoslavia's foreign trade (and therefore in the structure of her economic system) (see Table 21.1). In 1985, for example, Yugoslavia bought 46.4% of her imports from the OECD countries but only delivered 31.7% of her exports there. On the other hand, 48.9% of Yugoslavia's exports were sold to the COMECON countries but only 31.7% of her imports purchased from them. During the period 1981–3 Yugoslavia's foreign-trade surplus with the COMECON countries amounted to 12% of her overall trade deficit for the same period, and in 1985 this figure increased to a remarkable 96%. On the other hand, for the period between 1981 and 1983 Yugoslavia's deficit with the OECD countries was 9.7% greater than the arithmetic total deficit for that period and in 1985 this figure increased to 25.4%. Since trade with the COMECON countries (with the exception of Hungary, Romania and Poland, who pay wholly or partly in convertible currency) is settled in clearing units, the reduction in the overall deficit which trading with these countries brings about does not lead to an equal improvement in the country's foreign-currency position or a reduction in her debts to the OECD region.

Reductions in her foreign-trade deficit after 1983 enabled Yugoslavia to realize modest, but growing, current-account surpluses. The deficit had stood at US$1.8 billion in 1981 and at US$1.4 billion in 1982, but in 1983 Yugoslavia realized a surplus of US$0.1 billion; this increased in 1984 to US$0.5 billion and in 1985 to US$0.8 billion. The country's increasing interest and loan-capital (re)payment commitments (US$3.7 billion in 1981, US$4.5 billion in 1982, US$4.9 billion in 1983, US$5.3 billion in 1984, US$5.5 billion in 1985 and US$6.0 billion in 1986) meant, however, that Yugoslavia was able to reduce her external debt only slightly. In 1981 this debt stood at US$20.8 billion, and in 1985 it was still US$20.7 billion. Not until 1986 could it be reduced to US$19.8 billion.

However, although relatively successful, Yugoslavia's policies for eradicating her debt set off unfavourable trends in almost every domestic economic indicator. Both tendencies have similar causes: for example, the inflationary effects of dinar devaluations of over 50% on average between 1981 and 1985 carried out (under pressure from the IMF!) in order to boost exports and the consequences of import restrictions for capacity utilization, profitability and worker productivity in processing industries dependent on imported raw materials.

On average, the increase in Yugoslavia's National Product from 1981–5 was –0.6% per annum, against +6.0% from 1973–9. For industrial output the corresponding figures are 2.8% and 7.25%. Worker productivity in industry fell between 1981 and 1985 by an average 1.8%; not until 1984 was there an increase of 0.2%. Measured against the National Product, net investment in fixed assets was 31.1% in 1981, but by 1985 had fallen, steadily over the 4 years, to 20.9%. The rate of investment in fixed assets fell during the same period by an average of 8.6% per annum. In the light of this trend, Yugoslavian economists feared, quite rightly, that industry, which was in need of modernization, would fall behind technologically to such an extent that catching up again would prove difficult. Whereas in 1981 Yugoslavian concerns still had an average of 62.9% of their net proceeds at their disposal, by 1985 this figure had fallen to 50.4%. In the face of the government's intentions, it proved impossible for concerns to overcome their non-liquidity, indebtedness and negligible accumulation capacity.

The greatest failure of all was the failure of Yugoslavia's stabilization policies to reduce the rate of inflation: both retail prices and the cost of living had been rocketing throughout the 1980s; in 1985 the rate of inflation passed the 100% mark.

Increases in the earnings of direct employees were unable to keep pace with the galloping depreciation of the currency, something which the government had wanted in the interests of restricting demand and the IMF had recommended in the interests of relieving businesses of some of the burden. From 1981–4 real income fell by an average 6.2% per annum; in 1985 it rose again, for the first time since 1979, by 2.8%.

One result which is particularly remarkable considering the restrictive nature of Yugoslavia's stabilization policies after 1980 is that employment did not fall in nationalized sectors of the economy. In fact, it actually rose from 1981–5 by an average 2.3% per annum. These rates were not, however, sufficient to guarantee school and college leavers employment, and as early as the beginning of the 1980s the unemployment figures exceeded the 1 million mark. In March 1986 the number of people registered as seeking employment was 1,107,374.

The social costs of Yugoslavia's debt crisis and the stabilization policies designed to overcome it are unmistakable, though the extent to which their true scale and manifestations are revealed in statistical data is limited. There is much to suggest that real income actually fell by considerably more than is officially reported. When assessing the consequences, it is also necessary to remember that before the outbreak of the crisis real average income levels were barely above subsistence level. All the same, if one does not get the impression of widespread impoverishment in the country today then this is partly because of possible perceptual deficiencies and partly because of the huge dimensions of Yugoslavia's shadow or parallel economy, which enables people to earn a main or supplementary income either legally, semi-legally or illegally. Poorest of all are those who are forced to live without, or on below-average, incomes in economically backward regions and who have neither access to such sources of income nor land of their own to cultivate on the side. In addition to the wage differentials which exist within the republics, between different occupations and as a result of status, there are also differences in average wages between the republics. Wages in Slovenia, for example, are double those in Macedonia. Considering the extent to which living conditions have deteriorated, a matter upon which we have only briefly touched, and the extent to which the little developed and retrogressive state of the system of social benefits has contributed to that deterioration, social protest has been surprisingly limited. Although strikes, which are neither banned nor completely legalized in Yugoslavia (384 strikes were recorded in 1984, 699 in 1985 and 847 in 1986), are on the increase, such actions have so far been isolated to individual firms and have tended not to last long since the Yugoslavian workforce is split into syndicates. Despite this, the number of strikes taking place increased to such an extent in March 1987 as a result of the failure to freeze prices as well as wages that in Croatia one might even talk in terms of a wave of strikes. For the first time attempts were made to reach agreement between firms on the demands which should be made and the action which should be taken.

The biggest threat which the Yugoslavian state could face in the future as a result of the debt crisis may well be an intensification, as seen in the 1970s, of the traditional rivalry between various sections of the population and increased attempts at regional separation, both of which serve to augment existing ethnic, religious and socio-cultural differences with differences in socio-political orientation. The economically prosperous (1% unemployment against a national average of 16%), formerly unmistakably pro-Yugoslavian republic of Slovenia has recently lodged demands for independence in a whole range of areas and with a stridency which raises suspicions of separatist endeavours.

In general because she has for two decades pursued an inappropriate economic strategy, and in particular as a result of the debt crisis which this has triggered, Yugoslavia now faces structural, social and domestic political problems for which she has so far found no solution. The pronounced egoism of the individual republics and the lack of essentially well-grounded, compatible and consistently implemented economic and social policies have been the major reasons that no way out of the chaos has yet been found. There is nothing to suggest that anything is about to change.

Recommended Reading

Bošković, B. (1984) 'Das Programm der ökonomischen Stabilisierung und seine Durchsetzung in der Selbstverwaltungspraxis', *Sozialistische Theorie und Praxis*, Belgrade, May.

Conert, H. (1982) 'Bedingungen und Konsequenzen der Weltmarktorientierung nachkapitalistischer Gesellschaften', *PROKLA* 3.

OECD Economic Survey (various editions) sections on Yugoslavia.

Yugoslav Economic Review, (1986) 'How Much is the IMF Helping Yugoslavia?', II.

22. Zaire: Indebtedness and Kleptocracy

Peter Körner

In terms of its surface area (roughly ten times the size of Britain) and population (35 million), Zaire is one of the largest countries in Africa south of the Sahara. In 1986, with overseas liabilities amounting to around US$6 billion, it was also one of the most heavily indebted, exceeded only by Nigeria, Sudan and Ivory Coast. Between 1976 and 1987, Zaire was forced to restructure her external debt eight times through the Paris Club and once through the London Club, and to conclude eight agreements (with strict conditionality) with the IMF. The conditions were intended to restore Zaire's international credit-worthiness and to rehabilitate her shattered economy. By 1987 all attempts of this kind had failed: partly due to the inadequacy in economic, social and development-policy terms of the IMF's rehabilitation programmes; partly due to the chasm between the stated economic policy and the actual deeds of the Mobuto regime, which has ruled since 1965; and partly due to the gap between the timing and the amount of the external financing which Zaire needed and the loans and development aid actually granted. The crisis and the way in which it has been managed has impoverished the mass of the urban and rural population of Zaire so seriously that despite the country's fabulous natural resources its per capita income of US$140 (1984) is one of the lowest in the world.

When the debt crisis erupted in 1975 the bulk of Zaire's overseas liabilities consisted of private, mainly publicly-guaranteed financial loans and trade credit, but 12 years later, as a consequence of restructuring, the withdrawal of private creditors and a shift in the allocation of funds, they were predominantly bilateral public loans. The mountain of debt is chiefly the result of the large-scale industrial and infrastructure projects with which the Mobuto regime intended to develop Zaire into the Brazil of Africa (that is into an NIC). The regime hoped that this plan would boost the industrialization drive, win it prestige domestically and abroad, and secure national unity in a state which in the 1960s, primarily because of the attempts of Shaba to secede, had been threatened with disintegration. In particular the 1,800 kilometre-long high-voltage transmission line between the Inga fill dam near the mouth of the River Zaire (Congo), the point at which it flows into the Atlantic, and Kolwezi in Shaba, where the bulk of Zaire's major export, copper, is produced, was intended to bring the region which obtains a large part of Zaire's foreign currency under stricter government control. In 1986 the Inga–Shaba Complex — the Inga Hydro-Electric Power Station, the Inga–Shaba Line and related industrial plants producing steel, cement and copper — represented more than half of the country's external debt.

Table 22.1
Zaire: The structure of the external debt
(US$ m)

	1970	1975	1980	1985	1986
External debt	416	2,354	4,817	5,851	6,534
bilateral	89	404	2,216	3,366	3,874
multilateral	6	164	702	1,414	1,613
IMF	—	86	376	801	856
World Bank and IDA	6	50	246	415	506
private creditors	216	1,236	1,603	762	729
short-term	105	550	296	309	318

Source: IMF; World Bank; own calculations.

In the early 1970s, Zaire had offered external financiers, in particular the multinational banks, attractive opportunities for excess capital which could not be invested profitably inside the industrialized world. It appeared that any debt service which might accrue from the country's ambitious, externally financed projects could be covered without any difficulty by Zaire's vast mineral reserves (amongst them copper, cobalt, diamonds, crude oil, uranium, manganese and coal), exportable agricultural raw materials (such as coffee, rubber, palm oil, cocoa, cotton, tea), wood and waterpower.

Both the debtor government and the creditors had allowed themselves to be dazzled by the country's economic boom of the late 1960s and early 1970s. This boom had been financed by the high world-market price of copper and had seduced them into making an irrational projection of future growth rates for the years up to the 1980s. Their optimism was founded primarily on the (totally unrealistic) assumption that the production of copper could be expanded from around 500,000–800,000 tonnes per annum and that in the medium term the price of that raw material would remain high.

The rude awakening came in 1975, when the terms of trade worsened suddenly as a result of the collapse in copper prices; the situation was aggravated by the world recession of 1974/5 when the major importing countries' demand for raw materials fell. Since imports, already made more expensive by the (OPEC) oil price shock and the upward trend in the prices of manufactured goods and foodstuffs could not be reduced in line with dwindling export earnings, Zaire's balance of payments position became rapidly untenable. By mid-1975 the debtor nation was incapable of paying her debts and lacked credit-worthiness. At the very moment when she needed external loans more urgently than ever before she received none. Zaire now had no option but to tread the path to the IMF.

Table 22.2
Zaire: The balance of payments
(US$ m)

	1970	1975	1980	1985
Current account	−64	−593	−294	−218
Trade balance	126	−283	508	518
Balance of capital transactions	35	141	57	−126
Balance of payments	−29	−451	−235	−429
Financing	29	451	235	429
IMF loans	–	55	17	66
Restructuring	–	–	1,613	417
Foreign-currency reserves	29	78	−48	−2
Arrears	–	318	−1,347	−52

Source: IMF: World Bank; own calculations.

For Zaire the debt crisis would have become unavoidable sooner or later even if the world-market shock had hit the country less unexpectedly and less dramatically than it did; Zaire's ability to service her debts was fundamentally limited by the structures established under Belgian colonialism, which had been consolidated and accentuated by the self-serving policies of independent Zaire's ruling class.

Zaire's debt crisis should be regarded primarily as a development crisis caused by kleptocracy. The term describes the form of rule adopted by Zaire's corrupt and parasitical ruling class, which was bent on feathering its own nest regardless of the country's development-policy needs and which, since it was not controlled by any democratic authority, used its power of disposal over the Zairean state to privately amass what were largely public resources. This plundering of resources by the ruling class, which had been born out of the colonial puppet class (the *évolués*), takes the form of sumptuous overseas immovables, numbered bank accounts in the world's flight-capital haven, Switzerland, and elsewhere, and unbridled luxury consumption. The value of public resources taken into private ownership by the Mobuto clan and other members of the ruling class can be estimated as roughly equivalent to Zaire's external debt.

Zaire's kleptocracy survived by bleeding the country of its mining and agricultural surplus produce; between 1973 and 1975 the ruling class sought to consolidate its economic basis through a ruinous process of Zaireanization (reversed in 1976) and nationalization. Its unlimited appetite for foreign exchange led this class to promote those sectors which could (or seemed to be able to) increase their exports most in the short term, which were the most prestigious and/or which could strengthen national cohesion. The bulk of state investments and external loans flowed into the mining industry and its accompanying infrastructure. When investing capital borrowed overseas, the Mobuto regime ignored every rule governing the use of productive capital. The external loans did not benefit projects which would have helped expand output, foreign-currency earnings and the country's debts-servicing capacity. Instead they were squandered on schemes of dubious developmental value. The gigantomania of projects such as Inga–Shaba proved developmentally destructive since it created useless, unproductive excess capacity. It tied up financial resources which had to be diverted from productive sectors, above all mining and agriculture and which were then unavailable for productive and/or socially necessary projects.

The ruling class' disastrous industrialization policies and its practice of granting itself privileges were encouraged by the alliance which the Mobuto regime forged specifically for this purpose with prominent representatives of Western banks, industrial firms and states (in particular Belgium, the USA and France). They provided capital, dubious advice and bribes. The only beneficiaries were the investors, advisors, financiers and slush-money recipients who took part. The costs were borne by the Zairean state (as public authorities) and the mass of the population, which drew no benefit from the projects but was selected to work to service the debts which these projects required. Protest was brutally repressed.

The demand for foreign currency with which to enrich the ruling class and to service the country's external debt consolidated and tightened up Zaire's export structure, which had been pre-formed by colonialism and was largely monocultural. In 1985 almost 90% of Zaire's export proceeds came from the sale of five raw materials: copper, cobalt, crude oil, diamonds and coffee.

For several years an average of approximately two-thirds of the country's export earnings were generated by just one state-owned firm GECAMINES, which was born out of the 1967 nationalization of the colonial, private capitalist *Union Minière du Haut-Katanga.* Without this single-track orientation of Zaire's export economy, for which the self-enrichment and industrialization policies of the ruling class were responsible, external shocks would not have had such disastrous consequences.

This dependence on the world market was intensified by the IMF's management of the crisis between 1976 and 1987. The years of playing tug-of-war with the Fund (and the World Bank) over the terms of its rehabilitation policies manoeuvred the Mobuto regime into a potentially explosive conflict of interests (both socially and in terms of domestic policy) between:

- the creditors' right to interest and loan-capital (re)payments;
- the endeavours of the ruling class to line its own pockets; and
- the right of the disadvantaged and exploited mass of the population to an existence fit for human beings.

During this wrestling match the IMF helped to further the interests of the creditors in a punctual and regulated debt service by: imposing conditions aimed at liberalization of the domestic market and foreign trade; the restriction of government spending and of the budget deficit; the (re)privatization of state-owned firms; the checking of inflation; reductions in Zaire's current-account deficit and arrears; and the restructuring of the country's vast overseas

Table 22.3
Zaire: Export structure and major outlets (%)

	1970	1975	1980	1985	1987
Share of export proceeds:					
Copper	66	50	46	37	n.a.
Cobalt	6	11	17	13	n.a.
Diamonds	5	6	5	11	n.a.
Crude oil	–	–	10	17	n.a.
Coffee	5	6	7	10	n.a.
Major outlets:					
Belgium	52	41	50	32	37
USA + Canada	5	7	15	25	20
West Germany	6	7	5	12	11
Italy	11	15	6	8	11
France	8	7	5	5	6
Copper Price Index	100	43	49	39[a]	n.a.

[a] = 1983

Source: IMF; World Bank; own calculations.

liabilities. In addition, after 1978 the IMF attempted, through sources in the Zairean central bank, to curb administratively the private access of the ruling class to the country's foreign-currency reserves, although without much success. The ruling class still found enough loopholes to obstruct IMF control.

It was the underprivileged Zaireans who picked up the bill: urban waged and salaried workers in private firms, state-owned industry and the public authorities, whose real incomes were cut in order to give the regime room for manoeuvre, first for self-enrichment and then to meet the creditors' debt-servicing requirements; and the massive army of landless and (politically) uninfluential small farmers, whose surplus produce was creamed off to such an extent that the majority of the peasants retreated into a subsistence economy. The production strike of the peasants, provoked by the regime, resulted in a serious crisis in the domestic-foodstuffs sector and the export-led agricultural sector. This agricultural crisis stood at the heart of the development crisis. Unless the agricultural crisis can be resolved and a dynamic agricultural sector emerge, then attempts to find a solution to the debt crisis will inevitably remain a hotchpotch.

Recommended Reading

Körner, P., Maaß, G., Siebold, Th. and Tetzlaff, R. (1986) *The IMF and the Debt Crisis: A Guide to the Third World's Dilemma*, Zed Books.
World Bank (1985) *World Debt Tables*, Washington.

Part III
Epilogue and Glossary

Epilogue to the Second Edition

Elmar Altvater/Kurt Hübner

In 1988, after the crash of October 1987, the international debt crisis is entering its seventh year, and still there is no end in sight. Moreover, since the outbreak of the crisis in 1982, Third World indebtedness has almost doubled, from around US$640 billion to US$1,200 billion, even though in the period between 1984 and 1987 the poor debtor nations transferred capital with a net value of some US$95 billion to the rich countries of the First World. It is expected that in 1988 the total debt will rise to US$1,250 billion. Despite the fact that Africa's income from exports goes almost entirely on debt service, by the turn of the century the continent's current debt of around US$200 billion will have risen to at least US$500 billion.

Solutions or blind alleys?

For the foreseeable future it certainly cannot be expected that the indebted nations will be able to increase the production and transfer of loan capital and interest on their external debts. Restructuring will consequently continue to be necessary, although this has so far merely deferred the problem at the risk of intensification. Reducing the debts by means of loan-capital repayments would require transfers of capital quite different in dimension from those so far effected. Yet already per capita incomes in Latin America are on average 8–13% (estimates differ on this point) lower than in 1980; in the countries south of the Sahara the situation is worse still. 'The consequence', writes the World Bank in its *World Debt Tables* from the beginning of 1988, 'has been the backsliding of large sections of the population into poverty.' The 1980s? A decade of indebted impoverishment in the Third World.

Internally, the banks have already written off some or all of their loans to the Third World. Although no one outside the banks' closed circles is informed in any detail about the matter, well-founded suspicions suggest that this is the case. The World Bank, for instance, assumes that at the end of 1987 the 15 biggest US banks created provisions for 20–35% of their debts receivable from the Third World; for West German banks the figure is even thought to be 70%. In any case, it is certain that although the banks' debts receivable are still shown at their nominal value in the banks' balance sheets, internally they have not been included in the operating base at these values for a long time. One telling piece of evidence for this is to be found on the used-credit market, where the price of (bonded) Third World loans has been falling for some time: Brazilian debts receivable of US$100 now cost only US$39. One should not conclude from the fall in market prices for such loans that the debt crisis is already virtually solved. The marked difference between the market and nominal values of the debts receivable suggests that there is still a great deal of potential for damage to the international banking system, for the system could only undertake an immediate adjustment of its debts receivable to the market value if it were prepared to incur huge losses.

Today the major objective of the banks involved in the international debt crisis is still to gain time in which both to reduce the credit risks arising out of their dealings with the Third World through provisions and adjustments of value and to diversify those risks by exchanging debts receivable (through swap transactions of all kinds). This strategy is designed to maintain the flow of interest and, if possible, also loan-capital (re)payments, since this income, which has accounted for a large proportion of bank profits over the last few years, can itself be used to provide against risks.

The Mexico deal

The most recent Mexico deal, which has already been extolled by some commentators as the solution to the debt crisis, is a good example of this strategy at work. Indeed, half of Mexico's dollar debts (worth US$20 billion), which account for around a fifth of Mexico's total debt, are to be cancelled; in place of their old debts receivable the banks will receive new government bonds at half the value. This swap will be made palatable for them first by the somewhat higher interest rates receivable on the new debts (which will still mean Mexico paying less than she did at the lower interest rates charged on the original debt of US$20 billion); second, they may be tempted by the greater security, since the USA is guaranteeing to redeem money claims on Mexico when they fall due with the help of Zero Bonds. Mexico buys government bonds from the US Government today for US$2 billion; the interest on these bonds is then capitalized, so that at the end of their lives, after ten years, the USA has to pay exactly the US$10 billion which Mexico has to pay the banks.

The idea is clever, but limited. It was thought up by the Brazilians, who have a particular flair for a *jeito* (a little trick). Yet when Finance Minister Bresser Pereira himself arrived at the IMF conference in Washington in 1987 with the plan, it was classified as a non-starter by US Secretary of the Treasury James Baker. The reason for this unequal treatment of Mexico and Brazil is not difficult to discern: anyone can see that this solution is not possible for every US$1,200 billion debt, since not even the USA (in conjunction with Japan and West Germany) could extend the US$10 billion guarantee which she has granted the creditor banks to US$1,000 billion, or even half of that. No bank could take seriously the guarantee given on behalf of Mexico if it were extended to cover the total debt of every country.

Moreover, once limits have been specified then these must be exploited politically: Mexico is being rewarded for her previous good conduct as a debtor, and Brazil punished as a rebellious debtor which in February 1987 dared to declare a unilateral moratorium on interest payments. The Mexico deal may therefore be less of an ideal solution to the international debt crisis than yet another form of the divide and rule strategy which has been a lasting element of the policies pursued by the banks, governments and international institutions since the public outbreak of the debt crisis in August 1982.

The risks of limited crisis management

The Mexico deal illustrates another change in the way in which the crisis is being managed. At first glance it appears that the USA with her credit guarantee is willing once again to take on the role of lender of last resort. One might also suspect, quite rightly, however, that the US Government will use the case of Mexico to oblige the surplus countries in the capitalist world economy, namely West Germany and Japan, to similar guarantee transactions and in this way will raise more financial resources for crisis management. The Mexico deal may also help to draw other developed capitalist countries more firmly into the management of the crisis.

Nevertheless, limits have been set for even this limited reduction strategy, both by the debtors and the creditors. Although Mexico has rid herself of US\$10 million in debts, she has had to make concessions, and not only on the question of paying higher rates of interest on the smaller amount of credit. For several of the creditor banks, the adjustment in the value of debts worth US\$20 billion to half that amount is unproblematic because of the reserves which they have already built up. What happens, however, if the bank regulatory authorities demand that now all debts receivable from Mexico, or from other countries with which such a deal might be on the cards, should be corrected in the same way? Although the debt remission feared by many (and indeed supported by individual bankers such as Alfred Herrhausen) would then take place, it would not pass off without causing liquidity problems. The stock exchange crash of October 1987 may have greatly limited the scope for such market-based solutions. The fall in price of bank shares quoted on the stock exchange and the credit risks which arose for the banks in the course of the crash in respect of non-Third World customers have helped to reduce drastically the possibility of more provisions being created. For example, the British Midland Bank, which is involved in Third World business to the tune of US\$7 billion, ended 1987 with a loss of almost US\$1 billion. This was the result of losses on bond trading and the creation of provisions for Third World business.

A total or partial debt remission is now being demanded widely, not only by representatives of the debtor nations, and this demand is being made with reference to the fact that the banks have in fact already, as the 'second-hand market' price of debts receivable from the Third World proves, written off the vast majority of loans extended to Third World countries. Under no circumstances should we forget, however, that we are not talking merely about the size of the loans themselves. The income from interest is far more important to the banks, and at the moment that income is not there to enable the banks to pay interest to their depositors, not to mention the matter of bank profits. If income from interest is lost, then share prices will inevitably fall. From the point of view of the banks, possible solutions therefore revolve around how their credit risks can be reduced to a normal level, how the flow of interest from the countries on the periphery can be maintained at the highest possible level and how the banking system's dependence on receipts from the Third World can be reduced, or if possible eradicated, through the banks finding new customers, the debtors of the 1990s. In view of recent poor accumulation in the industrialized world, the search will not be an easy one, especially since the indebtedness of the public sector in the USA has reached its limits and some investments in such things as bonds and real estate have fallen in value as a result of the 1978 crash. Of course, even after a serious fall in value it is always possible to start again; the money has not been burned to ashes, merely damaged by the fire. However, the next debt crisis is already waiting in the wings: that of the USA, which has risen to the rank of the world's major net external debtor, with around US$400 billion in debts. The indebtedness of this supreme power now threatens the stability of international financial relations as much as, if not more than, the Third World debt crisis.

Despite the risks which the banks have faced, the international debt crisis has so far generally been good for business in the industrialized world. Nor is it only the banks which have profited. So too have importers and buyers of raw materials and other primary products from the Third World. They have been able to increase their profit margins substantially as a result of both the debt-induced pressure on the Third World to increase quantities and the related fall in prices on the international markets. Ultimately, the governments of the developed capitalist countries have also profited so far, for the fall in prices of raw materials has enabled them to take credit for successfully reducing the rate of inflation. Admittedly, there have been victims too in the industrialized world: exporters, since the debtor nations have not had the foreign currency to pay for imports; and those producers who have had to compete with goods from the debtor nations. It was, in fact, this front which prevailed upon US Senator Bill Bradley to call for a solution to the debt crisis: the sacrifices being made in some US industries were, and are, simply too great. It is also clear that the conflicts of interest which have arisen during the debt crisis have done so not only between creditors and debtor nations but also within the industrialized nations themselves: for example, between the financial sector and the export sector.

A word in favour of political regulation

What is the solution if swap transactions and the model Mexico deal either have too many disadvantages or are still not far-reaching enough to bring the debt crisis to its long-awaited end? However one looks at the problem, there is no chance of even a partial debt remission (for example, of the 'non-legitimate' part of the debt, as Castro describes it). Consequently, it is immaterial whether or not a debt reduction would mean that only the developing nations' ruling classes, which having erected the tower of debt now do not wish to go in, would be disencumbered. There are more meaningful measures which could be taken in order to make them responsible for their mistakes and their criminal acts than the maintenance of a debt obligation which is met primarily at the expense of the prospects for survival and development of the poor sections of their countries' population.

This immediately raises the question of who would bear the cost, for although debt remission is not a game in which one party can only win what another has lost and vice versa, there would nevertheless be losses. What is clear is that the banks should write off the Third World debts which have to date proved so profitable for them. Both Neo-Liberals like Milton Friedman and many solidarity groups on the Left are agreed on this demand. Yet such a strategy only makes sense if the use of bank provisions and bank profits to finance any write-offs is regulated, that is, politically controlled. This would necessarily require financing for banks whose solvency would be threatened by writing off debts, either through redistribution within the banking sector or possibly through public allocations. The fact that it is so difficult to find a solution to the debt crisis demonstrates the enormous need for regulation of the international credit system and the various national financial sectors. After the decades of Neo-Liberal deregulation, we must now consider again how the world economic system can be controlled politically in such a way that the next crisis will not be generated immediately a solution, of whatever kind, has been found for the present one.

Glossary

Adjustment of value: Every now and again banks have to assess their outstanding loans and give an account of their short-term and medium-term solvency. The rules governing the supervision of banks are different in each of the Western nations: in the USA loans have to be written-down (have their value adjusted) as 'non-performing' as soon as interest payments are overdue for longer than three months; in West Germany there is no such regulation.

ASEAN (Association of South-East Asian Nations): Founded in 1967 in order to promote co-operation, economic growth, social progress and political stability in five Southeast Asian states (including Thailand and the Philippines).

Austerity: According to a former chancellor of the exchequer in the British Labour Cabinet of 1948, Sir R. Stafford Cripps, the term describes a policy of 'extreme severity in budgeting'. Whereas in those days attention was focused on policies designed to fight inflation for the purposes of avoiding a devaluation in the currency, today the term is generally understood to cover all actions necessary to check upward trends in prices and costs by means of restrictive measures in both the national budget and wages policy. IMF conditions normally include elements of strict austerity.

Bail-out: The withdrawal, by commercial banks in particular, from previously profitable credit business with debtor nations. In general, it is the smaller banks, those for which only a small part of their total volume of business is lending to debtor nations, which bail-out, despite opposition from the big banks. For the developing nations bail-out means ever greater difficulty in obtaining fresh money.

Baker Plan: Named after US Secretary of the Treasury James Baker, who in the autumn of 1985 encouraged the joint annual meeting of the IMF and World Bank in Seoul to make available US$20 billion in new bank loans plus US$9 billion from Western governments and international institutions for a period of three years for the 15 (later 17) most heavily indebted nations. The condition imposed on access to this money was the willingness to implement reforms of the kind favoured by the IMF: privatization of state-owned concerns, encouragement of investment from abroad, liberalization of trade, and austerity programmes. The developing nations criticized the plan, saying that it

244 Glossary and Epilogue

did not adequately meet the indebted nations' liquidity requirements and therefore gave an exclusively monetary response to a structural problem.

Balance of payments: The balance of payments combines all domestic and foreign-trade transactions, commercial transactions relating either to goods (trade balance) and services (balance of services, including interest service). These two part-balances combine to make the current account, which gives details of real performance. Capital transactions appear either in the balance of long-term or short-term capital transactions, depending on the period over which the transaction extends. The difference between the balance of capital transactions and the current-account balance is represented by a change in the value of a country's stock of foreign exchange (gold, dollars, SDRs — balance of foreign-exchange payments). The balance of payments always balances in book-keeping terms; it is the balances of its component parts which indicate possible foreign-trade imbalances.

BIS (Bank for International Settlements): An international institution founded in 1930 and entrusted primarily with the task of managing German reparation payments. Its headquarters is in Basle. All of the European issuing banks (except those of the GDR, the USSR and Albania) and the central banks of the USA, Japan, Canada, Australia and South Africa have since joined. The BIS promotes co-operation between the central banks and assumes fiduciary relationships or acts as a representative for international financial agreements. In 1982 the BIS played an important part in temporarily warding off Mexico's inability to pay her debts.

B-loans: B-loans are granted to Third World nations by private commercial banks and linked to the transactions of the World Bank. B-loans can be of two sorts: bank loans which are part of a World Bank loan package and which only become payable at a later point in time; and bank sureties covering amortization instalments on World Bank loans. For the developing nations B-loans have the advantage that they do not preclude the recipient from continuing to obtain private loans; for the banks the risk involved in granting loans is reduced, because loans are linked with World Bank programmes.

BMwZ (Bundesministerium für Wirtschaftliche Zusammenarbeit): The West German Federal Ministry for Economic Co-operation is responsible for West German development aid and policy. For several years this aid has been shifting more and more away from the poorest nations of the Third World towards the already partially industrialized (NICs). The BMwZ has been criticized for this, since it illustrates a trend towards giving less priority to development aid and more to both the procurement of financial concessions for West German exporters and making development-aid payments conditional upon the purchase of West German goods.

Board of Governors: The senior committee of the IMF. The Board of Governors rules on whether to accept would-be new members, sets membership quotas and allocates SDRs. In general, IMF members are represented on the Board of

Governors by the minister responsible for monetary policy or by the president of their issuing bank.

Bond: A mortgage debenture, a stock at a fixed rate of interest.

Bretton Woods system: Created in 1944 under the Bretton Woods Agreement, it became the basis of the international monetary order in the period after World War II. The agreement was shaped largely by ideas put forward by the USA (as set out in the White Plan) and was a mark of that country's position as the world's strongest economic and political power, and most powerful creditor nation at the time. The 45 nations which joined the IMF, which was established at Bretton Woods, agreed to fix an exchange rate to be maintained by national monetary authorities through the application of interventionist monetary and economic policy measures (for example, the restoration of equilibrium to the balance of payments). The US dollar took on the role of the world currency and could, in principle, be converted on the basis of a guarantee issued by the US Government against gold (US\$35 = 1 ounce). It was the job of the IMF to see that the rules were observed and make available agreed amounts of credit to countries which faced short-term balance of payments problems.

Cartagena Group: The first meeting of the Latin American debtor nations took place in June 1984 in Cartagena, Columbia. The countries involved subsequently formed themselves into the Cartagena Group. Although the Western press regarded this union as a move towards a debtors' cartel, the federation has so far functioned instead as a forum for discussion of the member countries' large variety of interests and views as these apply to the solution of the debt crisis.

CEPAL (Comisión Económica para América Latina) — ECLA (Economic Commission for Latin America): In terms of development policy and strategy, this commission is the most influential of the economic commissions (for Europe, Asia and Africa) of the UN.

Chicago School: The School, which is resident at the University of Chicago, was founded by Frank H. Knight in the 1920s. Its guiding light was Nobel Prize winner and leading Neo-Liberal monetarist ideologue, Milton Friedman. Representatives of this School exercised a great deal of practical political influence over the economic policies of the Pinochet dictatorship in Chile ('Chicago boys'), and the Chicago credo of 'freeing up market forces' in order to speed up economic growth has been pursued also in other Latin American countries. The School has taken a leading role in the economic-policy debates conducted in the industrialized nations since the 'change of paradigm from Keynesianism to monetarism'.

COMECON (Council for Mutual Assistance): An Eastern Bloc organization founded in 1949 to co-ordinate economic development within its member states: the members of the Warsaw Pact organizations, Cuba, Vietnam, Mongolia and (to a limited extent) Yugoslavia.

Comparative Cost, Theory of: In 1776, Adam Smith illustrated that the well-being of a nation increased if it had absolute cost advantages in international trade. On the other hand, the Theory of Comparative Cost, elaborated by David Ricardo in 1817, maintains that international trade itself brings (cost) advantages for all countries taking part if one country has absolute cost disadvantages in its production of all traded goods and another therefore has absolute cost advantages — since the specialization in the production of all traded goods which takes place as a result of international trade offers trading partners the opportunity to employ the factors of production in such a way that fewer units of product X have to be given for product Y if it is bought abroad than if it is produced domestically. The precondition for realizing the advantages is an appropriate flow of money (between the trading partners) which causes the level of prices to fall (for the partner with the higher production costs) or rise (for the partner with comparatively lower production costs). The theory has been developed further since its conception, but also criticized: it has always been used to justify the advantages of free trade as opposed to nationalist isolation or other forms of state intervention.

Comptroller of the Currency: In the private sector this is the chartered accountant or chief accountant. In the USA it is the authorities responsible for supervising the banks and which make up the Fed.

Conditionality: The conditions placed upon the granting of IMF loans (IMF conditions). The type of conditionality depends on the type of drawing and becomes stricter the more a country's drawings exceed its quota.

Convertibility: A currency is convertible if it is exchangeable freely and without restriction at the effective exchange rate. At the moment, around a third of the member countries of the IMF have freely convertible currencies. The rest have currencies which are convertible to a limited extent.

Country lending-exposure service: The classification of the risks involved in granting loans to a country by the lenders according to that country's previous record on raising debt service, economic growth, inflationary trends and export strength. The worse the classification, the more expensive the loans (the higher the spread or surcharge over and above the normal interest rate).

Credit facility (see *Facility*)

Crony capitalism: The specific variant of favouritism practised in the Philippines under Marcos under which preference was consciously given to certain individuals, especially to businessmen who were not particularly successful but who were granted monopolies in key areas of the economy after the imposition of martial law in 1972.

Cross-default clause: The undertaking given by a borrower to a creditor that he will not fall into arrears with other loans granted by third parties. Any default may be seen by a creditor, even one who is not directly affected, as a default on agreed payments and as grounds for calling his own loans in.

Current Account (see *Balance of payments*)

Cut and run: The tendency of smaller commercial banks to disengage from credit commitments, in particular to heavily indebted nations, despite the cost of withdrawal, on the grounds that the risks of continuing and the cost of making available fresh money are estimated to be still greater.

Debt ratio: The relationship between a country's total external debt and GDP or exports.

Debt service ratio: Generally, the relationship between a country's interest and/or loan capital (re)payments on external debts and that country's income from exports. From the creditor's point of view, the ratio illustrates a debtor nation's capacity to transfer debt service, and from the debtor's point of view it illustrates the level of domestic vulnerability: the higher the ratio, the more vulnerable the country, the lower the ratio, the more capable that country is of servicing its debts.

Debt-equity-swap/scheme: Describes the practice of converting external debts into equity capital (shares) in the domestic concerns of an indebted country. By participating, the lending bank takes a share in the risk. Conversions of this kind have been tried out (since profitable equity capital to the value of the external debt is not generally available) in various Latin American countries with moderate success, and PINs (Philippine Investment Notes) have been offered on the capital markets in the Philippines since 1987. These enable interested parties to buy up Filipino concerns with foreign currency.

De-industrialization: The term describes a fall in the level of industrial output and employment. In a number of indebted countries de-industrialization and 'distorted industrialization' have been caused by an excessive burden of debt service, which not only limits the consumption of the masses and the state but also means that investment and even vital imports have to be cut if the country concerned is to realize a balance of trade surplus.

Dependency theory: Developed in Latin America in the late 1960s as a response to failed attempts at modernization in that region and the shortcomings of CEPAL's concept of *desarrollismo*. According to Theotonio dos Santos, the theory describes the underdevelopment and dependence of the periphery as a result of the structural influence of the metropole. In the course of capitalist expansion all domestic markets are internalized and therefore subjugated to the economically superior and politically all-powerful societies of the centre (penetration of the periphery by developed capital from the metropole). As a result of the structural heterogeneity caused from outside in this way, the dependent societies lack internal forces capable of transforming under-development into development. Attempts have been made to overcome these internal obstructions through the concept of the modes of production and the way in which they are connected. The political consequences of the theory have been seen in the alliances which peasants and the proletariat have forged in the hope of a socialist revolution. The leading exponents of the approach are

André Gunder Frank, Fernando Henrique Cardoso, Enzo Faletto and Roger Bartra.

desarrollismo: (from *desarrollo* — development). Describes a theoretical concept which was elaborated in the late 1950s and early 1960s within CEPAL, particularly under the leadership of its Argentinian director, Raúl Prebisch. Underdevelopment in Latin America was regarded as being disadvantageous for the periphery in terms of the structures of free world trade and the changing terms of trade. It was held that the negative influence of the world market should be countered with national import-substitution policies combined with major land reforms and a redistribution of income in favour of the poor population. It was expected that an expansion in the domestic market as a result of the increased purchasing power of the rural and poor urban population would generate a stronger, internal process of development.

Deutsche Bundesbank (DBB): Established by statute in 1957 as West Germany's issuing bank in succession to the Bank Deutscher Länder. It determines monetary and credit policy through its various organs (the Central Bank Council, the Board of Directors, and the management committees of the Land Central Banks). In this respect it is subject neither to the instructions of the federal government nor to parliamentary control. However, the Bank does co-ordinate its policies with the economic policies of the federal government, and the president and the directors are appointed at the suggestion of the federal government. The Bank's top policy priority is to secure the domestic and international value of the DM ('guardian of the currency'). The DBB is a member of BIS and both enjoys the rights and meets the obligations arising out of West Germany's membership of the IMF.

Development Committee: A joint committee of the World Bank and the IMF which, according to the function allocated to it by the governors of both institutions, is concerned with the question of transferring resources to the developing nations. The 20 members of the committee are nominated in the same way as the IMF's and World Bank's executive directors.

Dollar standard: (see *Gold standard)*

*ECLA (*see *CEPAL)*

EFF (Extended Fund Facility): In 1974 the recognition that the balance of payments deficits sustained by the developing nations' during the 1970s as a result of rises in the price of oil could only be eradicated in the medium to long term prompted the IMF to establish the EFF. This increased the member nations' scope for drawing credit from 125–140% of their shareholding. The facility was important too for the fact that it extended the period within which applications for loans could be submitted from the normal one year to two or three years.

Equity: A firm's own capital funds or share capital.

Euromarkets: International credit markets where transactions are effected in foreign currencies which do not have the status of central bank currencies. Only sight deposits are traded. The Eurodollar market, a market for dollar loans outside the USA's currency area, developed when convertibility restrictions were lifted at the end of the 1950s. Today all major world currencies are traded on the Euromarkets. People talk in terms of a Eurotransaction when, for example, a German bank in Luxemburg runs a dollar account for a non-American customer or grants the customer a dollar loan. Originally, the banks which operated in the Euromarkets were concentrated in London or Luxemburg, but the expansion of the international credit business and the deregulation of national banking systems have meant that participants are now just as likely to be found in New York, the Bahamas and other off-shore locations, or in Hong Kong or Singapore (free banking zones). The monies sold on the Euromarkets are described as Eurodollars, Euro-DM, and so on.

EIB (European Investment Bank): Founded in 1958 as part of the EC with its headquarters in Luxemburg. Its functions include encouraging a balanced expansion in the Common Market through the granting of loans to concerns or to states associated with the EC.

EPU (European Payments Union): Predecessor of the European Monetary Agreement. The EPU was established in 1950 with the aim of both facilitating the liberalization of trade between the OECD countries by enabling them to settle their balance of payments surpluses and deficits and of reintroducing convertibility. This was effected in 1958; the EPU was dissolved by the European Monetary Agreement.

Export production zones (free industry zones): These have sprung up in a number of developing countries as a result of the development of a New International Division of Labour since roughly the end of the 1960s. They are part of the global production processes operated by transnational concerns whereby manufacturing stages which are labour-intensive or which entail heavy labour costs are relocated in Third World countries in order to cut costs. In this way even underdeveloped countries are incorporated into the global process of industrialization, although admittedly in a subordinate role and through the formation of enclaves whose spread in their economies is, in fact, generally negative rather than stimulating. Export production zones are characterized by inadequate socio-political protection for the workers, largely unregulated working conditions, union-free areas and therefore low labour costs and a lack of environmental regulations, tax concessions and the possibility of profit repatriation ('bloody Fordism'). (See *World-wide sourcing*).

Facility: Refers to the various types of credit available to the individual member countries from the IMF. Facilities have been established for various purposes and now enable non-crude-oil producers among the developing nations to borrow up to 600% of their original quotas. In view of the fact that a large part of world trade is transacted in just a few hard currencies, it is important for countries to be able to obtain the hard currency which they need. The credits provided by the IMF are therefore not denominated in the currency used to pay the recipient's quota, but have to be effected in one of the major trading currencies, that is in a currency in which obligations, for example to exporters abroad, can be settled.

Factoring: The sale of debts receivable at a discount (assessed according to the 'goodness' of the debt) to firms which settle the debt on behalf of the debtor. Although these firms bear the risk of possibly not being able to redeem the loans, they also make hefty profits in the form of interest, since the debtor has to pay interest on the face-value of the debt.

FAKTURIERUNG: The setting of the terms (for example, the currency) under which an international commercial transaction is to be conducted.

Fed., the (Federal Reserve System): The central bank of the USA, consisting of 12 federal banks. Around 40% of all US banks are members and responsible for underwriting the Fed.'s original capital.

Floating: Used to describe flexible exchange rates which are determined by supply and demand on the foreign-exchange markets without monetary authorities being obliged to intervene by buying or selling. In 1973, after the collapse of the fixed exchange-rate system set up at Bretton Woods, it was expected that floating the exchange rates would result in the development of stable and fair market rates. However, because of the enormous volume of international liquid resources traded on the international credit markets (more than US$200 billion daily), the rates are subject to repeated erratic fluctuations.

Fordism: An analytical term for a historically specific capitalist development of society which is characterized by a close connection between mass production and mass consumption and which creates specific cultural patterns and forms of social regulation. The basis of Fordism is considered to be steady rates of increase in worker productivity and real wages. Originating in the USA, this model of social development spread to Europe in nationally modified forms after World War II; it is possible to find forms of peripheral Fordism in some Third World countries, for example South Korea, Brazil.

Foreign-exchange control: A method of managing foreign exchange with the aim of stabilizing the exchange rate, and which the countries of the Third World, for example, often introduce in order to prevent both capital from leaving the country and speculation in foreign exchange.

Free trade: The principle of free trade provides for the creation of economic relations between countries which are similar to those found within a domestic market. Accordingly, international trade should be hampered neither by customs duties, quotas or taxes, nor by other regulatory instruments. The theory of foreign trade regards a world economy based on free trade as an opportunity to improve the well-being of all of the economies which are integrated into the world market. Every national economy would specialize in those products which it could produce most cheaply (see *Theory of Comparative Cost*). Free trade as a principle by which to order the world economy is, however, contradictory: participation in the process of the international division of labour brings with it forfeiture of national autonomy, which could have disadvantageous effects on individual sectors of a country's economy or even on entire economies.

Fresh money: New money, loans mobilized for indebted nations which are in danger of becoming short of liquid assets in order to enable them to pay debt service ('throwing good money after bad').

Futures: Transactions which provide for the purchase and delivery of goods or bonds at a future date (generally after three or six months), but which are effected at the rates or prices in use on the day when the contract is concluded.

G-10 (Group of Ten): Signatories to the General Agreement to Borrow (GAB): Belgium, Canada, France, Great Britain, Italy, Japan, the Netherlands, Sweden, the USA and West Germany. Later extended to Denmark, Eire and Luxemburg.

G-77 (Group of 77): Afro-Asian and Latin American developing nations organized in UNCTAD which joined together to form the G-77 and whose list of members now contains 109 UNCTAD Third World states. G-10 and G-77 are not the only such unions. Other groups of countries with different viewpoints have also joined forces to form the G-5 (the richest industrialized nations, which since 1975 have held regular economic summits), the G-7 (G-5 plus Canada and Italy), G-24 and G-30.

GAB (General Agreement to Borrow): Concluded in 1962 between the ten leading industrialized nations (G-10) and the IMF. It provides that, if necessary, the signatories will make available to the IMF at short notice around 6 billion SDRs in their own currencies over a period of five years for a country with balance of payments problems. The GAB is an attempt to mobilize government liquid resources as opposed to the increasing volume of private liquid resources on international capital markets since the establishment of currency convertibility in order to defend the exchange rates of currencies against which there is a lot of speculation.

GATT (General Agreement on Tariffs and Trade): Signed in 1947 and intended to supplement the monetary order established at Bretton Woods with a world-trade order (Havana Charter). In its final form, however, it was no more than a loose agreement on the achievement of a world-wide liberalization of trade policy. Quotas and overt export promotion were banned. The GATT principle of the most favoured nation (trading advantages granted to one country should also apply to all other member states) was jeopardized by a multitude of different forms of non-tariff obstructions to trade, especially in the industrialized nations.

GDP (Gross Domestic Product): The value (in the national currency) of the total goods and services produced by a country in the course of a year. In order to avoid double counting, the value of primary products is subtracted from the gross output value. The GDP includes all write-offs. If these are taken into account then the result is the Net Domestic Product at market prices. Whereas the GDP counts only domestic transactions, the GNP contains transfers of income to and from abroad. If indirect taxes are subtracted from and subsidies added to GNP (at market prices) the result is GNP at factor costs, and this is identical to the national income.

Gold convertibility: The exchangeability, as a matter of principle, of US dollars for gold through the US issuing bank at fixed and guaranteed parities. Gold–dollar convertibility existed until 1971.

Gold standard: A monetary system in which the world currency must be convertible into gold at a fixed parity. The other currencies are also tied either to gold or to the world currency. Attempts were made to establish a monetary system of this kind after World War I (at the Conference of Genoa in 1922) with sterling as the world currency. It only functioned for a few years and had to be abandoned as early as 1931. The Bretton Woods monetary system is also described as the gold standard, since only one national currency (the dollar) officially performed the function of a world currency. The abandonment of gold–dollar convertibility in August 1971 therefore meant the abandonment of the gold standard.

GNP (Gross National Product) — see *GDP*

Hermes Guarantee: Export-credit guarantees provided by the Hermes Kreditversicherungs-AG, founded in 1917. The concern grants export guarantees and export securities on behalf of the West German Government in order to make the economic and political risks, for example the irretrievability of debts receivable, more calculable for individual exporters.

HWWA (Hamburger Welt-Wirtschafts-Archiv): Now the *Institut für Wirtshaftsforschung*. An economic science research institute founded in 1908 which specializes in economic systems and policies, development policy and international monetary policy.

IDB (Inter-American Development Bank): A finance institute founded in 1959 under the auspices of the Organization of American States (OAS) and which grants economic and technical assistance for development projects in Latin America. Some of its members are non-American, for example West Germany and Japan.

IFC (International Finance Corporation): A sister organization of the World Bank. It promotes private-sector economic initiatives in the developing nations by creating favourable conditions for private investment. The IFC only undertakes part-financing of private investment projects if insufficient private capital is available on suitable terms.

Import substitution: In general the replacement of imports by products which are the result of domestic production built up during the course of industrial development. Import substitution is thus an industrialization strategy and was used in Latin America during the 1930s and in the Southeast Asian NICs in particular after World War I.

Informal sector: A term coined by the International Labor Organization (ILO) in a study on the labour market in Kenya at the beginning of the 1970s and which was used to define, in a negative sense, all employment relationships other than formal ones (with a contract of employment and standard remuneration for regular hours). Positive definitions of the informal sector are still controversial. It is equated often with such terms as shadow economy, black economy, work done 'on the side', underground economy and moonlighting. Studies on informal employment relationships in Third World countries indicate: that employees switch regularly between the formal and the informal sector, with the result that demarcation problems arise; the predominance of the small business economic form; and a high degree of dependence on the market. Unlike formal work, subsistence labour, very often done by women, does not produce for the market but for the family organization or district. Subsistence labour is, as a rule, a prerequisite for the existence of the informal sector and this, as a supplier of cheap primary products, is in turn a precondition for the profitability of the capitalist-dominated formal sector.

Institute of International Finance: Washington-based, founded in 1982 and financed by numerous private bankers and international monetary specialists. The think tank of the commercial banks. In 1984, 189 commercial banks belonged to the institute, of which around a third were US banks.

Interest earned and payable: The various rates of interest earned/charged by the banks. The lower is the rate paid on money deposited with the banks and the higher the rate charged on money lent by them. The difference is known as the spread. This is the basis for the profits earned from banking operations and gives banks the ability to create reserves and provisions.

Joint venture: Ventures undertaken jointly by domestic and foreign business partners.

Keynesianism: Describes an economic policy programme (or model) which is based on the work published by John Maynard Keynes in 1936: *The General Theory of Employment, Interest and Money*. In this, Keynes substantiates the theory that a capitalist society can be in balance even where there is underemployment, and maintains that full employment can be achieved only with the help of government measures known as deficit spending in both the field of investment and in consumption expenditure. The starting point for anti-cyclical control through economic policy is 'effective demand'. In the wider sense, Keynesianism also describes a 'compromise between the classes'. The state has the task of maintaining full employment, but the trades unions, like the state, forego intervention in the autonomy of entrepreneurs to make investment decisions which suit them. During the period between World War II and the beginning of the 1970s, until the change of paradigm to monetarism (see *Monetarism*), Keynesianism was the undisputed guiding concept of national and international economic policy in the Western industrialized nations.

Keynes Plan: Put forward in 1943 as the British contribution to the reform of the international monetary order. It provided for stable exchange rates, convertibility and control over the movement of capital. In addition, it suggested multilateral clearing (an international equalization of the balance of payments) through a clearing union, with settlement being effected in an artificial currency, the bancor. Particularly important was the planned regulation under which surpluses would be devalued over time (negative rates of interest) in order to force countries with balance of trade surpluses to repeatedly transform their reserves into demand with international purchasing power. The Keynes Plan was not able to win support away from the US White Plan.

*Laissez-faire (*also *laissez-passer)*: Dates back to the liberal economic theory of the nineteenth century which demanded far-reaching restrictions on the activities of the state in economic matters. *Laissez-faire* is based on the conviction that humans are active chiefly in their own interests and that there are natural rules which create harmony through the operation of the 'invisible hand' of the market. If individuals were left to themselves to pursue their interests (producing, buying and selling) then everyone would profit from the result. The laws of supply and demand would ensure the best use (allocation) of capital and labour. Historically, *laissez-faire* was an expression of a new form of individualism geared to industry and which in the sixteenth century turned against church and state interference in the economy and trade.

Lender of last resort: The last lender willing to lend, that is an institution, such as an issuing bank, which provides the national economy with money through the commercial banking system and which, for example, discounts acceptance credits drawn upon the commercial banks by businesses. In this way the issuing bank is able, to a limited extent, to regulate the amount of money and credit in circulation (discount policy, open-market policy and minimum-reserve policy). On the international money and credit markets there is no official lender of last resort and therefore no authority capable of controlling the international credit system in the same way as national monetary and credit systems are controlled.

*Letter of intent (*see *Stabilization programme)*

LIBOR (London Inter-bank Offer Rate): The interest rate at which banks lend each other money; more precisely, the interest rate at which one bank is prepared to deposit Eurodollars with another for a period normally lasting three or six months. After the USA's prime rate, LIBOR is the key rate on the basis of which interest rates are set in the international debt and credit business. The surcharge (spread) added to LIBOR depends on the period over which debts are to be repaid, the reliability of the debtor and the risks involved in dealing with the country in question.

LIFFE (London International Financial Futures Exchange): A market for financial futures, established in 1982.

LLDCs (least developed countries): Often also known as the Fourth World. GDP per head stands at less than US$250, the proportion of GDP accounted for by industrial output at less than 10% and the rate of literacy at under 20%. At present, 36 countries are covered by this definition, which was suggested by the World Bank.

Low Income Countries: According to the World Bank, low income countries are defined as those with per capita incomes of less than US$405. The list of such countries contains Afghanistan, India and Zaire.

Metrodollar: The money capital deposited with internationally-operating banks by the business sector of the developed capitalist nations. The term was created in analogy to the Petrodollar and refers to the fact that since the 1970s the business sector of the OECD countries has been the major net depositor in the Eurobanking system.

Middle Income Countries: According to the World Bank definition, these are countries with a per capita income of more than US$405 (using 1981 dollar levels).

MIGA (Multilateral Investment Guarantee Agency): Founded in 1985 by the governments of various developed and underdeveloped nations. Its function is to promote overseas investment in the developing nations; it guarantees non-commercial, that is basically political risks.

Monetarism (see *Chicago School*)

Moratorium: Temporary suspension by a country of its debt service payments (interest and/or loan capital).

MYRA (Multi-Year Rescheduling Agreement): A rescheduling agreement which extends over several years (rather than just a few months).

Net exporter of capital: The fact that a country is a net exporter of capital signifies that the value of that country's short- and long-term capital investments abroad is greater than the capital investment in that country from abroad at the same point in time. One of the common characteristics of a leading nation is that it exports more short- and long-term capital than it imports, in order in this way to make available liquid funds and credit to the world economy. The USA until the beginning of the 1980s was a classic example.

NICs (Newly Industrialized Countries): Third World countries with a relatively developed industrial structure, for example South Korea, Taiwan, Singapore, Yugoslavia, Argentina or Brazil, and whose industrial goods are competitive on the world market. Examples are South Korean shipbuilding, electronic goods from Taiwan, Brazilian arms and Indian steel products.

ODA (Official Development Assistance): Can either be bilateral (between two countries) or multilateral (effected through international organizations such as the World Bank and the IFC). In the industrialized nations, development assistance is regarded as any measure designed to stimulate the developing nations in the economic, social and cultural spheres. West Germans tend to talk less of development aid and more of economic co-operation, which corresponds with the name of the ministry responsible (the BMwZ) in that country. West Germany, like almost every other industrialized nation, has never achieved the target set by the UN whereby the industrialized nations are supposed to make 0.7% of their GNPs available in the form of development aid.

OECD (Organization for Economic Co-operation and Development): Evolved out of the Organization for European Economic Co-operation (OEEC) in 1960 and is based in Paris. It is the Western industrialized nations' advisory and co-ordinating body on almost all economic, budgetary and monetary policy matters (compilation of analyses, information exchange, advice and joint recommendations).

Oil facility: Special drawing opportunities introduced in 1974 by the IMF as a result of rises in the price of oil and which were intended to make it easier for non-crude-oil producers among the developing nations to finance current account deficits caused by the rise in price of crude oil. The oil facility existed until 1976.

Paris Club: An informal body based in Paris. It gathers together representatives of the major Western lending countries (which are essentially the same countries as belong to G-10) at the request of a debtor nation in order to discuss debt service difficulties, and possibly to negotiate restructuring and its terms. The role of the Paris Club in restructuring or promising new credit has increased since the beginning of the debt crisis. One reason for its importance is that the countries which are represented there also have a majority of the votes in the IMF.

Petrodollar: The extra funds earned by the OPEC states in the 1970s as a result of increases in the price of crude oil and which they deposited with the private Eurobanks. Having no use for the enormously increased dollar income from oil exports on the import side of their trade balances, the 'oil and sand states' (W. Hankel) of the Middle East became major exporters of capital. The way in which the Eurobanks recycled the Petrodollar was regarded as a great achievement. The funds were transformed into loans for the Third World and used also by international organizations such as the IMF.

Portfolio: The financial investments held by private firms. These might include shares, investment certificates and bonds, as well as other bonded debts. Firms aim to amass an optimal portfolio by balancing liquidity, risks and profits.

Principal: Original capital or capital investment, also the face-value of a bond without accrued interest.

Revenue: Income, takings.

SAL (Structural Adjustment Loan): A loan granted by the World Bank but comparable in its function and terms to the structural adjustment facility (see *Structural adjustment programme*) of the IMF.

SDRs (Special Drawing Rights): SDRs were created at the end of the 1960s in order to relieve the dollar of its role as the world currency. They serve as reserves for the central banks, and balances between countries can be settled with them through the appropriate issuing banks. SDRs play virtually no role at all in commercial transactions. As a unit of account, they are valued by reference to a basket of currencies containing the US dollar, the DM, the yen, the French franc and the pound sterling. SDR assets can be exchanged for hard currency through the appropriate issuing banks, international monetary institutions and some development banks. The allocation of SDRs is related to the quotas paid by IMF members, who have the right to draw foreign exchange without conditions either through the IMF or directly from other central banks for the temporary financing of balance of payments deficits up to the value of the SDRs allocated to them.

Secondary market: The market for bonds or unbonded debts owed by indebted nations and which are already in circulation. (See *factoring*)

Speculation in foreign exchange: Speculation on the foreign-exchange market. That is monetary transactions the aim of which is to exploit differences in interest rates or exchange rates on the various markets or over a period of time (forward business). The growth in volumes traded on the international financial markets and the higher profitability of financial capital compared to productive invested capital (especially in conjunction with trends in the dollar rate and international interest rates at the beginning of the 1980s) stimulated speculation in foreign exchange. It is now not only foreign-exchange dealers who participate, but also and increasingly the large transnational concerns (speculative losses of Volkswagen).

*Spread (*or *margin) (*see *LIBOR)*

Stabilization programme: A package of economic policy measures accepted by IMF borrowers in a Letter of Intent and which is generally based on suggestions put forward by the IMF. The implementation of a stabilization programme is always a precondition for obtaining stand-by credits from the IMF or fresh money from the private banks, which means that indebted nations have hardly any choice as to the economic policy measures contained in the programmes. As a rule, these are geared towards improving a country's foreign-trade position in order to eradicate an imbalance in the balance of payments. Of crucial importance here is the fight against inflation, which according to IMF estimates is essentially the result of excessive budget deficits and excess demand caused by real incomes which are too high. The IMF rarely discusses structurally-caused imbalances in North–South economic relations, for example the worsening of the terms of trade and the increased need for funds which is associated with this. The instruments with which the IMF attempts to eradicate imbalances can be divided into foreign- and domestic-trade policy measures. Foreign-trade measures include: the devaluation of the currency in order to boost exports and reduce imports; the limiting of credit from abroad and the setting of upper limits for new loans; the restriction of imports, for example by setting a scale of priorities; and increases in the level of interest rates in order both to discourage capital from leaving the country and to stimulate its import. Domestic-trade policy measures can be: conditions relating either to monetary policy (such as compliance with upper limits for increases in the money supply and limits on government spending in order to reduce the deficit) or to budgetary policy (including the withdrawal of subsidies and social-welfare benefits); increases in the charges levied for public services; and the freeing-up of administered prices (such as the withdrawal of subsidies on foodstuffs). Furthermore, there are generally conditions relating to wages policy which are designed to reduce the level of wages. A number of Third World countries have put up resistance to IMF stabilization programmes, some of which have even led to 'IMF revolts'.

Stand-by arrangement: With the Stand-by Agreement of 1968 the IMF created a budgetary policy instrument of intervention and sanction for use in its dealings with countries seeking credit. A stand-by arrangement is a prerequisite for any agreement between the IMF (and therefore other potential lenders) and member countries which need loans. A stand-by agreement, whose conditionality is determined by the Board of Directors of the IMF, contains the obligation of the Fund to make foreign-currency loans available over a period of one to three years, and a Letter of Intent from the country concerned, in which that country commits itself to applying a catalogue of measures intended to eradicate its balance of payments deficit. Since loans are paid in instalments under the phasing system, the IMF is able to check adherence to the budgetary, monetary and exchange-rate policy target dates and if necessary effect a cancellation of further payments. For heavily indebted nations the granting of official and private loans is always tied to the conclusion of a stand-by agreement. These are thus the vehicles used to enforce IMF conditionality.

Structural adjustment programme: A facility established by the IMF in March 1986 in order to help low-income developing countries with balance of payments difficulties on particularly easy terms. Between 1985 and 1991, 2.7 billion SDRs are to be made available under this facility.

Subsistence labour (see informal sector)

Swaps: In general, these are financial transactions by means of which debts receivable from third parties can be exchanged or sold at a discount. By swapping debts receivable, the banks are able to spread their credit risks by distributing their debts receivable between several countries. Among the best known swap transactions are debt-equity swaps.

Syndicated loans: A Euro-currency loan made available jointly by several banks. Usually the sums involved are large (US$1 billion or more) and granted to a single customer.

Terms of trade: In general: the relationship between import and export prices or the relationship indicated by the actual quantity of a country's exports which have to be given in return for a certain quantity of imports. Calculation of the terms of trade is based on a comparison between export and import price indices: if import prices rise and export prices remain constant or fall, or if export prices fall and import prices remain constant, then the terms of trade worsen, because fewer goods can be imported for the same quantity of exports, and vice versa. The terms of trade have worsened for a whole series of developing nations as a result of the fall in the price of many raw materials; measured against the price of manufactured goods, raw-materials prices were just as low in 1986 as they were after the world economic crisis in the 1930s. Consequently, many raw-materials-exporting developing nations have found their development options seriously threatened.

Trade balance (see *balance of payments*)

Trilateral Commission: A body inspired in 1972 by a then professor of political sciences and later security advisor to Jimmy Carter, Brzezinzski, which in 1973 brought together for the first time the economic and political élites of North America, Western Europe and Japan in order to discuss international management of the Western world's 'crises of democracy'. The commission meets once a year and in 1987 concerned itself, among other things, with the debt crisis. Its political significance was, however, blunted with the rise of Thatcherism and Reaganomics.

UN or *UNO*: United Nations (Organization)

UNCTAD (United Nations Conference on Trade and Development): The organization within the General Assembly of the United Nations whose task it is to promote world trade and economic development. Unlike GATT, UNCTAD also calls for *dirigiste* intervention in world trade and market structures in the belief, for example, that fixed raw-materials prices (raw-materials agreements) could help to stabilize export proceeds. The New World Economic Order proposed repeatedly by G-77 within UNCTAD has, however, never materialized because of opposition from the industrialized nations.

UNIDO (United Nations Industrial Development Organization): Founded in 1967 by the General Assembly of the United Nations to promote the industrialization of the developing nations. UNIDO designs industrial-development programmes and advisory plans relating to information, education and research. Its declared aim (defined at the UNIDO conference in Lima in 1975) of increasing the Third World's share of world industrial output to 25% is being placed in jeopardy by the de-industrialization caused by the debt crisis.

White Plan (see *Keynes Plan, Bretton woods system*)

World-wide sourcing: The world-wide reorganization of capitalist production, which exploits differences in the cost of workers and other resources and tends towards the creation of a world market for production sites. The aim of such a business strategy is to cut production costs and increase flexibility without altering any other commercial parameters. One result of the strategy is world-market-oriented part-industrialization in the countries of the Third World ('new international division of labour').

Chronology of the Debt Crisis (1980–87)

US$13.8 billion restructured between 1975 and 1980

1980
War breaks out between Iran and Iraq
Interest rates: 15%
Total third world foreign debt: US$573 billion
World raw materials price (1975 = 100): 280

1981
The price of crude oil begins to fall
IMF drawing rights are extended to a maximum of 600% of each country's quota
Representatives from 15 Western governments discuss a new restructuring agreement for Poland: in December martial law is declared
Saudi Arabia lends the IMF US$16 billion
The IMF blocks a loan to Romania
Interest rates: 21.5%–20.5%
Brazil's debt service reaches US$8 billion within the first nine months of the year
Latin America's GNP falls by an average of 2%, having increased between 1977 and 1980 by an average of 5%
Total third world foreign debt: US$666 billion
A large deficit is recorded on the USA's current account and continues in subsequent years
World raw materials price (1975 = 100): 300
Debts restructured:
* Poland (US$3.1 billion)
* Bolivia (US$455 million)
* Sudan (US$600 million)
* Madagascar (US$140 million)
* Central African Republic (US$72 million)
* Zaire (US$3.8 billion)
* Senegal (US$75 million)
* Uganda (US$30 million)
* Liberia (US$30 million)

1982

The Soviet Union announces financial difficulties

In April war breaks out between Britain and Argentina over the Malvinas (Falklands). Argentina is defeated. The dictatorship ends

Serious unrest in the Sudan over the IMF conditions imposed on new loans (IMF revolts)

Bolivia is denied further loans

Because of high rates of interest in the USA, the World Bank enters (primarily) the European market

Total third world foreign debt: US$738 billion

Interest rates: 16.5%

In August Mexico is incapable of paying her debts: the debt crisis officially breaks out

Hungary joins the IMF

In November Brazil suspends import licences and some debt service payments

The USA blocks fresh money for the IDA

Cuba requests the restructuring of its US$3 billion external debt

World raw materials price (1975 = 100): 290

Debts restructured:
* Madagascar (US$107 million)
* Sudan (US$105 million)
* Poland (US$500 million)
* Romania (US$2.9 billion)
* Malawi (US$225 million)
* Morocco (US$120 million)
* Senegal (US$74 million)
* Uganda (US$19 million)

1983

The non-aligned states hold a summit in Delhi and call for all outstanding loans extended to the least developed nations to be converted into gifts

The Sixth United Nations Conference on Trade and Development votes for a proposed reform of the IMF

Debtor nations from Latin America meet to discuss joint action

The BIS calls for commercial banks to increase their provisions for bad debts

Brazil cannot raise loan capital repayments for several months

The Philippines is incapable of paying her debts

Total third world foreign debt: US$797 billion

Third World nations are in arrears to the tune of US$250 billion with their payments

Regulation of the US banks' international obligations is stepped up. The loans extended by the ten biggest US banks to the three major Latin American debtors exceed those banks' capital funds

The international banks begin to take the view that their outstanding debts can only be rescued with several billion in fresh money

Interest rates: 10.5%–11.0%

Brazil cannot meet the IMF's conditions. New loans are blocked
World raw materials price (1975 = 100): 248
Debts rescheduled:
* Mexico (US$20 billion)
* Costa Rica (US$200 million)
* Sudan (US$536 million)
* Cuba (US$415 million)
* Togo (US$300 million)
* Zambia (US$375 million)
* Romania (US$195 million)
* Chile (US$16 billion)
* Peru (US$400 million)
* Ecuador (US$200 million)
* Malawi (US$30 million)
* Brazil (US$2.7 billion)
* Niger (US$46 million)
* Zaire (US$1.6 billion)

1984
Argentina is incapable of paying her debts
The US big bank Continental Illinois is insolvent
The US big bank Manufacturers Hanover is saved from bankruptcy
Total third world foreign debt: US$832 billion
The indebted Latin American nations meet in Cartagena, Colombia. One day later the US banks raise their interest rates
Brazil, Mexico, Argentina and Colombia protest jointly against high US interest rates
Interest rates: 13%
Economic recovery in Brazil and Mexico fuels hopes for an end to the debt crisis
World raw materials price (1975 = 100): 250
Debts restructured:
* Sierra Leone (US$22 million)
* Ivory Coast (US$360 million)
* Sudan (US$280 million)
* Yugoslavia (US$600 million)
* Peru (US$800 million)
* Zambia (US$250 million)
* Cuba (US$250 million)
* Jamaica (US$120 million)
* Mozambique (US$400 million)
* Philippines (US$800 million)

1985
June: the Austral Plan in Argentina — wage and price freezes, reduction in the national deficit, high real interest rates, a new currency

In September, Mexico restructures US$40 billion in debts. A couple of days later an earthquake devastates Mexico City. The country is once again incapable of paying its debts

Total third world foreign debt: US$892 billion

Brazil's New Republic is born after 20 years of military dictatorship

The new Peruvian president (Alan García) sets an upper limit for debt service at 10% of income from exports

The Baker Plan is presented in Seoul: US$20 billion in new loans to the 15 most heavily indebted nations in three years

The USA becomes a net external debtor for the first time in recent history with external debts of more than US$60 billion

The Cartagena Group calls for a reduction in interest rates and describes the Baker Plan as inadequate

Interest rates: 10.5%–9.5%

World raw materials price (1975 = 100): 247

Debts restructured:
* Argentina (US$2.2 billion)
* Senegal (US$80 million)
* Somalia (US$85 million)
* Costa Rica (US$190 million)
* Ecuador (US$400 million)
* Mauritania (US$60 million)
* Dominican Republic (US$290 million)
* Yugoslavia (US$850 million)
* Zaire (US$350 million)

1986

Following Peru's lead, Nigeria sets an upper limit for debt service

Total third world foreign debt: US$952 billion

The Marcos regime in the Philippines is toppled

February: the *Plano Cruzado* in Brazil
— a battle against inflation
— economic activity stimulated

The IMF declares Vietnam, Guyana, Liberia, the Sudan and Peru uncreditworthy

A debt market for 'dodgy' loans develops (factoring)

A debate begins on the subject of converting loans into interests (debt-equity swaps)

Crude oil prices fall to 1973 levels (in real terms). Most other raw materials prices fall

Interest rates: 8.5%–7.5%

World raw materials price (1975 = 100): 112

Debts restructured:
* Bolivia (US$100 million)
* Brazil (US$30 billion)
* Congo (US$800 million)

* Madagascar (US$130 million)
* Nigeria (US$10 billion)
* Poland (US$3.4 billion)
* Uruguay (US$2 billion)
* Venezuela (US$21 billion)

1987

Total third world foreign debt: US$1,010 billion

Mexico, Argentina and the Philippines conclude long-term restructuring agreements with a number of years grace

The major US banks considerably increase provisions for their Latin American loans

Hyperinflation in Brazil. Brazil declares a moratorium on interest payments in February and on loan-capital repayments in June

Unrest in South Korea. Political reform

The Baker Plan is regarded as having failed

Interest rates in the USA increase again for the first time since 1984

Interest rates: 8.25%

World raw materials price (1975 = 100): 103

Africa south of the Sahara: the burden of debt (1985)

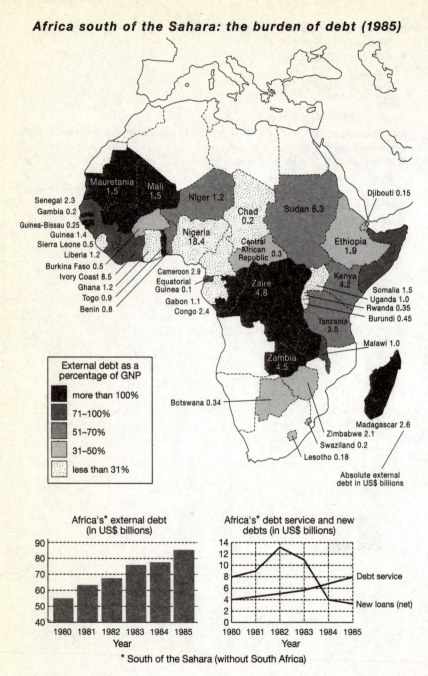

Mauretania 1.5
Mali 1.5
Niger 1.2
Chad 0.2
Sudan 6.3
Djibouti 0.15

Senegal 2.3
Gambia 0.2
Guinea-Bissau 0.25
Guinea 1.4
Sierra Leone 0.5
Liberia 1.2
Burkina Faso 0.5
Ivory Coast 8.5
Ghana 1.2
Togo 0.9
Benin 0.8

Nigeria 18.4
Central African Republic 0.3
Ethiopia 1.9

Cameroon 2.9
Equatorial Guinea 0.1
Gabon 1.1
Congo 2.4

Zaire 4.8
Kenya 4.2
Somalia 1.5
Uganda 1.0
Rwanda 0.35
Burundi 0.45
Tanzania 3.6

Malawi 1.0

Zambia 4.5

Botswana 0.34

Madagascar 2.6
Zimbabwe 2.1
Swaziland 0.2
Lesotho 0.18

Absolute external debt in US$ billions

External debt as a percentage of GNP

- more than 100%
- 71–100%
- 51–70%
- 31–50%
- less than 31%

Africa's* external debt (in US$ billions)

Year: 1980 1981 1982 1983 1984 1985

Africa's* debt service and new debts (in US$ billions)

Debt service
New loans (net)

Year: 1980 1981 1982 1983 1984 1985

* South of the Sahara (without South Africa)

Source: World Debt Tables; World Bank

Eastern Europe's External Debt (1985)

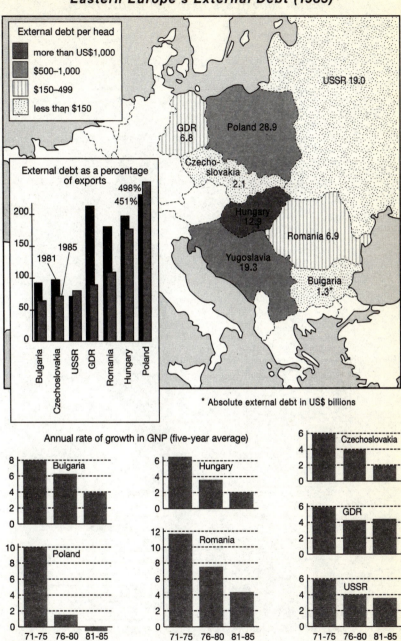

External debt per head
- more than US$1,000
- $500–1,000
- $150–499
- less than $150

USSR 19.0

GDR 6.8

Poland 28.9

Czecho-slovakia 2.1

Hungary 12.9

Romania 6.9

Yugoslavia 19.3

Bulgaria 1.3*

External debt as a percentage of exports

498%
451%

1981

1985

Bulgaria
Czechoslovakia
USSR
GDR
Romania
Hungary
Poland

* Absolute external debt in US$ billions

Annual rate of growth in GNP (five-year average)

Bulgaria

Hungary

Czechoslovakia

Poland

Romania

GDR

USSR

71-75   76-80   81-85

Source: World Debt Tables; *The Economist*

Latin America's External Debt (1985)

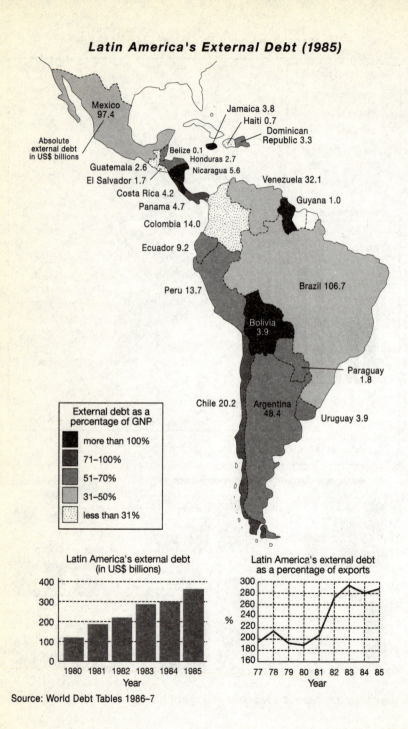

Absolute external debt in US$ billions

Mexico 97.4
Jamaica 3.8
Haiti 0.7
Dominican Republic 3.3
Belize 0.1
Honduras 2.7
Guatemala 2.6
Nicaragua 5.6
El Salvador 1.7
Venezuela 32.1
Costa Rica 4.2
Guyana 1.0
Panama 4.7
Colombia 14.0
Ecuador 9.2
Brazil 106.7
Peru 13.7
Bolivia 3.9
Paraguay 1.8
Chile 20.2
Argentina 48.4
Uruguay 3.9

External debt as a percentage of GNP

- more than 100%
- 71–100%
- 51–70%
- 31–50%
- less than 31%

Latin America's external debt (in US$ billions)

400
300
200
100
0
1980 1981 1982 1983 1984 1985
Year

Latin America's external debt as a percentage of exports

%
300
280
260
240
220
200
190
180
170
160
77 78 79 80 81 82 83 84 85
Year

Source: World Debt Tables 1986–7

Recommended Further Reading

BIS, Bank for International Settlements: annual reports, Basle, ongoing. These publications are among the most important official sources on current trends on the international financial markets.

Brandt, Willi (ed.) (1983) *Hilfe in der Weltkrise. Ein Sofortprogramm.* The second report of the Brandt Commission, Reinbek. An alarming call for action which was written in the shadow of the Mexican crisis of 1982. It puts forward proposals for economic policy measures oriented towards humanitarian goals.

Branford, Sue and Kucinski, Bernardo (1988) *The Debt Squads: The US, the Banks and Latin America*, Zed Books. A Brazilian writer and British financial journalist have produced a striking and up-to-date analysis that puts a cogent case for debt repudiation.

Castro, Fidel (1985) 'Die Verschuldungskrise der Weltwirtschaft und die aufhaltsame Zerstörung des Kapitalismus durch die Banken: Vom Verschuldeten Kapitalismus und von der Sozialisierung der Schulden' (with an introduction by Elmar Altvater), in *Leviathan* 13 (3). This is a German translation of an interview with Fidel Castro available in all of the major languages of the world. It is significant for the theory that indebtedness is not only strangling the indebted nations and their development prospects, but might also cause a serious crisis on the capitalist world market as a whole. The solution to the debt crisis therefore lies in rescuing the international banks.

CEPAL/ECLA (1985) 'Crisis and development in Latin America and the Caribbean' in *CEPAL Review* 26, August. The most current summary of the development strategies favoured by the UN Economic Commission for Latin America.

Dam, Kenneth W. (1982) *The Rules of The game: Reform and Evolution in the International Monetary System*, Chicago. A thorough analysis of the development of the world monetary system from the gold standard, through the inter-war period, to the Bretton Woods system and its collapse.

Folker, Fröbel; Heinrichs, Jürgen and Kreye, Otto (1986) *Umbruch in der Weltwirtschaft*, Reinbek. Using updated material, the authors confirm the findings of their 1977 thesis on *The New International Division of Labour* (Cambridge University Press, 1980), into which the countries of the Third

World are incorporated only as subordinates. The debt crisis is merely an expression of this basic tendency.

George, Susan (1988) *A Fate Worse the Debt*, Penguin. A highly readable account by a prominent American author on development questions.

Ghai, Dharam (ed.) (1991) *The IMF and the South*, Zed Books/UNRISD. The United Nations Research Institute on Society and Development has assembled prominent Third World social scientists to examine the impact and implications of the IMF's structural adjustment programmes for particular social groups in Africa, the Caribbean and Latin America.

Hankel, Wilhelm (1984) *Gegenkurs. Von der Schuldenkrise zur Vollbeschäftigung*, Berlin. A Keynesian-inspired study of the link between the debt crisis and the employment crisis of the 1980s. It proposes a Marshall Plan for the Third World.

Horsefield, John K. (ed.) (1969) 'The IMF 1945–1965', Vol. 3, *Documents*, Washington. An official IMF publication containing documents relating to the founding of the IMF, including the plans conceived by Keynes and White.

IMSF (Institut für Marxistische Studien und Forschungen) and ASK (Antiimperialistisches Solidaritätskomitee) (eds) (1986) *Die Dritte Welt in der Schuldenkrise — Rolle der Bundesrepublik — Diskussion um Alternativen*, Frankfurt/Main. The volume gathers together contributions which were presented at a conference in 1986. Though the analytical range leaves a little to be desired, the contributions are nevertheless most useful; they demonstrate the range of assessments of the causes and course of, and possible solutions to, the debt crisis. Particularly recommended are the accounts of the role of the West German economy in the debt crisis.

Jahrbuch Lateinamerika: analyses and reports, Hamburg, ongoing. This publication regularly contains major analyses of the economic and political situation in the Latin American countries; in the last few years it has focused increasingly on the question of external debt.

Körner, Peter, Maaß, Gero, Siebold, Thomas and Tetzlaff, Rainer (1986) *The IMF and the Debt Crisis: A Guide to the Third World's Dilemma*, Zed Books. A well-documented volume on IMF crisis management. As well as an account of the creation and functioning of the IMF, there is also a series of analyses of individual countries (Brazil, Portugal, the Sudan, Jamaica, Zaire and Ghana). The authors suggest that the way out of the debt crisis is a reform of the IMF and the World Bank and the formulation of development-policy conditionalities which are oriented towards social and ecological objectives.

Loeschner, Ernst (1983) *Souveräne Risiken und internationale Verschuldung*, Vienna. This work deals rather technocratically with the question arising from the debt crisis as to the possible ways in which states can react. It is interesting for its historical retrospect of debt crises and thoughts on how national bankruptcy should be dealt with.

Nuscheler, Franz (1987) *Lern- und Arbeitsbuch Entwicklungspolitik*, Bonn. Using well-documented data, this work outlines in comprehensible fashion the problems faced by the Third World today. Within this, the debt crisis is only one aspect of the whole development-strategy crisis. Thoroughly recommended for anyone who wishes to be informed about not only the debt crisis but also the fundamental strategic problems of development out of underdevelopment.

Onimode, Bade (ed.) (1989) *The IMF, the World Bank and the African Debt: Vol. 1: The Economic Impact. Vol. 2: The Political and Social Impact*, Zed Books. African scholars present country case studies and analyses of general issues relating to the impact of structural adjustment on the continent hit hardest by the debt crisis.

Payer, Cheryl (1991) *Lent and Lost*, Zed Books. This prominent American critic of the IMF and the World Bank develops a seminal argument as to why poor countries which borrow cpaital from overseas on a large scale are doomed to experience a debt crisis sooner or later.

Roddick, Jackie (ed.) (1988) *The Dance of Millions: Latin America and the Debt Crisis*, Latin America Bureau.

Schatan, Jacobo (1987) *World Debt: Who is to Pay?* Zed Books. This Chilean economist spells out the environmental implications of pressure on Third World countries to repay their debt.

Schubert, Alexander (1987) *Die internationale Verschuldung. Die Dritte Welt und das Trasnationale Bankensysteme*, Frankfurt. (2) One of the German language's standard works on the subject. The Third World debt crisis is interpreted as part of the increasing tendency to crisis of the global monetary world-market development and the system of supremacy after World War II. In addition to a detailed analysis of the transnational banking system, the work contains case studies of Mexico, Brazil, Chile and Argentina.

Simonis, Udo-Ernst (ed.) (1984) *Externe Verschuldung — interne Anpassung. Entwicklungsländer in der Finanzkrise*, Berlin. This work documents the contributions presented to a meeting of the *Verein für Sozialpolitik* and looks in particular at controversy over the IMF's policy on conditionality. Studies of Mexico, Venezuela, South Korea, Turkey and Eastern Europe.

Tetzlaff, Rainer (1980) *Die Weltbank: Machtinstrument der USA oder Hilfe für die Entwicklungsländer?* Munich. A standard work on the history of the World Bank. A meticulous and well-documented account of the history of both the World Bank and its development-policy strategies. A good supplement to the understanding of events since 1980 is given by Cheryl Payer (1986) 'The World Bank: A new role in the debt crisis', in *Third World Quarterly* 8 (3).

World Bank (1985) *World Development Report 1985*, Washington DC. This work contains the World Bank's official view of the debt problem. Essential for anyone who is concerned with the whole issue, since it is rich in material, and often critical.

Contributors

Elmar Altvater, Professor of Political Science at the Free University of Berlin, member of the editorial board of the journal *PROKLA*.

Niña Boschmann, journalist on *Tageszeitung*.

Tatjana Chahoud, Dr. rer. pol., lives in Berlin.

Hansgeorg Conert, professor at the University of Bremen.

Claudia Dziobek, research assistant to the Greens in the *Bundestag*.

Folker Fröbel, researcher at the Starnberg Institute for Research into Global Structures, Trends and Crisis.

Wolfgang Hein, research assistant at the Latin America Institute of the Free University of Berlin, currently working on a project in Costa Rica.

Jürgen Heinrichs, researcher at the Starnberg Institute for Research into Global Structures, Trends and Crises.

Kurt Hübner, research assistant in the Department of Political Science at the Free University of Berlin, member of the editorial board of the journal *PROKLA*.

Thomas Hurtienne, research assistant at the Latin America Institute of the Free University of Berlin.

Gerd Junne, professor in the *Fachgruppe für Internationale Beziehungen und Völkerrecht* (a team of specialists studying international relations and public law) at the University of Amsterdam.

Peter Körner, doctor in the Department of Political Science at the University of Hamburg.

Otto Kreye, researcher at the Starnberg Institute for Research into Global Structures, Trends and Crises.

Jochen Lorentzen, formerly of the Department of Political Science at the Free University of Berlin, and the American University Washington DC; now teaching at the European University Institute, Florence.

Ulrich Menzel, instructor at the Johann–Wolfgang–Goethe University in Frankfurt.

Dorothea Metzger, graduate political ecnomist, works as a freelance researcher in Munich.

Theo Mutter, research assistant at the Latin America Institute of the Free University of Berlin, currently working on a project in the Cape Verde Islands.

Manfred Nitsch, professor at the Latin America Institute of the Free University of Berlin.

Claudia Preußer, graduate of political science, currently working on a project on Amazonas at the Free University of Berlin.

Raúl Rojas, research assistant at the Technical University of Berlin.

Alexander Schubert, instructor in the Department of Political Science at the Free University of Berlin, has completed projects on several Latin American countries.

Gabriela Simon, graduate political economist, works as a freelance journalist in Berlin.

Rainer Tetzlaff, Professor of Political Science at the University of Hamburg.

Eugenio Rivera Urrutia, professor at the *Universidad de Costa Rica.*

Friedhelm Wachs, graduate political scientist and freelance journalist.

Index

Zed Books Ltd

is a publisher whose international and Third World lists span:

- **Women's Studies**
- **Development**
- **Environment**
- **Current Affairs**
- **International Relations**
- **Children's Studies**
- **Labour Studies**
- **Cultural Studies**
- **Human Rights**
- **Indigenous Peoples**
- **Health**

We also specialize in Area Studies where we have extensive lists in African Studies, Asian Studies, Caribbean and Latin American Studies, Middle East Studies, and Pacific Studies.

For further information about books available from Zed Books, please write to: Catalogue Enquiries, Zed Books Ltd, 57 Caledonian Road, London N1 9BU. Our books are available from distributors in many countries (for full details, see our catalogues), including:

In the USA
Humanities Press International, Inc., 165 First Avenue,
Atlantic Highlands, New Jersey 07716.
Tel: (201) 872 1441;
Fax: (201) 872 0717.

In Canada
DEC, 229 College Street, Toronto, Ontario M5T 1R4.
Tel: (416) 971 7051.

In Australia
Wild and Woolley Ltd, 16 Darghan Street, Glebe, NSW 2037.

In India
Bibliomania, C-236 Defence Colony, New Delhi 110 024.

In Southern Africa
David Philip Publisher (Pty) Ltd, PO Box 408, Claremont 7735,
South Africa.